1001 GREAT STORIES AND QUOTES

R. KENT HUGHES

Tyndale House Publishers, Inc.
Wheaton, Illinois

Visit Tyndale's exciting Web site at www.tyndale.com

Designed by Melinda Schumacher

Additional editorial work by Kathryn S. Olson, Anne Goldsmith

Library of Congress Cataloging-in-Publication Data

1001 great stories and quotes / [compiled by] R. Kent Hughes.
p. cm.
Includes index.
ISBN 0-8423-0409-6 (sc : alk. paper)
1. Anecdotes. 2. Quotations, English. I. Hughes, R. Kent.
PN6261.A17 1998
082—dc21 97-34836

Printed in the United States of America

03 02 01 00 99 98
7 6 5 4 3 2

For Pip

CONTENTS

Preface

This book contains the very best of the stories, anecdotes, and quotations culled from my files compiled from over thirty years of reading and preaching—and obsessive collecting.

Most of them are fresh. That is, you will not find them in other collections of illustrations. The few that do appear elsewhere have been deemed so good that it would be wrong to leave them out.

The use of a fitting illustration is a joy in itself. All speakers and teachers know this well: the delight of seeing the light of recognition in the hearers' eyes, indicating that they are with you; the pleasure of refocusing the listeners' attention on the truth being expounded; and the satisfaction of knowing that the truth of God's Word is being served. It is a humbling joy to realize that one has been used to help others plainly see the truth of God's Word. And this is the sole purpose of this book. May you find fresh expressions and windows through which to communicate God's truth.

The way to benefit from *1001 Great Stories and Quotes* is to spend an evening browsing and getting to know the contents. I promise, it will be fun! Many of the epigrams and famous lines will lodge in your mind for future reference. Read an entire section, say, on *love* or *sin* because that will give you a sense of the book's range on crucial subjects.

And by all means, follow the cross-references, because perhaps this will point you to just the right gem.

The Why of Illustrations

There are vital reasons why illustrations are a must. The first, of course, is because Jesus indulged in them. It has been calculated that one-half of Jesus' public instruction was given in the form of parables and comparisons and that there are 164 metaphors in the synoptic Gospels, with 56 in the Sermon on the Mount alone. Our Lord communicated the grand truths of salvation in terms that were familiar to the people.

Second, stories and illustrations make truth arresting. Preaching or speaking is far more difficult today than it was at the turn of the century, due to the modern culture's glut of words. Billions of words are spoken every second. And sometimes, it seems, they are all assaulting us through TV, radio, VCRs, and the multiple conversations around us. We are a distracted people. Our attention span has been shortened so that many have difficulty listening to reasoned discourse—apart from anecdotes and graphic images.

Third, illustrative materials can help to make truth concrete for hearers. For example, Paul's admonition in Colossians 3:14, "And over all these virtues put on love," has immense practical application that can be brought home with great power with a story like the one about the man who loved his wife enough to take her punishment (see page 264).

And fourth, illustrations serve to clarify the truth. Illustrations access the mental processes of the hearers. Abstractions (and many theological realities are abstract!) will fly by most hearers unless they are attached to concrete references and experiences of life. Illustrations serve to make the crucial connections.

The How of Illustrations

Communicators must understand that there is no such thing as a "good illustration." There are only good illustrations of what one is saying. An illustration is valuable only to the extent that it calls attention to the point being made and contributes to the momentum, clarity, and force of what is being said. If the illustration does not precisely illustrate the point, don't use it—no matter how gripping it may be. Resist the temptation that comes after reading or hearing a powerful story to think, *What a great illustration! Now I've got to find a place to use it!*

This becomes an intensely ethical matter when opening God's Word. Bottom line: If the illustration doesn't clarify and focus the truth of God's holy Word, forget it. Better to preach a sermon with no illustrations than to employ misleading or inaccurate illustrations. The more powerful an illustration is, the more careful one must be. In fact, a given illustration may perfectly illustrate the point of the text but be so dynamic that it overpowers the text. If so, it should not be employed.

Similarly, if an illustration becomes the message, it has gone awry. Praise God for the powerful story of Jim Elliot's love for the Auca Indians, but his love and death for them is not gospel. The gospel is the good news of Christ.

We must also keep before us the understanding that when people remember an illustration but not the truth it illustrates, we have failed.

Strive to employ illustrations naturally. They cannot be inserted ready-made into a message like pieces of a jigsaw puzzle. The craft of illustration demands that they be woven into the flow of the discourse. In this respect, an illustration that requires explanation is worthless. As J. H. Jowett said, "Illustrations are like streetlamps, scarcely noticed, but throwing floods of light upon the road."

Wisdom for Illustrations

- If you are presenting the illustration as true, make sure it is!
- Avoid hackneyed, overused illustrations like Hawthorne's "The Great Stone Face" or "He's not heavy; he's my brother" or "You should have seen this garden when only the Lord was working in it."
- Never begin an illustration with an apology—"If you will pardon the personal illustration . . ."
- Don't be predictably clichéd in introducing illustrations—"A story is told . . ."
- Refrain from personal anecdotes that demonstrate your own spirituality and accomplishments, "for we do not preach ourselves, but Jesus Christ" (2 Corinthians 4:5).
- Quote only poetry that is readily comprehensible to the average hearer.
- Commit your illustrations to memory so that they can be told with eye contact and involvement with your hearers.

Acknowledgments

Sincerest thanks to Dr. Ken Taylor and Dr. Wendell Hawley for the original vision for the book and continued encouragement to do it.

Deepest appreciation to Mrs. Lorraine Triggs, whose deft and discriminating editor's eye has sorted through thousands of stories, anecdotes, and quotations to find only the best. Lorraine, this is *your* book!

ACTION

When all is said and done, there is more said than done.
Anonymous

ADULTERY

Adultery is the escape of the disappointed man.
Walter Trobisch

AFFLICTION

The good of trouble is not generally while we are in trouble, but when we get out of trouble.
Charles H. Spurgeon

Jesus promised three results for those who would follow him. They will be absurdly happy, entirely fearless and always in trouble.
William Russel Maltby

I had a secret satisfaction in the greatness of the difficulties. So far from being cast down on account of them, they delighted my soul. I did nothing but pray. Prayer and faith helped me over the difficulties.
George Mueller

God appoints his ministers to be sorely exercised, both from without and within, that they may sympathize with their flock, and know in their own hearts the deceitfulness of sin, the infirmities of the flesh, and the way in which the Lord supports and bears all who trust in Him.
John Newton

It was only when I lay there on rotting prison straw that I sensed within myself the first stirrings of good. . . . So bless you, prison, for having been in my life.
Aleksandr Solzhenitsyn

Life Goes Better with Affliction

In *A Twentieth-Century Testimony,* the late Malcolm Muggeridge wrote:

I can say with complete truthfulness that everything I have learned in my seventy-five years in this world, everything that has truly enhanced and enlightened my existence, has been through affliction and not through happiness, whether pursued or attained. In other words, if it ever were to be possible to eliminate affliction from our earthly existence by means of some drug or other medical mumbo jumbo, as Aldous Huxley envisaged in *Brave New World,* the result would not be to make life delectable, but to make it too banal and trivial to be endurable. This, of course, is what the Cross signifies. And it is the Cross, more than anything else, that has called me inexorably to Christ.

Dark Threads the Weaver Needs

See page 406

AGING

The only way not to reject eternal values is to submit willingly to the erosion of temporal ones. . . . A spirit of graceful submission is required of every person in life, and there can be no peace without it. For one way or another we must all be humbled, even unto death. One way or another we must all die a little every day, and in the process we will all suffer unspeakably.

Mike Mason

Age has a word for any day and generation. Some things would be in better shape today if some older men had spoken out a few years ago. . . . The Scriptures tell us that when the Spirit is poured out, young men shall see visions and old men shall dream dreams. It is as proper for an old preacher to be a dreamer as for a young preacher to be a seer so long as his dream is not a nightmare!

Vance Havner

There Goes His Memory

Samuel Johnson once observed that "there is a wicked inclination in most people to suppose an old man decayed in his intellects. If a young or middle-aged man, when leaving a company, does not recollect where he laid his hat, it is nothing; but if the same inattention is discovered in an old man, people will shrug up their shoulders and say, 'His memory is going.'"

James Boswell, The Life of Johnson *(London: Penguin, 1979), 289.*

The Traits of Late Middle Age

Says writer John Updike:

In myself I observe the very traits that used to irritate me in men of late middle age whom I have known: a forgetfulness, a repetitiveness, a fussiness with parcels and strings, a doddery of deliberation of movement mixed with patches of inattention and uncertainty that make my car-driving increasingly hazardous and—other, younger drivers indicate with gestures and honking—irritating to others. I feel, also, I am not innocent of self-absorption, a ruminativeness that makes me blind and deaf and indifferent to the young, invested as these passing twitches are with their own emerging identity and sexuality. My brain cells have accepted their program and are full. I used to find it difficult to talk to my first wife's father, an intelligent and sensitive man, because he didn't seem to be *up* on anything. Now, as I look over *The New Yorker,* its cartoons and "The Talk of the Town" bristle with allusions I don't quite catch, and a psychic music that isn't mine, any more than Thurber and White's was mine.

John Updike, Self-Consciousness *(New York: Fawcett Crest, 1989), 259.*

The Unfolding Murder Mystery
See page 105

The Big Difference
See page 434

AMBITION

My own ego needs drove me compulsively in my work. Just serving God faithfully was not enough. I had to be leading the pack or, at the least, promising to lead the pack in time. Somewhere along the line, to make matters worse, I had equated church work as being the measure of my love for God.

Lane Adams

All-Consuming Choice
See page 429

You're Getting ahead of Me
See page 402

General Preference
See page 244

ANGELS

The Voice of an Angel

We so often hear the expression "the voice of an angel!" that I got to wondering what an angel would sound like. So

I did some research, and discovered that an angel's voice sounds remarkably like a person saying, "Hurry up!"

Until the time I took over, research had been blocked because it was based on the delusion that the voice of an angel would always be beautiful. The words "Get up" are rarely beautiful, never less so than at 7 A.M. Yet, that is always what the angels say when they are talking to me, as reported in the Bible. I can't think of anything an angel ever said but, "Get up and hurry!" An angel comes to Peter in jail and says, "Rise quickly." An angel says to Gideon, "Arise and go in this thy might." An angel says to Elijah, "Arise and eat." An angel appears to Joseph in a dream, when Herod is slaughtering the infants, and says, "Go quickly." An angel appears to Philip and says, "Arise and go."

Really, the angels are monotonous talkers! They always say the same thing—"Arise, hurry!" But so is a fireball monotonous. If we are to be saved, it will be by monotony, the reiterated command, "Get up and get going!" Listen carefully and you can hear the voice of angels above the contemporary din of the world, a voice that ought to get us out of lounge chairs and comfortable beds. "Arise, go quickly!"

It might be a good idea to allow an angel to occupy the pulpit on Sunday. An irate hearer said to Samuel Barnett when he was canon of Bristol Cathedral in England, "I come to church to be comforted, and you sound like a fire alarm." Perhaps there was a fire.

Halford E. Luccok, The Christian Century.

Hundreds of Men in Shining Garments

In a dark night, about a hundred years ago, a Scottish missionary couple found themselves surrounded by cannibals intent on taking their lives. That terror-filled night, the couple fell to their knees and prayed that God would protect them. It was a horrible time. Intermittent with their prayers, the missionaries heard the cries of the savages and imagined the specters coming through the door to take their lives. As the sun began to rise, to their astonishment they found that the natives were retreating into the forest. The missionaries were absolutely amazed and filled with joy. Their hearts soared in praise to God. It was a day of rejoicing.

The couple bravely continued their work. A year later, the chieftain of the tribe was saved. As the missionary spoke with him, he remembered the horror of that night. He asked the chieftain why he and his men had not killed them. The chieftain replied in surprise, "Who were all those men with you?" The missionary answered, "Why, there were no men with us. There were just my wife and myself." The chieftain began to argue with him, saying, "There were hundreds of tall men in shining garments with drawn swords circling about your house, so we could not attack you."

This story, recorded in Billy Graham's book *Angels,* is one of the greatest stories of missionary history. The missionary was the nearly legendary John G. Paton of the New Hebrides.

Billy Graham, Angels *(New York: Galahad, 1993).*

Jesus Stopped the Cars

One evening a southern California pastor's wife was driving down the Santa Ana Freeway, which is always busy. As she drove, somehow the car door opened and her four-year-old child tumbled out onto the freeway in the middle of the high-speed traffic. With her heart pounding and with horrible expectations, she came to a screeching stop and ran frantically back along the freeway. But she didn't expect to see what she saw. Her child was sitting up in the fast lane of the freeway, amidst the glare of headlights. His only injuries were a few abrasions. The first words that came out of his mouth were, "Mommy, Mommy, I saw Jesus put up his hands and stop the cars!" None of the drivers saw anyone; they just managed to stop their cars and miss hitting him.

ANGER

The Unrecognizable Sinner

Sin makes the sinner unrecognizable.

I experienced this once myself, and I remember it because it frightened me. I became an animal. This sinful experience occurred—as so many do—around the occasion of a dinner party. It was a hot August afternoon. I was having 10 people [over] for dinner that evening. No one was giving me a bit of help. I was, of course, feeling like a victim, as everyone does in a hot kitchen on an August day. (It is important to remember that the angry person's habit of self-justification is often connected to his habit of seeing himself as a victim.) I had been chopping, stirring, bending over a low flame, and all alone, alone! The oven's heat was my purgatory, my crucible.

My mother and my children thought this was a good time for civil disobedience. They positioned themselves in the car and refused to move until I took them swimming. Now my children were at tender ages at that time, 7 and 4. My mother was 78 and, except for her daily habit of verbal iron-pumping, properly described as infirm. They leaned on the horn and shouted my name out the window, well within hearing of the neighbors, reminding me of my promise to take them to the pond.

There are certain times when a popular cliché disgorges itself from the dulled setting of overuse and comes to life, and this was one of them. *I lost it.* I lost myself. I jumped on the hood of the car. I pounded on the windshield. I told my mother and my children that I was never, ever going to take any of them anywhere and none of them were ever going to have one friend in any house of mine until the hour of their death, which, I said, I hoped was soon. I couldn't stop pounding on the windshield. Then the frightening thing happened. I became a huge bird. A carrion crow. My legs became hard stalks; my eyes were sharp and vicious. I developed a murderous beak. Greasy black feathers took the place of arms. I flapped and flapped. I blotted out the sun's light with my flapping. Each time my beak landed near my victims (it seemed to be my fists on the windshield, but it was really my beak on their necks) I went back for more. The taste of blood entranced me. I wanted to peck and peck forever. I wanted to carry them all off in my bloody beak and drop them on a rock where I would feed on their battered corpses till my bird stomach swelled.

I don't mean this figuratively: I became that bird. I had to be forced to get off the car and stop pounding the windshield. Even then I didn't come back to myself. When I did, I was appalled. I realized I had genuinely frightened my children. Mostly because they could no longer recognize me. My son said to me, "I was scared because I didn't know who you were."

I understand that this is not sin of a serious nature. I know this to be true because it has its comic aspects and deadly sin is characterized by the absence of humor, which always brings life. But because of that experience and others I won't tell you about, I understand the deadly sin of anger. I was unrecognizable to myself and, for a time, to my son, but I think I still would have been recognizable to most of the rest of the world as human. Deadly sin causes the rest of the human community to say: "How can this person do this thing and still be human?"

Mary Gordon, "The Fascination Begins in the Mouth," New York Times, *13 June 1993, 31.*

A Bitter Buildup

See page 166

ANXIETY

No man ever sank under the burden of the day. It is when tomorrow's burden is added to the burden of today, that the weight is more than a man can bear.
George Macdonald

APATHY

The things of religion are so great, that there can be no suitableness in the exercises of our hearts, to their nature and importance, unless they be lively and powerful. In nothing is vigor in the actings of our inclinations so requisite, as in religion; and in nothing is lukewarmness so odious.
Jonathan Edwards

The hottest places in hell are reserved for those who remain neutral in a time of great moral crisis.
Dante

None are so unholy as those whose hands are cauterized with holy things.
C. S. Lewis

APOSTASY

The evangelical church is sick—so sick that people are crowding in to join us. We're a big flock, big enough to permit remarriage of divorced people (beyond the exceptions of the Word of God), big enough to permit practicing homosexuals to pursue their lifestyle, big enough to tolerate almost anything pagans do. We're no longer narrow; it's a wide road of popular acceptance for us.
Joseph Bayly

We do not believe in *God*. But we believe in the supremacy of hu-*man*-ity. We do not believe in life after *death*. But we believe in *immortality* through good deeds.
Bertrand Russell, "The Atheist's Creed."

Prone to Wander

Few people know it, but both sets of Ernest Hemingway's grandparents were committed evangelical Christians. In fact, his paternal grandparents were both graduates of Wheaton College and very close friends of D. L. Moody. His maternal grandfather was such a godly patriarchal figure that his grandchildren called him "Abba." Furthermore, one of Hemingway's uncles was a missionary to China. Yet Ernest Hemingway, after leaving his evangelical rearing in Oak Park, Illinois, became the worldwide emblem of the lost generation who said, "I live in a vacuum that is as lonely as a radio tube when the batteries are dead and there is no current to plug into"—and who took his own life.

Daniel Pawley, "Ernest Hemingway, Tragedy of an Evangelical," Christianity Today, *23 November 1984, 20–22.*

Purging the Jewish Element

Joachim Hossenfelder, head of the German Christians and a Berlin pastor, presided in his Nazi uniform. After the usual parade of swastika-bedecked flags, a fanfare of trumpets and throaty chorus of "Now Thank We All Our God," Hossenfelder announced that in his diocese the Aryan paragraph, dismissing all Jews from church office, was being put into effect immediately. He also announced that Niemoller and other leaders of the Pastors' Emergency League would be suspended, since their activities were entirely foreign to the true spirit of Germany. At each announcement the crowd erupted into a resounding cheer.

The main speaker of the evening was a senior Nazi official who demanded that everything un-German be purged from the church. His final admonition was that the Bible be reexamined for non-German elements: "liberation from the Old Testament, with its Jewish money morality and these stories of cattle-dealers and pimps." It also meant purging the New Testament of its Jewish elements, especially the unheroic theology of the apostle Paul with his "inferiority complex." A proud, heroic Jesus must replace the model of a "suffering servant."

His speech was interrupted again and again by applause. Not one of the bishops or church leaders stood to disagree. Instead, when the speaker had finished, resolutions were enthusiastically passed supporting his words and calling for Jewish Christians to be forced into "ghetto churches."

Charles Colson, Kingdoms in Conflict *(Grand Rapids, Mich.: William Morrow/Zondervan, 1987), 138.*

Far from the Original Plan

In 1896 the Victorian-minded planners of St. John the Divine in New York City envisioned a great Episcopal cathedral that would bring glory to God. Nearly a century later, though the immense structure is still under construction, it is in use—in a way that its planner might well have regarded with dismay.

St. John's Thanksgiving service has featured Japanese Shinto priests; Muslim Sufis perform biannually; Lenten services have focused on the ecological "passion of the earth" (one gathers that Christ's passion is passé). The cathedral has featured "Christa," a huge crucifix with a female Christ, and St. John's pulpit welcomes everyone from the Rev. Jesse Jackson to Norman Mailer, rabbis, Imam, Buddhist monks, secular politicians, atheist scientists, and during the feast of St. Francis in October 1985, an arkload of animals received blessings from the high altar, including a llama, an elephant, and a goose.

Logistical questions such as curbing your elephants within the cathedral notwithstanding, St. John the Divine seems to have ceased to be a house of the one God of Scriptures, and has become instead a house of many gods. Novelist Kurt Vonnegut Jr. wrote for the cathedral's centennial brochure that "the Cathedral is to this atheist . . . a suitable monument to persons of all ages and classes. I go there often to be refreshed by a sense of nonsectarian community which has the best interests of the whole planet at heart."

Charles Colson, Kingdoms in Conflict *(Grand Rapids, Mich.: William Morrow/Zondervan, 1987), 222–223. The information and citations concerning St. John the Divine Cathedral are drawn from Kenneth L. Woodward and Deborah Witherspoon, "The Awakening of a Cathedral,"* Newsweek, *16 June 1986, 59–60.*

God Is Cold

See page 13

ATHEISM

The existentialist finds it extremely embarrassing that God does not exist, for there disappears with Him all possibility of finding values in an intelligible heaven.

Jean Paul Sartre

Among the repulsions of atheism for me has been its drastic uninterestingness as an intellectual position. Where was the ingenuity, the ambiguity, the humanity (in the Harvard sense) of saying that the universe just happened to happen and that when we're dead we're dead?

John Updike

The crisis of all primitive mankind comes with the discovery of that which is fundamentally not-holy, the a-sacramental, which withstands the methods, and which has no "hour," a province which steadily enlarges itself.

Martin Buber

The science to which I pinned my faith is bankrupt. Its counsels, which should have established the millennium, led instead directly to the suicide of Europe. I believed them once. In their name I helped to destroy the faith of millions of worshipers in the temples of a thousand creeds. And now they look at me and witness the great tragedy of an atheist who has lost his faith.

George Bernard Shaw

Atheism turns out to be too simple. If the whole universe has no meaning, we should have never found out that it has no meaning. Just as, if there were no light in the universe and therefore no creatures with eyes, we should never know it was dark. "Dark" would be without meaning.

C. S. Lewis

Massive Defection

The startling spread of secular theory continues as a major phenomenon of the twentieth century. No Christian statesman foresaw in 1900 that our era would be marked by a massive defection, unparalleled in history, by descendants of Christian parents; instead, evangelicals spoke of winning the world for Christ in a single generation. From a mere 0.2 percent of the world population in 1900, atheists grew in number to 20.8 in 1980; increasing by 8.5 million a year, atheists by 1984 totaled one billion, a number that includes liberal humanists and skeptical nonbelievers as well as dialectical materialists. More rather than less countries than in 1970 are now officially atheistic; in fact, during the last fifteen years atheism added sixty million adherents.

Carl F. H. Henry, Twilight of a Great Civilization *(Westchester, Ill.: Crossway Books, 1988), 25.*

God Is Cold

Stephen Crane somehow brought to focus in his person, in his work, the sudden skepticism of a generation that had seen religion's authority weakened by science and conventional patriotism abandoned for American imperialism and saber rattling in the 1890s. . . . And if "God was dead," as they first began to hint in the nineteenth century, his absence was marked by writers principally in the 1890s, the "clever decade" in which Crane did all his principal work. Nowhere in American writing was a godless world expressed with so much terseness and finality as in the work of Stephen Crane. He was to write in one of his astonishingly chilling, totally skeptical poems that "God is cold," and he repeated this in stanza after stanza as if to assure the reader that he meant it.

The Modest Fool

A pastor once entered a tavern where a man, wishing to embarrass him, rose and suddenly called out quite loudly, *"Es gibt keinen Gott!"* ("There is no God!").

The pastor went to him, calmly laid his hand on his shoulder, and said, "Friend, what you have said is not at all new. The Bible said that more than two thousand years ago."

The man replied, "I never knew that the Bible made such a statement."

The pastor informed him, "Psalm 14, verse 1, tells us, 'The fool says in his heart, "There is no God."' But there is a great difference between that fool and you. He was quite modest and said it only in his heart; he didn't go about yelling it out in taverns."

The UN Meditation Room

See page 241

ATONEMENT

The world was checkmated by the devil, but the Redeemer of man made the one move that could free us from gloom in life and doom in eternity—he died to free us from Satan's bondage.

John Wesley White

Barabbas was the only man in the world who could say that Jesus Christ took his physical place. But I can say that Jesus Christ took my spiritual place. . . . I deserved Hell; Jesus took my Hell; there is nothing left for me but his Heaven.

Donald Grey Barnhouse

Mystery of mysteries, God forsook God.
Martin Luther

The Blood-Bought

There is a story of an African slave whose master was about to slay him with a spear, when a chivalrous British traveler thrust out his arm to ward off the blow, and it was pierced by the cruel weapon. As the blood spurted out, he demanded the person of the slave, saying he had bought him by his suffering. To this the former master ruefully agreed. As the latter walked away, the slave threw himself at the feet of his deliverer, exclaiming, "The blood-bought is now the slave of the son of pity. He will serve him faithfully."

A Great Debt, Who Can Pay?

There is a story about Czar Nicholas I of Russia that tells us something of Jesus' atoning love. As the story goes, the czar was greatly interested in the welfare of a young man whose father had been the czar's friend. When that young man came of age, Czar Nicholas gave him a fine position in the army and stationed him in a place of responsibility at one of the great fortresses of Russia. The young man was responsible for the monies and finances of a particular division of the army.

The young man did quite well at first, but as time went on, he became a gambler. It wasn't long until he had gambled his entire fortune away. He borrowed from the treasury and gambled that money away, a few rubles at a time. One day he heard there was going to be an audit of the books the next day. He went to the safe, took out his ledger, figured out how much money he had, and then subtracted the amount that he had taken. He discovered that he had an astronomical debt. As he sat at that table, he took out his pen and wrote this phrase: "A great debt, who can pay?" Not willing to go through the shame of what he would face the next day, he took out his revolver and decided that at the stroke of midnight he would take his life.

It was a warm and drowsy night and, as the young man sat at the table, he dozed off. Now Czar Nicholas had a habit of putting on a soldier's uniform and visiting some of his outposts. On that very night he came to the great fortress. As he inspected it, he saw a light on in one of the rooms. He knocked on the door. No one answered. He tried the latch, opened the door, and went in. There was the young man. The czar recognized him immediately. When he saw the note on the table, "A great debt, who can pay?" and the ledger opened, his first impulse was to wake the young man and arrest him. But Czar Nicholas was overwhelmed with a wave of generosity. Instead, he took the pen that had fallen from the soldier's hand, wrote one word on the same sheet of paper, and quietly left the room.

About an hour later, the young man woke up and reached for his revolver, realizing that it was long past midnight. Then he saw his note: "A great debt, who can pay?" And there was one more word added: "Nicholas." The young man dropped the gun, ran to the files, thumbed through the correspondence, and found the czar's signature. The note was authentic. Suddenly it dawned on him—the czar had been there that night and knew his guilt, but he had undertaken the young man's debt, and he would not die. The young man trusted the czar's word, and sure enough the debt was paid.

The czar's love was an atoning love; he paid the price for his guilty young friend. But it was only a faint shadow of the atoning love of Christ. It was a beautiful gesture, and it does Nicholas great credit. But it was an easy matter for him, as easy as signing his name. The atoning love of Jesus is superior because it cost him everything!

H. A. Ironside, Illustrations of Bible Truth *(Grand Rapids, Mich.: Zondervan), 67–69.*

Covering the Fine

Mr. La Guardia, one of the famous mayors of New York City, used to be a judge at a police court. One day they brought a trembling old man before him charged with stealing a loaf of bread. The old man said he had to do it because his family was starving.

"Well, I have to punish you," said Mr. La Guardia. "The law makes no exceptions, and I can do nothing but sentence you to a fine of ten dollars."

Then he added, after reaching into his pocket, "And here's the ten dollars to pay your fine.

"Furthermore," he said as he threw another dollar into his hat, "I am going to fine everyone in the courtroom fifty cents for living in a town where a man has to steal bread in order to eat."

So he passed the hat around, and the old man, with the light of heaven in his eyes, left the courtroom with $47.50.

Christ Crucified
See page 97

Painful Pride
See page 195

Royal Water
See page 390

Checkmated
See page 365

ATTITUDE

> They [the Nazis] could take everything from me except one thing—and that was the attitude with which I chose to respond to the situation.
>
> *Victor Frankl*

The Response to Failure

Perhaps the most impressive and memorable quality of leaders is the way they responded to failure. Like Karl Wallenda, the great tightrope aerialist—whose life was at stake each time he walked the tightrope. . . .

Shortly after Wallenda fell to his death in 1978 (traversing a 75-foot-high wire in downtown San Juan, Puerto Rico), his wife, also an aerialist, discussed that fateful San Juan walk, "perhaps his most dangerous." She recalled: "All Karl thought about for three straight months prior to it was falling. It was the first time he'd ever thought about that, and it seemed to me that he put all energies into not falling rather than walking the tightrope." Mrs. Wallenda added that her husband even went so far as to personally supervise the installation of the tightrope, making certain that the guide wires were secure, "something he had never even thought of doing before."

. . . It became increasingly clear that when Karl Wallenda poured his energies into not falling rather than walking the tightrope, he was virtually destined to fail.

Warren Bennis and Burt Nanus, Leaders *(New York: Harper & Row, 1986), 69–70.*

Negative Test Results

I heard this story from Dr. Kenneth Chapin, pastor of the Main Street Baptist Church in Houston, Texas. Dr. Chapin is a dynamic preacher, and at one time he was the Billy Graham Chairman of Evangelism at Southwestern Baptist Theological Seminary.

When Dr. Chapin was a professor of homiletics he gave a

test to his young students, men who were going to be preachers. It was a scientifically designed word-association test. Dr. Chapin said that he was appalled to find bitterness and resentment in those men who were preparing for the ministry. Key words such as *truck driver* would invariably elicit derogatory responses such as *lazy*. Chapin said that he came to realize through this test—and subsequent conversations—that very often those who went into the ministry were negative, highly competitive people. In fact, they particularly did not like preachers!

The Beggar Is a King

One day Tauler, the fourteenth-century mystic and preacher, met a beggar. "God give you a good day, my friend," he said. The beggar answered, "I thank God I never had a bad one." Then Tauler said, "God give you a happy life, my friend."

"I thank God," said the beggar, "I am never unhappy." Tauler in amazement said, "What do you mean?"

"Well," said the beggar, "when it is fine, I thank God; when it rains, I thank God; when I have plenty, I thank God; when I am hungry, I thank God; and since God's will is my will, and whatever pleases him pleases me, why should I say I am unhappy when I am not?" Tauler looked at the man in astonishment. "Who are you?" he asked. "I am a king," said the beggar. "Where then is your kingdom?" asked Tauler. And the beggar answered quietly, "In my heart."

The Pastor's Story File, *vol. 3, no. 8 (June 1987): Attitude, 3/32.3.*

Paganini and One String

The great concert violinist Niccolò Paganini was standing before a packed house, surrounded by a full orchestra. He was playing a number of difficult pieces, and he came to one of his favorites, which was a violin concerto. Shortly after he was under way and the Italian audience was sitting in rapt attention, one of the strings on his violin snapped and hung down from the instrument. Relying on his genius, he improvised and played on the next three strings. To his surprise (and the conductor's as well), a second string broke. Now there were two dangling as he again began to improvise and play the piece on the two remaining strings. You guessed it! Almost at the end of this magnificent concerto, a third string snapped. Now there were three dangling, and he finished the piece on one string. The audience stood to their feet and applauded until their hands were numb. They never thought to ask for an encore; they expected to leave. But Paganini held his instrument high in the air and said, "Paganini and one string," and he proceeded to play an encore with the full orchestra. He made more music from one string than many violinists ever could do on four. The difference, of course, aside from his superb abilities, was one of attitude. Instead of falling to despair and self-pity, Paganini's splendid attitude allowed him to take a very difficult situation and turn it into a triumph. As we go through life, no matter what we pursue—music, athletics, education, business, homemaking, politics—attitude makes a world of difference. With reasonable qualifications, the saying "Attitude is everything" is amazingly true.

The Attitude of the Soul

A wise man once commented: "There is an invisible sculptor who chisels the face into conformity with the attitude of the soul!"

The In"sight" of Fanny Crosby

Fanny Crosby, that marvelous writer of many of our hymns, lived to be ninety-five years old. She was blind all her life, but what a perspective on life she had. When she was eight years old, she wrote,

Oh what a happy child I am although I cannot see,
I am determined that in this world, contented I will be.
How many blessings I enjoy that other people don't.
To weep and sigh because I'm blind I cannot and I won't.

On her grave in Bridgeport, Connecticut, there is a simple little headstone with the name "Aunt Fanny" and these words: "Blessed assurance, Jesus is mine. Oh, what a foretaste of glory divine."

A Slightly Opposed Wind
See page 42

Just Pretend We Won
See page 344

AUTHENTICITY

Seen on a card: "Old fishermen never die—they only smell that way." That surely describes false Christianity. It never dies; it only smells that way.

Ray Stedman

AUTHORITY

When masters and mistresses do not perceive: "We are not better than others and [yet] God has willed to honor us, not only by creating us in his image, but in addition by giving us a position which is above those who are subject to us." [I say] when people cannot grasp all of that, isn't it fitting to say that they have become entirely stupid?

John Calvin

AWARENESS

If we are keenly aware of the rock and what we are doing on it, if we are honest with ourselves and our capabilities and weaknesses, if we avoid committing ourselves beyond what we know is safe, then we will climb safely. For climbing is an exercise in reality. He who sees it clearly is on safe ground, regardless of his experience or skill. But he who sees reality as he would like it to be may have his illusions rudely stripped from his eyes when the ground comes up fast.

Royal Robbins, professional rock climber

B

BELIEF

A theological dogma might be refuted [to a person] a thousand times, provided, however, he had need of it. And he again and again accepts it as true.

Sigmund Freud

Those who believe that they believe in God, but without passion in their hearts, without anguish in mind, without uncertainty, without doubt, without an element of despair even in their consolation, believe only in the God idea, not God Himself.

Unamuno y Jugo, Spanish philosopher and writer

I believe in Christianity as I believe that the sun has risen, not only because I see it but because by it I see everything else.

C. S. Lewis

Believe what you believe . . . points to one of the great needs of Christians—which is not to believe more and better things but to believe what we already believe.

R. Kent Hughes

The Absolute Demand and Final Succor
See page 150

THE BIBLE

Become a man of the Book. Let everyone you work with see how much you love the Word of God.
Robert Coleman

John Owen and John Calvin knew more theology than John Bunyan or Billy Bray, but who would deny that the latter pair knew their God every bit as well as the former? All four, of course, were beavers for the Bible, which counts for far more anyway than a formal theological training.
J. I. Packer

I preached to . . . a thronged assembly. After I had done prayer and named my text, the rustling made by opening the Bibles all at once, quite surprised me: a scene I never was witness to before.
George Whitefield

One of the reasons why it needs no special education to be a Christian is that Christianity is an education itself. That is why an uneducated believer like Bunyan was able to write a book that has astonished the whole world.
C. S. Lewis

There are times when I have thought that the Bible was being read [in public readings] with less preparation than the notices—and with considerably less understanding.
John Blanchard

Now what is food for the inner man: not prayer, but the Word of God; and here again not the simple reading of the Word of God so that it only passes through our minds, just as water runs through a pipe, but considering what we read, pondering over it, and applying it to our hearts.
George Mueller

Take time to read His Word in His presence, that from it you may know what He asks of you and what He promises you. Let the Word create around you, create within you a holy atmosphere, a holy heavenly light, in which your soul will be refreshed and strengthened for the work of daily life.

Andrew Murray

The modern scientist has lost God amid the wonders of His world; we Christians are in real danger of losing God amid the wonders of His Word.

A. W. Tozer

God did not give us the Scriptures to increase our knowledge, but to change our lives.

D. L. Moody

A Bible which is falling apart usually belongs to someone who is not.

Charles H. Spurgeon

I want to know one thing—the way to heaven. . . . God Himself has condescended to teach the way. He hath written it down in a book. O give me that Book! At any price, give me the Book of God!

John Wesley

It is hard to understand Christians who think they can live a Christian life without ever reading their Bibles. It is impossible. Our memories do not retain and maintain what we need to know. We are built in such a way that we need refreshment and reminder—again and again.

Ray Stedman

If there be any mistakes in the Bible, there may well be a thousand. If there be one falsehood in that book, it did not come from the God of truth.

John Wesley

Here is the call in black and white; and I do but speak according to common sense when I say that if the Lord's call to you be written in the Bible, and it certainly is, you did not speak the truth when you said, "I would listen to it if it were spoken, but I cannot listen to it because it is written."

Charles H. Spurgeon

If thou art a learned man, take care lest with all thy erudite reading (which is not reading God's Word) thou forgettest perchance to read God's Word.

Karl Barth, imitating a biblical warning

If you have never been hurt by a word from God, it is probable that you have never heard God speak.

Amy Carmichael

Scripture Twist

An art enthusiast in New York had on the walls of his office an outstanding collection of etchings, including one of the Leaning Tower of Pisa. For a long time he noticed that it persisted in hanging crooked, despite the fact that he straightened it every morning. At last he spoke to the lady who cleaned up the room each night, asking her if she was responsible for its lopsided condition. "Why, yes," she said, "I have to hang it crooked to make the tower hang straight!" In the same fashion some twist the Scriptures in order to justify their own opinions or to make their imperfect lives appear right. Let us beware of thus deceitfully handling the Word of God, for to distort its meaning in order to fit our preconceived ideas is a dangerous practice and a terrible sin.

Our Daily Bread, *reprinted by Walk Thru the Bible Press, Inc., 1978.*

The License-Plate Trust

Author Frederick Buechner writes:

I remember sitting parked by the roadside once, terribly depressed and afraid about my daughter's illness and what was going on in our family, when out of nowhere a car came along down the highway with a license plate that bore on it the one word out of all the words in the dictionary that I needed most to see exactly then. The word was

TRUST. What do you call a moment like that? Something to laugh off as the kind of joke life plays on us every once in a while? The word of God? I am willing to believe that maybe it was something of both, but for me it was epiphany. The owner of the car turned out to be, as I'd suspected, a trust officer in a bank, and not long ago, having read an account I wrote of the incident somewhere, he found out where I lived and one afternoon brought me the license plate itself, which sits propped up on a bookshelf in my house to this day. It is rusty around the edges and a little battered, and it is also as holy a relic as I have ever seen.

Frederick Buechner, Telling Secrets *(San Francisco, Calif.: Harper San Francisco, 1991), 49–50.*

Let the Fool Choke on Them

This story is about an Episcopal clergyman who took a seat in a dining car on a train traveling along the Hudson River. It happened that opposite him was an atheist. Seeing the clerical collar of his companion, he set out to argue with him and began thus: "I see, sir, that you are a clergyman."

"Yes," was the reply. "I am a minister of the Gospel."

There was a pause, after which the atheist said: "I suppose, then, that you believe the Bible."

Now the clergyman was a man of sound, scriptural faith, so that he replied: "I do believe the Bible to be the Word of God."

Immediately there came the query: "But don't you find things in the Bible that you can't understand?"

The minister answered humbly: "Yes, there are places in the Scripture too hard for me to understand."

Whereupon the atheist retorted with an air of triumph, thinking he had his companion cornered: "Well, what do you do then?"

Quietly the minister went on eating his luncheon, which happened to be Hudson River shad, a delicious fish, but noted for the over-development of its bony structure. Then he looked up and said: "I do, sir, just as I do when eating this shad. When I come to the bones, I put them to the side of the plate and go on enjoying my lunch, leaving the bones for some fool to choke on."

Frank E. Gaebelein, The Practical Epistle of James *(Great Neck, N.Y.: Channel Press, 1955), 65–66.*

Saturated with the Word of God

Under his mother's guidance, Harry Ironside began to memorize Scripture when he was three. By age fourteen, he had read the Bible fourteen times, "once for each year." During the rest of his life he read the Bible through at least once a year. A pastor recalled a Bible conference at which he and Ironside were two of the speakers. During the conference the speakers discussed their approaches to personal devotions. Each man shared what he had read from the Word that morning. When it was Ironside's turn, he hesitated, then said, "I read the book of Isaiah." He was saturated with the Word of God.

Warren Wiersbe, Listening to the Giants *(Grand Rapids, Mich.: Baker, 1980), 198.*

The Passages That We Do Understand

Mark Twain once said: "Most people are bothered by those passages of Scripture which they cannot understand; but as for me, I have always noticed that the passages in Scripture which trouble me most are those which I do understand."

The Word Transforms

Dr. E. V. Rieu was a classical scholar and translator for many years. He rendered Homer into very modern English for the Penguin Classics. Rieu was sixty years old and a lifelong agnostic when the same firm invited him to translate the Gospels. His son remarked: "It will be interesting to see what Father makes of the four Gospels. It will be even more interesting to see what the four Gospels make of Father."

The answer was soon forthcoming. A year later, Rieu, convinced and converted, joined the Church of England.

In an interview with J. B. Phillips, Rieu confessed that he had undertaken the task of translation because of "an intense desire to satisfy himself as to the authenticity and spiritual content of the Gospels." He was determined to approach the documents as if they were newly discovered Greek manuscripts. "Did you not get the feeling," asked Canon Phillips, "that the whole material was extraordinarily alive?" The classical scholar agreed. "I got the deepest feeling," he replied. "My work changed me. I came to the conclusion that these words bear the seal of the Son of Man and God."

J. B. Phillips, The Ring of Truth *(New York: Macmillan), 74–75.*

The Silence of Science

It is said of Charles Haddon Spurgeon that one Sunday when the time for reading Scripture came, he left the Bible closed. "Some have found fault with me," he said, "contending that I'm too old-fashioned. I am always quoting the Bible and do not say enough about science. Well, there's a poor widow here who has lost her only son. She wants to know if she will ever see him again. Let's turn to science for the answer: Will she see him? Where is he? Does death end all?" There was a long pause. "We are waiting for an answer," he said. "This woman is anxious." Another long pause. "Nothing to say? Then we'll turn to the book!" Spurgeon clinched his point by reading the wonderful promises concerning Heaven and eternal life.

Our Daily Bread *(Grand Rapids, Mich.: Radio Bible Class).*

No Other Book

I have guided my life by the Bible for more than sixty years, and I tell you there is no book like it. It is a miracle of literature, a perennial spring of wisdom, a wonder of surprises, a revelation of mystery, an infallible guide of conduct, and an unspeakable source of comfort.

Pay no attention to people who discredit it, for I tell you that they speak without knowledge. It is the Word of God itself.

Study it according to its own direction. Live by its principles. Believe its message. Follow its precepts.

No man is uneducated who knows the Bible, and no one is wise who is ignorant of its teachings.

Samuel Chadwick

What You Read in the Light

See page 255

BLASPHEMY

God remains dead. How shall we, the murderers of all murderers, comfort ourselves? Must not we ourselves become gods simply to seem worthy of it?

Nietzsche

The "Dechristianization" of France

Historians of religion sometimes chart curious phases of a powerful "dechristianization" movement that has rolled over France. One of the explicit phases of dechristianization was launched in 1793–94 during the French Revolution. The dechristianizers wanted to abolish all vestiges of the Christian religion. Sundays were eliminated; Roman Catholic and Protestant clergy were ordered to abdicate their ministries, and churches by the hundreds were closed. So-called priestesses of "Reason" (i.e., local prostitutes) danced on the altar in Notre Dame before Robespierre called for another religion to replace the "Cult of Reason." He proposed as the new national religion the "Cult of the Supreme Being," which of course denied the divinity of Christ.

D. A. Carson and John D. Woodbridge, Letters along the Way *(Wheaton, Ill.: Crossway, 1993), 61–62.*

Blank Verse versus [Blank] Verse

David Mamet, of Chicago, and William Shakespeare, of Stratford-on-Avon, are playwrights separated by four centuries.

But to compare Mamet's *Glengarry Glen Ross,* also made into a movie, and Shakespeare's *Julius Caesar . . . is to note that while human greed and ambition remain fertile subjects for drama, writing styles change over 400 years. . . .*

Typically modern in its foul language, the original *Glengarry Glen Ross* contains 232 obscenities, including 152 variations of a favored four-letter word.

Old-fashioned *Julius Caesar* has somehow muddled through without a single blankety-blank.

Paul Galloway, "Blank Verse versus [Blank] Verse," Chicago Tribune, *12 October 1992.*

Dear Believer

"Dear Believer" is a "non-tract" published by the Freedom from Religion Foundation, of Madison, Wisconsin. Here are excerpts from the so-called tract:

Dear Believer,

You ask me to consider Christianity as the answer for my life. I have done that. I consider it untrue, repugnant, and harmful. . . .

If Christianity were simply untrue, I would not be too concerned. Santa is untrue, but it is a harmless myth that people outgrow. But Christianity, besides being false, is also abhorrent. It amazes me that you claim to love the God of the Bible, a hateful, arrogant, sexist, cruel being who can't tolerate criticism. I would not want to live in the same neighborhood as such a creature!

The biblical God is a macho male warrior. Though he said, "Thou shalt not kill," he ordered death for all opposition. He punished offspring to the fourth generation; ordered pregnant women and children to be ripped up; was partial to one race of people; judged women inferior to men; was a sadist who created a hell to torture unbelievers; created evil; spread dung on people's faces; sent bears to devour forty-two children who teased a prophet; punished people with snakes, dogs, dragons, swords, axes, fires, famine, and infanticide; and said fathers should eat their sons. Is that nice? Would *you* want to live next door to such a person?

And Jesus is a chip off the old block. He said, "I and my father are one," and he upheld "every jot and tittle" of the Old Testament Law. He preached the same old judgment: vengeance and death, wrath and distress, hell and torture for all nonconformists. He never denounced the subjugation of slaves or women. He irrationally cursed and withered a fig tree for being barren out of season. He mandated burning unbelievers. (The church has complied with relish.) He stole a horse. You want me to accept Jesus, but I think I'll pick my own friends, thank you.

I also find Christianity to be morally repugnant. The concepts of original sin, depravity, substitutionary forgiveness, intolerance, eternal punishment, and humble worship are all beneath the dignity of intelligent human beings. . . .

Harper's Magazine, *January 1991.*

Selective Selection

The Orthodox Church excommunicated writer Tolstoy in February 1901 . . . in view of the fact that he not only denied the divinity of Jesus Christ but asserted that to call him God or pray to him was the "greatest blasphemy." The truth is Tolstoy selected from the Old and New Testaments, the teachings of Christ and the Church, only those bits he agreed with and rejected the rest. He was not a Christian in any meaningful sense. Whether he believed in God is more difficult to determine since he defined "God" in different ways at various times. At bottom, it would seem, "God" was what Tolstoy wanted to happen, the total reform.

Paul Johnson, Intellectuals *(New York: Harper & Row, 1988), 130–131.*

Far from the Original Plan
See page 11

God Is Cold
See page 13

BODY OF CHRIST

Passing Fellowship

Writes Allan Emery in *A Turtle on a Fencepost:*

Thirtieth Street Station Philadelphia was as usual a scene of movement and activity. As I stood on the designated platform for "The Washington Express" I had time to notice those about me. A mother held a baby in her arms. An active three-year-old was being restrained from falling over the edge of the platform. All about this woman were suitcases and boxes. I knew she'd need help in boarding. . . .

Behind my conscious thoughts was the heaviness of heading off on a two-week selling trip. I liked selling, but today my two calls had been fruitless. New York was not buying cloth. I thought of Marian and her having to handle the affairs at home as well as our three children. . . . How much happier it would be to be heading home, but the trip was just beginning and my responsibility now was to sell and service my customers who were also my friends. . . .

Suddenly I realized that there was a beautiful whistling over the public address system. I knew the song. It was "How Great Thou Art." The words formed in my mind as the whistling continued. Where was the whistler? I looked about. Three minutes more before my train would be rushing into the station. Leaving my sample cases and bag, I raced up the stairs. I asked the stationmaster's assistant where the train announcer was. Then I ran down the stairs to the platform indicated, and there in a small glass cubicle was the whistler. . . . I smiled, and he nodded his head. The whistling ended abruptly. He announced: "The Washington Express . . ." I had to run back up to the concourse and down to the platform for my train. I waved, and the whistler waved while he was still announcing—but in that brief interchange there was membership. I had shared my appreciation, and he knew he was a blessing to a fellow believer and member of the family of God.

Allan Emery, A Turtle on a Fencepost *(Waco, Tex.: Word, 1979).*

The Smallest Bones in the Body

Do you know which bones are the smallest in the human body? There are three of them, and they are located in your middle ear. The average medical student finds them only with difficulty: the malleus, incus, and the stapes. You hear through these three bones only when they are in proper functioning order.

One of the most exciting surgeries I have ever witnessed is what is called a stapedectomy. It's an operation performed on the third smallest of these bones. I watched a man operated on who had not heard anything in 26 years. The patient was under partial anesthesia, and as the surgeon was about to join the bones, he said, "Howie, keep talking as I join the bones, and keep your eyes glued to his eyes." The instant the surgeon joined those bones, the man's eyes got like saucers. He said, "W-w-hat's that? Who's talking? Why . . . that's me! That's my voice I hear?" Tears streamed down the man's face, and a nurse wiped them away with some gauze.

You know, in the body of Christ size does not determine the significance of the members. A Christian may belittle himself because he's not an "arm." But he may be as a "stapes" for clearly transmitting communications, and he is an essential part of the body.

Howard G. Hendricks, Say It With Love *(Wheaton, Ill.: Victor), 40.*

A Can of Worms

In his book *Management for Your Church,* Norman Shawchuck remembers this incident from his childhood:

As a small boy I spent many hours with my father sitting on the banks of a river with nothing between us but a can of worms. Time after time, I used to view the worms with amazement. It always seemed, no matter how large the can, that they always would be found at the bottom, a tight, confused ball of wiggling, squirming worm-flesh. The ball seemed to be moving in every direction, but it really never went anywhere. I could never tell where one worm began and another ended, and when I reached in to grab one, the whole ball would react as though I had touched every one of them.

Often in my haste I would grab one and pull, only to wind up with a torn end of the worm, too small to use; and always my Dad would tell me I shouldn't jerk a worm out of the ball, but that I should take a firm grip on one and apply a steady pull, allowing the worm time to work itself free from the rest.

A local church is very much like a can of worms.

BOLDNESS

Offended by Boldness

Hugh Latimer, the great English Reformer, once preached before Henry VII and offended Henry with his boldness. Latimer was commanded to preach the following weekend and make an apology. On the following Sunday, after reading the text, Latimer addressed himself as he began to preach:

"Hugh Latimer, dost thou know before whom thou art this day to speak? To the high and mighty monarch, the king's most excellent majesty, who can take thy life if thou offendest; therefore, take heed that thou speakest not a word that may displease; but then consider well, Hugh, dost thou not know from whence thou comest; upon whose message thou art sent? Even by the great and mighty God, who is all-present, and who beholdeth all thy ways, and who is able to cast thy soul into hell! Therefore, take care that thou deliverest thy message faithfully."

He then gave Henry the same sermon he had preached the week before—only with more energy.

Charles H. Spurgeon, Metropolitan Tabernacle Pulpit, *vol. 10 (Pilgrim Publications), 407.*

The Stronger God

John G. Paton, a missionary to the New Hebrides Islands, often lived in danger as he worked among the aborigines who had never heard the gospel. At one time, three witch doctors, claiming to have the power to cause death, publicly declared their intentions to kill Paton with their sorcery before the next Sunday. To carry out their black art they had to get possession of some food he had partially eaten. Knowing this, Paton bravely asked for three plums. He took a bite out of each and then handed the fruit to the men who were plotting his death. Sunday dawned peacefully, and the missionary entered the village with a happy smile and a spring in his step. The natives looked at each other in amazement, thinking it couldn't possibly be Paton. Their "sacred men" admitted that they had tried by all their incantations to kill him. When asked why they had failed, they replied that the missionary was a sacred man like themselves but that his God was stronger than their demon helpers and had protected him! From then on, Paton's influence grew, and soon he was joyfully leading souls to the Lord.

BUSYNESS

Unbearable mental fatigue. Work alone could rest me; gratuitous work, or play . . . I am far from that. Each thought becomes an anxiety in my brain. I am becoming the ugliest of all things: a busy man.

Andre Gide

Mary had a little lamb,
'Twas given her to keep,
But then it joined the Baptist Church,
And died for lack of sleep!

Many churches judge their basis of success by the number of activities they have going.

Ray Stedman

The reason why so many of us are overwrought, tense, distracted, and anxious is that we have never mastered the art of living one day at a time. Physically we do live a day at a time. We can't quite help ourselves. But mentally we live in all three tenses at once—past, present, and future. . . . And that will not work! The load of tomorrow, added to that of yesterday, carried today makes the strongest falter.

William M. Elliott Jr.

The fastest time in modern existence is the instant when the traffic light turns green and the car behind you honks its horn.

Lloyd Perry

A Caravan of Complications

In her book *Gifts from the Sea,* Anne Morrow Lindbergh writes on the life of a homemaker:

The life I have chosen as wife and mother entrains a whole caravan of complications. . . . It involves food and shelter: meals, planning, marketing, bills and making the ends meet in a thousand ways. It involves not only the butcher, the baker, the candlestick maker, but countless other experts to keep my modern house with its modern "simplifications" (electricity, plumbing, refrigerator, gas stove, . . . dishwasher, radios, car, and numerous other labor-saving devices) functioning properly. It involves health: doctors, dentists, appointments, medicine, . . . vitamins, trips to the drugstore. It involves education, spiritual, intellectual, physical: schools, school conferences, car pools, extra trips for basketball or orchestra practice, tutoring, camps, camp equipment and transportation. It involves clothes: shopping, laundry, cleaning, mending, letting skirts down and sewing buttons on, or finding someone else to do it. It involves friends: my husband's, my children's, my own, and endless arrangements to get together: letters, invitations, telephone calls and transportation hither and yon.

C

CARE (GOD'S)

He Who Hath Led Will Lead

In firm, clear handwriting, Amy Carmichael's mother wrote "My Precious Child":

He who *hath* led *will* lead
All through the wilderness,
He who hath fed will surely feed. . . .
He who hath heard thy cry
Will never close His ear,
He who hath marked thy faintest sigh
Will not forget thy tear.
He loveth always, faileth never,
So rest on Him today—forever.

Elisabeth Elliot, A Chance to Die *(Old Tappan, N.J.: Fleming H. Revell, 1987), 55.*

Divine Radar

One night as Howard and Clarence Jones were driving along in a blizzard, suddenly C. W. felt compelled to stop the car right in the middle of the highway. And the next moment, scarcely six feet in front of their stopped vehicle, like a ghost in the silent whiteness, a train swooshed past.

The astonished pair again could only praise God for his unmistakable guidance, the unfailing "Divine Radar."

Lois Neely, Come up to This Mountain *(Wheaton, Ill.: Tyndale, 1980), 142.*

The Tender Care of the Shepherd

What does the Lord mean by referring to himself as the door? There is a beautiful story about the great preacher G. Campbell Morgan traveling across the Atlantic. As he was on the steamer, he noticed that among the passengers was Sir George Adam Smith, who was at that time the most famous Old Testament scholar. The greatest preacher of the day (Morgan) and the greatest Old Testament scholar (Smith) had a great time as they traveled together. Morgan said that among the tales Sir George told of the East was this one:

"He was one day traveling with a guide, and came across a shepherd and his sheep. He fell into conversation with him. The man showed him the fold into which the sheep were led at night. It consisted of four walls, with a way in. Sir George said to him, 'That is where they go at night?' 'Yes,' said the shepherd, 'and when they are in there, they are perfectly safe.' 'But there is no door,' said Sir George. 'I am the door,' said the shepherd. He was not a Christian man; he was not speaking in the language of the New Testament. He was speaking from the Arab shepherd's standpoint. Sir George looked at him and said, 'What do you mean by the door?' Said the shepherd, 'When the light has gone, and all the sheep are inside, I lie in the open space, and no sheep ever goes out but across my body, and no wolf comes in unless he crosses my body; I am the door.'"

G. Campbell Morgan, The Gospel According to John *(Old Tappan, N.J.: Fleming H. Revell, 1934), 177.*

God's Unusual Care

There are times when God chooses to protect his trusting children in unusual ways. Felix of Nola found this to be true when he was fleeing from his enemies. Calling on God for help, he took refuge in a cave. He had scarcely entered when a spider began to spin a web over the opening. The pursuers saw the spider's lacy veil blocking the entrance and didn't bother to look inside. They figured that no one could have entered without disturbing that delicate curtain of silk. So they left, and the life of one of God's noble men was spared for additional service for Christ. Felix of Nola later summed up his experience in these words, "Where God is, a spider's web is a wall; where He is not, a wall is but a spider's web."

Mother Hen

See page 58

Who Died?

See page 122

V. Raymond Edman's Funeral-to-Be

See page 394

The License-Plate Trust

See page 26

CARING

How May I Serve You?

Some of the most effective leaders and movements of evangelical Christianity have been birthed through Henrietta Mears's influence. She may well have been among the greatest Christians of the twentieth century. I am told by those who knew her that when she entered a room, people often had the feeling that she was saying to each person, "Where have you been? I've been looking all over for you." You would never have caught her walking into a room and saying in contrast, "I'm Henrietta Mears, Miss Sunday School. Anyone want my autograph?" Her secret? Like Christ, she was always asking, "How may I serve you?"

Gail MacDonald, High Call, High Privilege *(Wheaton, Ill.: Tyndale, 1981), 86.*

A Passion for Prisoners
See page 67

Banking on the Inner City
See page 68

CHALLENGE

The Red-Shirt Challenge

A few months after Giuseppe Garibaldi marched into Rome, the French government dispatched an army that would total forty thousand by June 1849, when it broke through the barricades and advanced into the papal city. Sitting on his horse and wearing a bloodstained red shirt as his enemy drew nearer, Garibaldi paused and addressed his loyalists in Saint Peter's Square: "This is what I have to offer those who wish to follow me: Hunger, cold, the heat of the sun. No wages, no barracks, no ammunition. Continued skirmishes, forced marches, and bayonet fights." Then, his voice resounding with confidence, he added: "Those of you who love your country and love glory, follow me!"

Gay Talese, Unto the Sons *(New York: Alfred A. Knopf, 1992), 155.*

A Slightly Opposed Wind

A ship, like a human being, moves best when it is slightly athwart the wind, when it has to keep its sails tight and attend to its course. Ships, like men, do poorly when the wind is directly blowing, pushing them sloppily on their way so that no care is required in steering or in the management of sails; the wind seems favorable, for it blows in the direction one is heading, but actually, it is destructive, because it induces a relaxation in tension and skill. What is needed is a wind slightly opposed to the ship, for then tension can be maintained, and juices can flow and ideas can germinate; for ships, like men, respond to challenge.

The Pastor's Story File, *vol. 3, no. 8 (June 1987): Attitude, 5/32.5.*

CHANGE

So profoundly revolutionary is this new civilization that it challenges all our old assumptions. Old ways of thinking, old formulas, dogmas, and ideologies, no matter how cherished or how useful in the past, no longer fit the facts.

Alvin Toffler

CHARACTER

Since most of us would rather be admired for what we do, rather than for what we are, we are normally willing to sacrifice character for conduct, and integrity for achievement.

Sydney M. Harris

Tell me with whom you are contending, and I'll tell you who you are.

Goethe

Distance Makes One Great

Montaigne once remarked that at home he was reckoned as just a scribbling country laird, in the neighboring town as a man of recognized business ability, farther afield as a noted author, and that the longer one traveled from him the greater he became.

Right and Wrong Matter More than Life

Studdert-Kennedy, an Anglican minister, pastor at Worcester and a chaplain in the first World War, a man who interpreted the Christian life for so many, wrote from the trenches in France to his son: "The first prayer I want my son to learn to say for me is not 'God keep Daddy safe' but 'God make Daddy brave, and if he has hard things to do, make him strong to do them.' Life and death don't matter, my son. Right and wrong do. Daddy dead is Daddy still, but Daddy dishonored before God is something awful, too bad for words. I suppose you'd like to put in a bit about safety, too, old chap, and Mother would. Well, put it in, but afterwards, always afterwards, because it really does not matter near so much. Every man, woman and child should be taught to put first things first in prayer, both in peace and war, and that, I believe, is where we have failed."

W. A. Criswell, Daniel *(Grand Rapids, Mich.: Zondervan, 1968), 114.*

George Mueller's Secret

A story is told of George Mueller, a man who exercised a wide influence for God. When someone came to him and asked, "What has been the secret of your life?" Mueller hung his head and said, "There was a day when I died." Then he bent lower and said, "Died to George Mueller, his opinions, preferences, tastes, and will; died to the world, its approval or censure; died to the approval or blame even of brethren or friends. . . ."

Christian Character Counts

The following is from a Christian publication entitled *The Cross and the Flag:*

Max Jukes lived in New York state; he was an unbeliever. Jukes married a girl of like character and training. From this union came 1,029 descendants.

Three hundred died prematurely. Of the ones that lived 100 were sent to the penitentiary for an average of 13 years each. One hundred and ninety were public prostitutes, 100 were alcoholics. The family cost the state $1,200,000. They made no contribution to society.

Jonathan Edwards lived in the same state. He believed in God and Christian training; he married a girl of like character. From this union, 729 descendants were traced. Three hundred became preachers, 65 college professors, 13 presidents of universities, 60 became authors, 3 were elected to congress, and one became vice president of the United States.

If All Were Discovered

Sir Arthur Conan Doyle, author of *Sherlock Holmes,* used to playfully tell how he sent a telegram to each of twelve friends, all men of great virtue and reputation and considerable position in society. The message was worded: "Fly at once, all is discovered." Within twenty-four hours, the story goes, all twelve had left the country.

A Bribe and a Breach

The Great Wall of China is a gigantic structure that cost an immense amount of money and labor. When it was finished, it appeared impregnable. But three times the enemy breached it—not by breaking it down or going around it. They did it by bribing the gatekeepers.

Dr. Harry Emerson Fosdick, in referring to this historical fact, had this to say: "It was the human element that failed. What collapsed was character which proved insufficient to make the great structure men had fashioned really work."

Life Goes Better with Affliction

See page 2

The Strength of Character

See page 236

Deflower and Devour

See page 235

A Greater King

See page 210

A Wartime Romance

See page 231

CHARM

Charm is often despised, but I can never see why. No one has it who isn't capable of genuinely liking others, at least at the actual moment of meeting and speaking. Charm is always genuine; it may be superficial but it isn't false.

P. D. James

CHILDREN

When a child manages to assume that air of adult cynicism and élan, then nature is alarmed. A form of moral clowning has occurred. Funny maybe, but a little sinister.

Lance Morrow

We Are Men

Pastor Kent Hughes, senior pastor of College Church in Wheaton, is an avid fisherman. Once his then-four-year-old grandson Joshua was in the basement "helping" his father clean up from a construction project. As Joshua followed his dad around, he said, "We are men. We work and we fish!"

The Ultimate Business Venture

The education of children for God is the most important business done on earth. It is the one business for which the earth exists. To it all politics, all war, all literature, all money-making ought to be subordinated; and every parent especially ought to feel, every hour of the day, that next to making his own calling and election sure, this is the end for which he is kept alive by God—this is his task on earth.

Robert L. Dabney, Discussions: Evangelical and Theological, *vol. 1 (London: Banner of Truth, 1967), 691.*

When the Children Were Little

You will not be able to influence your children next year the way you can this year. Annie Dillard writes of a friend whose children had long been raised:

The children were all very young, very small, and they

were playing with buckets, and pouring water, and piling sand on each other's feet. I remember thinking, *This is it, now, when the children are little. This will be a time called "when the children were little."* I couldn't hear anything through the window; I just saw them. It was morning. They were all three blond and still curly headed then, and the sun was behind them.

Annie Dillard, Teaching a Stone to Talk *(New York: Harper & Row, 1982), 187.*

Nothing Doing!

Dr. Robert Coles, noted child psychiatrist, recalls this incident during his training at Children's Hospital in Boston. He was assigned to a ten-year-old boy, described to him as having a "learning problem." The boy's behavior was rude, impatient, demanding, and without self-control during their sessions together. Dr. Coles tried reasoning with him, hoping to discover why he was behaving as he was, but each session only increased his own feelings of helplessness. Weeks passed in the same fashion—the boy having his way in the doctor's office and the doctor without a clue about how to help.

One snowy day when the boy arrived, he casually took off his galoshes and threw them, dripping slush, onto the doctor's chair. Dr. Coles recalls that he instinctively felt rage welling up inside of him but at the same time heard an inner voice telling him that he must discover *why* the boy had acted as he had. Fighting to control himself, he walked to the chair, picked up the wet galoshes, put them in the hall outside his office, and slammed the door hard. When the boy responded that he wanted them inside the office, the doctor shouted, "Nothing doing!"

They were words the doctor had often heard his parents use during his own childhood when their patience had worn thin with his behavior. An astonishing thing happened: The boy sat down, looking as close to repentant as the doctor had ever seen him, and asked if there was something he could use to clean up the mess he had made. It was at that point that the doctor began to be able to help the boy.

Dr. Robert Coles had discovered something the Bible taught long ago: We do no favor to children when we let them get away with bad behavior.

Robert Coles, "Discipline," Family Weekly, *27 March 1983.*

Treated as Gods
See page 130

D. L. Moody's Two and a Half Conversions
See page 83

Immense Design
See page 89

CHOICES

Your choice is not a piece of theatre. You are not a thistledown in the wind. There are good and sufficient reasons in history to know that this is a choice you should make, and you are called upon to make it. Choose once and for all justification.

Francis A. Schaeffer

I am not a determinist. But I also believe that the decisive choice is seldom the latest choice in the series. More often than not, it will turn out to be some choice made relatively far back in the past.

Arnold Toynbee

It may be true that there are two sides to every question, but it is also true that there are two sides to a sheet of flypaper, and it makes a big difference to the fly which side he chooses.

Christian Medical Society Journal, *Spring 1977.*

CHRIST

There is more in Jesus, the Good Shepherd, than you can pack away in a shepherd. He is the good, the great,

the chief Shepherd; but he is much more. Emblems to set him forth may be multiplied as the drops of the morning, but the whole multitude will fail to reflect all his brightness. Creation is too small a frame in which to hang his likeness. Human thought is too contracted, human speech too feeble, to set him forth to the full. When all the emblems in earth and heaven shall have described him to their utmost, there will remain a someone not yet described. He is inconceivably above our conceptions, unutterably above our utterances.
Charles H. Spurgeon

Preach any Christ but a crucified Christ and you will not draw men for long.
R. A. Torrey

There were times when [Christ] did not behave as a Christian.
George Bernard Shaw

The impeccability of Jesus Christ can be illustrated as follows: Christ's human nature is described by a copper wire, which a man can bend; Christ's divine nature is described as a railroad track, which no man can bend; sin is described as bending; if the copper wire were welded to the railroad track, neither could be bent. In the same way, Christ, though He had a human nature, could not sin: He is impeccable.
J. D. Pentecost

Jesus is a V.I.P. to be honored but not believed or followed. In America, he is a custom but not the true Christ; a captured hero of casual civil religion but not Lord of our lives.
Lloyd Ogilvie

Christ Is Everything

One evening the great conductor Arturo Toscanini conducted Beethoven's Ninth Symphony. It was a brilliant performance. At the end of it, the audience went absolutely wild. They clapped, whistled, and stomped their feet, caught up in the greatness of the performance. As Toscanini stood there, he bowed and bowed and bowed, then acknowledged his orchestra. When the ovation finally began to subside, Toscanini turned and looked intently at his musicians. He was almost out of control as he whispered, "Gentlemen! Gentlemen!" The orchestra leaned forward to listen. Was he angry? They could not tell. In a fiercely enunciated whisper, Toscanini said, "Gentlemen, I am nothing!" This was an extraordinary admission since Toscanini was blessed with an enormous ego. He added, "Gentlemen, you are nothing." They had heard that same message before in rehearsal. "But Beethoven," said Toscanini in a tone of adoration, "is everything, everything, everything!"

When we truly believe and repent of our sins and realize all that Christ has done for us, we must say "I am nothing . . . but he is everything, everything, everything."

Vernon C. Grounds, "Faith to Faith Failure, or What's So Good about Success?" Christianity Today, *9 December 1977.*

Agnus Dei

Several years ago, while at a speaking engagement in San Diego, I visited the Timkin Art Museum.

I had heard they had an El Greco painting of St. Peter holding the keys to the kingdom. I paid my money, walked into the museum, located the painting, and looked at it in admiration. Then I turned around. On the opposite wall was a small, ancient, walnut-colored painting. The date said 1525. As I looked closely at the painting, I saw that it was a lamb almost photographically rendered. Around the lamb's head, barely perceptible, was a halo. As I looked more intently, I saw that the lamb's legs were tied, and, shrouded by the dark background, it was lying on a cross. The title of the painting was *Agnus Dei,* Latin for "Lamb of God."

Deprived of Rights

M. Dupin, in his tract on the trial of Jesus before the Sanhedrin, has satisfactorily shown that throughout the whole course of [Jesus'] trial the rules of the Jewish law of procedure were grossly violated and that the accused was deprived of rights belonging even to the meanest citizen. Jesus was arrested in the night, bound as a malefactor, beaten before his arraignment and struck in open court during the trial; he was tried on a feast day and before sunrise; he was compelled to incriminate himself, and this under an oath or solemn judicial abjuration; and he was sentenced on the same day of the conviction. In all these particulars the Jewish law was wholly disregarded.

Simon Greenleaf, An Examination of the Testimony of the Four Evangelists *(Boston: Little & Brown, 1946).*

CHRISTMAS

The Magical Day

If those who knew the Churchills could choose one moment of the year to relive, it would be Christmas. For them, in a nostalgic chamber of the mind, it will always be that magical eve when the entire family has gathered here, including Jack and Goonie and their young, with Randolph home from Eton, the girls rehearsing an amateur theatrical, Clementine helping the servants build a snowman, and Churchill upstairs writing one of his extraordinary love letters to her. ("The most precious thing in my life is your love for me. I reproach myself for many shortcomings. You are a rock & I depend on you & rest on you.") Presents, hidden all week in an out-of-bounds closet, the "Genie's cupboard," are about to appear. Fires crackle; the house is hung with holly, ivy, laurel, and yew; the Christ child gazes down lovingly from a large Della Robbia plaque. Now the double doors between the library and the drawing room are flung open, and the Christmas tree is revealed in all its splendor, a hundred white wax candles gleaming, the scent of pine and wax like a breath of rapture, and Churchill, the benign sovereign in this absolutely English castle, leads the way across the threshold toward his annual festival of joy "with my happy family around me," as he would later write, "at peace within my habitation."

James Hastings, ed., The Speaker's Bible, *vol. 17 (Grand Rapids, Mich.: Baker, 1971), 782.*

There's Room Anyway

It was a children's Christmas play, and as the children portrayed the story of the birth of Christ, they came to the time when Joseph and Mary could find no room in the inn. At this particular place, the boy playing Joseph was carried away by the part, and he began to passionately plead with the innkeeper, pointing to Mary and explaining their difficult straits. Finally, the other boy who was playing the innkeeper said, "Aw, shucks, I'm not supposed to do this, but come in anyway."

Sankey's Song

The stocky, mustached man nervously paced the deck of a Delaware River steamer, unbuttoning his frock coat, and regularly removing his derby to wipe his brow. He looked much older than his thirty-five years.

It was unseasonably warm for a Christmas Eve.

The man stared at the passing Pennsylvania shoreline, thinking of his family in Newcastle, some three hundred miles to the west, whom he might not see this Christmas, unless he made his train connection in Philadelphia. Christmas 1875.

"Pardon me, sir."

"Aren't you Ira Sankey, the gospel singer?"

He smiled at the lady and her husband. . . . He thought

he was gracious to acknowledge that he was, indeed, Ira D. Sankey.

"We've seen your pictures in the newspapers."

He had not wanted to be recognized: Not today, not tonight. He was tired and fretful and warm. Fact of the matter was, he was angry and provoked with Mr. Moody.

"We thought you were still in England!" said the lady.

"We returned last week, Madam," Mr. Sankey replied in his resonant baritone voice. And if Mr. Moody hadn't insisted on more conferences and meetings, he thought, he would have been home by now for Christmas with his family. Instead he was a prisoner on a river steamer.

"Mr. Sankey, would you sing for us? It is Christmas Eve, and we'd love to hear you."

Mr. Sankey said he would sing, and his presence was announced loudly across the deck. As the people gathered, he pondered what he might sing. He wished he had his portable pump organ which had become an integral counterpart to his singing. But no matter. He would sing a Christmas carol or two, unaccompanied. Perhaps he would get the passengers to sing along with him.

He tried to shed his melancholy. He was a famous person, whether he liked it or not, and he was not normally shy about his gifts. He was known on two continents as the gospel singer, the song leader and soloist working with Dwight L. Moody, who was surely the greatest evangelist of the day. Perhaps God had intended it this way—for him to be in this place, on this boat, at this particular time.

"I thought I would sing a carol or two." Then he added, "But somehow I feel I should sing another song."

"Sing one of your own songs!" shouted someone unseen. "Sing 'The Ninety-And-Nine'!" commanded another.

"No, thank you very much, but I know what I must

sing." He was smiling broadly now, feeling much better about himself and the situation, enjoying his congregation. "I shall sing a song by William Bradbury. And if you know it, as I'm sure many of you do, hum along with me."

Sankey began to sing.

"Savior, like a shepherd lead us,
Much we need Thy tender care;
In Thy pleasant pastures feed us,
For our use Thy folds prepare:
Blessed Jesus, blessed Jesus!
Thou has bought us, Thine we are."

He sang all three verses. There was uncommon silence, and Ira Sankey felt it would be inappropriate to sing anything else. So he simply wished everyone a Merry Christmas, and the people murmured a greeting in return. The silence returned, and he was alone.

"Your name is Ira Sankey?"

"Yes." He recognized neither the voice nor the man.

The man came out of the shadows. He was about his own age, with a beard beginning to turn gray, and comfortably but not fastidiously dressed. Perhaps he was in sales. . . .

"Were you ever in the Army, Mr. Sankey?"

"Yes, I was. I joined up in 1860."

"I wonder if you can remember back to 1862. Did you ever do guard duty, at night, in Maryland?"

"Yes, I did!" Sankey felt a stab of memory and excitement. "It might have been at Sharpsburg."

"I was in the Army, too. The Confederate Army. And I saw you that night."

Sankey looked at him warily.

"You were parading in your blue uniform. Had you in my sights, you standing there in the light of the full moon, which was right foolish of you, you know." The man paused. "Then you began to sing."

Amazingly, Sankey remembered.

"You sang the same song you sang tonight, 'Savior Like a Shepherd Lead Us.'"

"I remember."

"My mother sang that song a lot, but I never expected no soldier to be singing it at midnight on guard duty. Especially a Union soldier." The man sighed. "Obviously I didn't shoot you."

"And obviously I am grateful." Sankey smiled.

"I always wondered who you were. Who it was I didn't kill that night, on account of his singing an old Sunday school song."

Sankey just shook his head.

"Frankly, up until tonight, the name of Ira Sankey wouldn't have meant much to me. Guess I don't read the paper like I should. I didn't know you'd turn out to be so famous!" The man smiled for the first time. "But I reckon I would have recognized the voice and the song anyplace."

Sankey reflected on what might have been.

"Do you think we could talk a mite?" asked the man. "I think you owe it to me. Very little has gone right for me. Not before the war. Not during it. And not since."

Ira Sankey put an arm around his former enemy. They found a place in a quiet corner of the deck to sit and chat. Sankey's impatience and anger had passed. He no longer fretted that he might be delayed in seeing his family. Christmas would soon be here. It always came but sometimes in the strangest of ways.

The night was still warm but it seemed filled with brighter stars. Sankey even thought he heard the sound of angels' voices: singing of course, and singing the Good News.

John Gillies, Christian Herald.

CHURCH

The great irony is that today we alleviate our disappointment with the contemporary Church by pointing back to the New Testament Church—which was a great disappointment to begin with!
Richard John Neuhaus

Tell me what the world is saying today, and I'll tell you what the church will be saying seven years from now.
Francis A. Schaeffer

It would seem that the church only prepares to move out after it has been run over from behind.
Leighton Ford

A church becomes institutionalized when its members are related primarily to it as an institution rather than to Christ.

A church becomes institutionalized when it becomes more concerned with the correctness of belief than with the quality of living that belief demands.
Richard Thomas

Outside this Christian church there is no salvation or forgiveness of sins, but everlasting death and damnation; even though there may be a magnificent appearance of holiness.
Martin Luther

Abandoning the Call

American pastors are abandoning their posts, left and right, and at an alarming rate. They are not leaving their churches and getting other jobs. Congregations still pay their salaries. Their names remain on the church stationery, and they continue to appear in pulpits on Sundays. But they are abandoning their posts, their *calling.* They have gone whoring after other gods. What they do with their time under the guise of pastoral ministry hasn't the remotest connection with what the church's pastors have done for most of twenty centuries.

A few of us are angry about it. We are angry because we have been deserted. Most of my colleagues who defined ministry for me, examined, ordained, and then installed me as a pastor in a congregation, a short while later walked off and left me, having, they said, more urgent things to do. The people I thought I would be working with disappeared when the work started. Being a pastor is difficult work; we want the companionship and counsel of allies. It is bitterly disappointing to enter a room full of people whom you have every reason to expect share the quest and commitments of pastoral work and find within ten minutes that they most definitely do not. They talk of images and statistics. They drop names. They discuss influence and status. Matters of God and the soul and Scripture are not grist for their mills.

The pastors of America have metamorphosed into a company of shopkeepers, and the shops they keep are churches. They are preoccupied with shopkeepers' concerns—how to keep the customers happy, how to lure customers away from competitors down the street, how to package the goods so that the customers will lay out more money.

Some of them are very good shopkeepers. They attract a lot of customers, pull in great sums of money, develop splendid reputations. Yet it is still shopkeeping; religious shopkeeping, to be sure, but shopkeeping all the same. The marketing strategies of the fast-food franchise occupy the waking minds of these entrepreneurs; while asleep they dream of the kind of success that will get the attention of journalists. "A walloping great congregation is fine, and fun," says Martin Thornton, "but what most communities really need is a couple of good saints." The tragedy is that they may well be there in embryo, waiting to be discovered, waiting for sound training, waiting to be emancipated from the culture of the mediocre.

Eugene H. Peterson, Working the Angles *(Grand Rapids, Mich.: Eerdmans, 1987), 1–2.*

The Church Costs Too Much
See page 179

CLARITY

The Idea Has Been Grasped
See page 65

No Va
See page 74

COMFORT

Mother Hen

A poultry owner in eastern Oregon had a mother hen of whom she was proud. One day a chicken hawk swooped down upon the band of baby fowls of which the old hen was the mother. The hen didn't squawk and run, calling upon her offspring to follow her; she faced the hawk to fight, and so fierce was her onslaught as she buried her bill beneath the hawk's left wing that the hawk seemed surprised and dazed. It feebly rose, flew aimlessly against a clothesline, and then dropped into the garden stone dead. Ordinarily the hen was timid. It was the "mother" in her that rose to the great emergency. How much it means when God says, "As one whom his mother comforteth, so will I comfort you" (Isaiah 66:13).

Louis Albert Banks, Windows for Sermons.

The Full Circle of Comfort

When their son died unexpectedly, author Joseph Bayly and his wife, Mary Lou, were comforted by a poem Dietrich Bonhoeffer wrote while imprisoned by the Nazis. The poem was sent to them by the young woman the Baylys' son loved and had planned to marry. Bonhoeffer had written the poem, "New Year, 1945," for the young woman he loved—just three months before he was executed.

Several years ago—thirty years after Bonhoeffer's death and twelve years after Joe Bayly's son's death—Joe received a letter from a young Massachusetts pastor whom he met. The pastor had been visiting a woman seriously ill in a Boston hospital over a period of time, and finally he gave the woman a copy of Bayly's book, *Heaven*. The next day, the woman said that she had stayed awake late the previous night to read it, and said that she was comforted and helped by the book. Shortly afterward, the woman died.

This woman, the pastor said, was Maria von Wedemeyer-Weller, Bonhoeffer's fiancée at the time of his imprisonment and death.

John 14—Comfort for Generations
See page 202

COMMITMENT

Very early I saw my parents working for their people, bearing their burdens. Day and night. They did not have to say a word to me about Christianity. I saw it in action.

Evangeline Booth, who took her parents' place in leading the Salvation Army

I am now about to take Orders and my degree, and go into the world. What will become of me I know not. All I can say is I look for perpetual conflicts and struggles in that life and hope for no other peace, but only a cross, while on this side of eternity.

George Whitefield

Some want to live within the sound
Of church or chapel bell.

I want to run a rescue shop
Within a yard of hell.
C. T. Studd

If God has really done something in Christ on which the salvation of the world depends, and if He has made it known, then it is a Christian duty to be intolerant of everything which ignores, denies, or explains it away.

James Denney

Father, take my life, yea, my blood if Thou wilt, and consume it with Thine enveloping fire. I would not save it, for it is not mine to save. Have it, Lord, have it all. Pour out my life as an oblation for the world. Blood is only of value as it flows before Thine altar.

Jim Elliot

Prayed a strange prayer today. I covenanted with the Father that He would do either of two things: either glorify Himself to the utmost in me or slay me. By His grace I shall not have His second best.

Jim Elliot

Church Hitchhikers

With his thumb, a hitchhiker says, "You furnish the gas, the car, attend to the repairs and upkeep, supply the insurance, and I'll ride with you. But if you have an accident, I'll sue you for damages."

It sounds pretty one-sided, but one wonders how many hitchhikers there are in many organizations—even churches. Many church members seem to say, "You go to the meetings, you serve on boards and committees, you do the paperwork, you study the issues and take care of things that need doing, and I'll just go along for the ride. If things don't suit my fancy, I will complain, criticize, and probably get out and hitchhike to another group."

Tested by Fire

St. Francis of Assisi, at the risk of his life, went with some of his followers to visit the Sultan. "Sire," said a number of the priests of Mahomet to the Sultan, "thou art expert in the law and art bound to maintain and guard it. We command thee by Mahomet, who gave it to us, that the heads of these men be cut off." Francis, who had already by his fearless yet loving, Christlike spirit, made a deep impression upon the Sultan, replied to him, "Your priests will not talk with me; perhaps they would be more ready to act. Have a fire lighted, and I will go into the fire with them, and you will see by the results which faith is the truest and the holiest." When Francis began to speak, there were a number of priests standing round him, but before he had finished, they had quietly taken themselves off. The idea had filled them with horror. The Sultan, perceiving their absence, remarked sarcastically, "I do not think that any of my priests are inclined to face flames and torture for the defense of their faith."

James Hastings, ed., The Speaker's Bible, *vol. 17 (Grand Rapids, Mich.: Baker, 1971), 219.*

No Turning Back

Here is a testimony of a young preacher from Zimbabwe:

I'm part of the fellowship of the unashamed. I have the Holy Spirit's power. The die has been cast. I have stepped over the line. The decision has been made; I'm a disciple of *His!* I won't look back, let up, slow down, back away, or be still.

My past is redeemed; my present makes sense; my future is secure. I'm finished and done with low living, sight walking, small plannings, smooth knees, colorless dreams, tamed visions, worldly talking, cheap giving, and dwarfed goals.

I no longer need preeminence, prosperity, position, promotions, plaudits, or popularity. I don't have to be right, first, tops, recognized, praised, regarded, or rewarded. I know life by faith, lean on His presence, walk by patience, am uplifted by prayer, and I labor with power.

My face is set, my gait is fast, my goal is heaven, my road is narrow, my way rough, my companions few, my guide reliable, my mission clear. I cannot be bought, compromised, detoured, lured away, turned back, deluded, or delayed. I will not flinch in the face of sacrifice, hesitate in the presence of the enemy, ponder at the pool of popularity, or meander in the maze of mediocrity.

I won't give up, shut up, let up, until I have stayed up, stored up, prayed up, paid up, and preached up for the cause of Christ. I am a disciple of Jesus. I must go 'til He comes, give 'til I drop, preach 'til all know, and work 'til He stops me. And when He comes for His own, He will have no problem recognizing me. . . . My banner will be clear.

No Reserve, No Retreat, No Regrets

Quite a few years ago, William Borden went to Yale University as an undergraduate and afterward became a missionary candidate planning to work in China. When he made his decision to invest his life in this service, many of his friends thought him foolish. He had come from a good family. He had wealth and influence. "Why are you going to throw away your life in some foreign country," they asked, "when you can have such an enjoyable and worthwhile life here?" But William Borden of Yale had heard the call of God. While in Egypt, on the way to China and even before he had much of a chance to do anything, he became sick. Soon it was evident to everyone, including himself, that he would die. At this point Borden could have said to himself, "What a waste. My friends were right. I could have stayed in New Haven." But Borden did not think this way.

As he lay on his deathbed in Egypt, he scribbled a farew note to his friends that was in some sense his epitaph. The note said, "No reserve, no retreat, and no regrets."

James Montgomery Boice, The Sermon on the Mount *(Grand Rapids, Mich.: Zondervan), 311.*

As Long As It Doesn't Rain

Too often we are like the young man who poured out his heart's devotion in a letter to the girl of his dreams. He wrote: "Darling, I would climb the highest mountain, swim the widest stream, cross the burning desert, die at the stake for you. PS I will see you on Saturday, if it doesn't rain."

Parable of the Wild Duck

The Danish philosopher Søren Kierkegaard has a parable of a wild duck that is a splendid illustration of how the soul declines from its ideals and becomes satisfied with lower standards.

With his mates this duck was flying in the springtime northward across Europe. During the flight he came down in a Danish barnyard where there were tame ducks. He enjoyed some of their corn. He stayed for an hour, then for a day, then for a week, then for a month, and finally, because he relished the good fare and the safety of the barnyard, he stayed all summer. But one autumn day when the flock of wild ducks were winging their way southward again, they passed over the barnyard, and their mate heard their cries. He was stirred with a strange thrill of joy and delight, and with a great flapping of wings he rose in the air to join his old comrades in their flight.

But he found that his good fare had made him so soft and heavy that he could rise no higher than the eaves of the barn. So he dropped back again to the barnyard and said to himself, "Oh, well, my life is safe here, and the food is good." Every spring and autumn when he heard the wild ducks honking, his eyes would gleam for a moment and he would begin to flap his wings. But finally the day came when the wild ducks flew over him and uttered their cry, and he paid not the slightest attention to them.

All of Me

Dr. Donald Hubbard, pastor of Calvary Baptist Church in New York City, told of spending a very difficult week at a youth camp some years ago. The teenagers from his church were at that time very cool and hardened toward the gospel. On the final night, they had a campfire where the idea was to toss a stick into the fire, symbolic of one's life and commitment to Christ. The evangelist spoke and the offer was made, and no one responded. There was a girl with a disability there who had been shunned by the group all week because she was so hard to talk to—not that the kids were mean to her, they simply ignored her. Finally, she stood and faced the group, looking at each one, and said, "I don't know why God made me this way, but he can have all of me."

No Retreat

When Cortez landed at Vera Cruz in 1519 to begin his conquest of Mexico with a small force of 700 men, he purposely set fire to his fleet of eleven ships. His men on the shore watched their only means of retreat sink to the bottom of the Gulf of Mexico. With no means of retreat, there was only one direction to move, forward into the Mexican interior to meet whatever might come their way. In paying the price for being Christ's disciple, you too must purposefully destroy all avenues of retreat. Resolve that whatever the price for being His follower, you will pay it.

Walter Henricksen, Disciples Are Made—Not Born.

We Died before We Came

When James Calvert went out as a missionary to the cannibals of the Fiji Islands, the captain of the ship sought to turn him back. "You will lose your life and the lives of those with you if you go among such savages," he cried. Calvert only replied, "We died before we came here."

David Augsburger, Sticking My Neck Out *(March 1979), 154.*

Total Commitment

See page 217

The Eyes of Faith

See page 155

COMMUNICATION

A man does not know what he is saying until he is not saying.

G. K. Chesterton

Conversation: A fair for the display of the minor mental commodities, each exhibitor being too intent upon the arrangement of his own wares to observe those of his neighbor.

Ambrose Bierce

Conversation: Something that starts the moment you put your foot through the television set.

Anonymous

The Idea Has Been Grasped

Gordon McDonald tells a story about a student in one of New England's private schools who was expelled by the headmaster. When the alumnus father of the boy heard what had happened, he took a plane to Boston, walked unceremoniously into the headmaster's office, and said these exact words: "You must damn well think you're the one who runs this place." The headmaster looked at him and replied, "Sir, your language is crass and your grammar is atrocious, but you have definitely grasped the idea."

Hardheaded Explanation

A man went into a bank and said he wanted some money. The teller asked him to sign a check. The man said that he wouldn't sign a check. The teller said, "If you won't sign a check, I won't give you any money."

So the man went across the street to another bank, and the same conversation took place. But after the exchange, the teller reached across the counter, took the man by the ears, and banged his head three times on the counter, at which time the man took out a pen and signed a check.

He then returned to the first bank and said, "They gave me money across the street."

"Why did they do that?"

"They explained it to me."

Elizabeth Barrett Browning's Love Letters

Elizabeth Barrett Browning's parents disapproved so strongly of her marriage to Robert Browning that they disowned her. Almost weekly Elizabeth wrote love letters to her mother and father asking for a reconciliation. They never once replied. After ten years of letter writing, Elizabeth received a huge box in the mail. She opened it. To her dismay and heartbreak, the box contained all of her letters to her parents. Not one of them had ever been opened! Today those love letters are among the most beautiful in classical English literature. Had her parents opened and read only a few of them, a reconciliation might have been effected.

The Alliance Witness, *14 January 1976, 5.*

If You Have One

George Bernard Shaw once wrote to Winston Churchill: "Enclosed are two tickets to the opening night of my play. Bring a friend . . . if you have one."

Churchill replied, "Dear Mr. Shaw, unfortunately I'll be unable to attend the opening night of your play due to a prior engagement. Please send me tickets for a second night . . . if you have one."

No Va
See page 74

COMPASSION

A Passion for Prisoners

Pascal was a university professor when he was thrown into a Madagascar prison after a Marxist coup. While in prison he became a Christian.

After his release, Pascal began a small import-export company, but he kept returning to prison to preach the gospel to the men he had met there and others who had arrived since. During one such visit in early 1986, he walked past the infirmary and was shocked to see more than fifty naked corpses piled on the screened veranda, identification tags stuck between their toes.

Pascal went to the nurse. Had there been an epidemic? he asked. Of sorts, he was told. Prisoners were dying by the dozens of malnutrition.

Pascal left the prison in tears. He tried to get help to feed the starving inmates, but his own church was too poor, and there were no relief agencies to assist. So he began cooking food in his own kitchen and taking it to the prison.

Today, Pascal and his wife feed prisoners every week, paying for the food out of the earnings from their small business. Without benefit of a government agency or even a theme song, this little platoon makes all the difference for seven hundred prisoners in Madagascar.

Charles Colson, Kingdoms in Conflict *(Grand Rapids, Mich.: William Morrow/Zondervan, 1987), 255.*

Banking on the Inner City

Robert Lavelle's neighborhood is one of the most isolated, forgotten, and helpless communities in America—the inner city.

"People tell me, 'You're crazy, man,'" says Lavelle, "but I have to do it." He is referring to his savings and loan and real estate operations in Pittsburgh's Hill District, an area where wrecking ball, drug dealer, and welfare check are a way of life. Many of Lavelle's bank loans go to people who would be unable to obtain credit elsewhere. Though federal regulators and others have urged him to move to a "better" location, Lavelle refuses.

Dwelling House Savings and Loan goes further than financial loans, however, for Lavelle takes a personal interest in his clients. If they fall behind in payments, he visits their homes to help them figure out budgets and challenges them to set an example of financial responsibility for their children. This appeal to self-respect and accountability is the key to helping needy people, he says. It is the only way to break the cycle of their poverty. Handouts enslave people. Teaching them how to manage and extend their resources helps set them free. . . .

Lavelle, who lives within walking distance of his office, is quick to tell his clients about spiritual freedom as well, but his faith is most evident by what he does, not by what he says. "For me," he says, "being a Christian is a matter of obedience—and that means helping people in need as the Holy Spirit leads."

Charles Colson, Kingdoms in Conflict *(Grand Rapids, Mich.: William Morrow/Zondervan, 1987), 258–259.*

Care for the Enemy

From *Through The Valley of the Kwai,* Ernest Gordon recalls this incident:

We found ourselves on the same track with several carloads of Japanese wounded (after the Kwai prison camp). These unfortunates were on their own without medical care. No longer fit for action in Burma, they had been packed into railway cars which were being returned to Bangkok.

They were in a shocking state. I have never seen men filthier. Uniforms were encrusted with mud, blood, and excrement. Their wounds, sorely inflamed and full of puss, crawled with maggots. The maggots, however, in eating the decaying flesh, probably prevent gangrene.

It was apparent why the Japanese were so cruel to their prisoners. If they didn't care . . . for their own, why should they care for us?

The wounded looked at us forlornly as they sat with their heads resting against the carriages, waiting for death. They had been discarded as expendable, the refuse of war. These were the enemy. They were more cowed and defeated than we had ever been.

Without a word, most of the officers in my section unbuckled their packs, took out part of their rations and a rag or two, and with water canteens in their hands, went over to the Japanese train.

Our guards tried to prevent us, bawling, *"No goodka! No goodka!"* But we ignored them and knelt down by the enemy to give water and food, to clean and bind up their wounds. Grateful cries of *"Aragatto!"* ("Thank you!") followed us when we left. . . .

I regarded my comrades with wonder. Eighteen months ago they would have joined readily in the destruction of our captors had they fallen into their hands. Now these same officers were dressing the enemy's wounds.

We had experienced a moment of grace, there in those bloodstained railway cars. God had broken through the barriers of our prejudice and had given us the will to obey His command, "Thou shalt love."

The Pastor's Story File *(July 1986): Love.*

There's Room Anyway
See page 52

A Generous Solution
See page 180

COMPASSIONLESS

I did not attend his funeral, but I wrote a nice letter saying I approved it.

Mark Twain

The Dead Weight of Humanity

Margaret Sanger . . . was in many ways a Social Darwinist throwback in her criticism of programs (both private and governmental) that provided "medical and nursing facilities to slum mothers." She complained that "the work of the maternity centers in the various American cities . . . is carried on among the poor . . . among mothers least able, through poverty and ignorance to afford the care and attention necessary for successful maternity." She opposed the "dysgenic tendency [of supporting] maternity among the very classes in which the absolute necessity is to discourage it." She argued that "such philanthropy . . . brings with it, as I think the reader must agree, a dead weight of human waste. Instead of decreasing and aiming to eliminate the stocks that are most detrimental to the future of the race and of the world, it tends to render them to a menacing degree dominant."

Marvin Olasky, Abortion Rites *(Wheaton, Ill.: Crossway, 1992), 257–258.*

The High Cost of Success
See page 402

COMPLACENCY

Martin Luther's Parable or Dream of Satan
See page 122

COMPROMISE

Some of you have just enough Christianity to be miserable in a nightclub, and not enough to be happy in a prayer meeting.
Donald Grey Barnhouse

Community Standards of Sin

A cartoon in *The New Yorker* magazine: Two clean-shaven middle-aged men are sitting together in a jail cell. One inmate turns to the other and says: "All along, I thought our level of corruption fell well within community standards."

Dynamic Preaching, *vol. 5, no. 2 (February 1990): 9.*

A Teachable, Compromising Spirit

Abraham Lincoln once got caught up in a situation in which he wanted to please a politician, so he issued a command to transfer certain regiments. When Secretary of War Edwin Stanton received the order, he refused to carry it out. He said the president was a fool. When Lincoln was told of Stanton's response, he replied, "If Stanton said I'm a fool, then I must be, for he is nearly always right. I'll see for myself." As the two men talked, the president quickly realized that his decision was a serious mistake. Without hesitation he withdrew it. A teachable, compromising spirit is often a major key in defusing conflict.

Purging the Jewish Element

See page 10

Freud's Departure from Vienna

See page 87

CONFESSION

We must lay before [God] what is in us, not what ought to be within us.
C. S. Lewis

> Tell [God] all that is in your heart, as one unloads one's heart to a dear friend. . . . People who have no secrets from each other never want for subjects of conversation; they do not . . . weigh their words, because there is nothing to be kept back. . . . Blessed are they who attain to such familiar, unreserved intercourse with God.
>
> *François Fenelon*

CONFIDENCE

We Shall Fight Them

Here is Winston Churchill's famous "We shall fight them . . ." speech in its context:

To the war cabinet [Churchill] said, "I have thought carefully in these last days whether it was part of my duty to consider entering into negotiations with that man," and concluded: "If this long island story of ours is to end at last, let it end only when each one of us lies choking in his own blood upon the ground." He spoke to them, to the House, and then to the English people as no one had before or ever would again. He said: "I have nothing to offer but blood, toil, tears, and sweat." Another politician might have told them: "Our policy is to continue the struggle; all our forces and resources will be mobilized." This is what Churchill said:

"Even though large tracts of Europe and many old and famous states have fallen or may fall into the grip of the Gestapo and all the odious apparatus of Nazi rule, we shall not flag or fail. We shall go on to the end. We shall fight in France, we shall fight on the seas and oceans, we shall fight with growing confidence and growing strength in the air, we shall defend our island, whatever the cost may be, we shall fight on the beaches, we shall fight on the landing grounds, we shall fight in the fields and in the streets, we shall fight in the hills; we shall never surrender."

William Manchester, The Last Lion *(Boston: Little Brown and Company, 1983), 6.*

Lie By till Morning

It happened a good many years ago aboard the steamship *Central America.* The *Central America* was steaming from New York to San Francisco, where she encountered difficulty in the high seas and became disabled. She sent out her distress signals, and another vessel close enough began to move and became disabled. She sent out her distress signals, and another vessel close enough began to move in her direction. It was nightfall when the would-be rescue ship arrived nearby and sent a message: "What is wrong?"

The captain of the *Central America* sent back word: "We are in bad repair. We may go down. Please lie by till morning."

And the would-be rescue ship sent another message back. The captain said, "Let me take your passengers on board now."

The captain of the *Central America* did not want to do that. It was nighttime. He feared some might be lost in all the confusion, and he simply replied, "Lie by till morning."

The captain of the would-be rescue ship sent word another time. "You had better let me take them now."

And a third time came the reply, "Lie by till morning."

Less than two hours later the lights disappeared because the *Central America* went down with loss of the total onboard count. Because it was thought that there was ample time later for a rescue. That points out the danger of delay. There was good news brought to the folks on the *Central America,* both crew and passengers, as a rescue vessel appeared and then said, "Can we take you on board?" And there was no doubt shouting and joy. Good news. But the good news delayed became tragedy.

Rev. David Meschke, "Good News," College Church in Wheaton, 28 October 1990.

Turning Out for Fools

While out in his carriage, John Wesley met another man in a carriage on the road. The man knew Wesley and disliked him, so he didn't turn out but kept in the middle of the road. Mr. Wesley cheerfully gave the man all the road, riding into the ditch instead. As they passed each other the man said, "I never turn out for fools," and Mr. Wesley said, "I always do."

Nothing Can Harm Me

See page 84

Tested by Fire

See page 61

CONFUSION

No Va

Former senator Paul Simon (D, Ill.) delighted in finding examples of trade opportunities lost because of the unwillingness of U.S. firms to speak the language of potential customers. For example, when trying to figure out why the Chevrolet Nova wasn't selling well in Latin America, General Motors discovered that *no va* in Spanish means "It does not go."

CONSCIENCE

> The conscience may be likened to a sundial that is made for the sun, even as the conscience, rightly directed, reflects God's will.
>
> *Donald Grey Barnhouse*

Guilt That Could Never Be Forgiven

Albert Speer was once interviewed about his last book on ABC's *Good Morning, America.* Speer, the Hitler confidant whose technological genius was credited with keeping Nazi factories humming throughout World War II, in another era might have been one of the world's industrial giants. The only one of twenty-four war criminals tried in Nuremburg to admit his guilt, Speer spent twenty years in Spandau prison.

The interviewer referred to a passage in one of Speer's earlier writings: "You have said the guilt can never be forgiven, or shouldn't be. Do you still feel that way?"

The look of pathos on Speer's face was wrenching as he responded: "I served a sentence of twenty years, and I could say, 'I'm a free man, my conscience has been cleared by serving the whole time as punishment.' But I can't do that. I still carry the burden of what happened to millions of people during Hitler's lifetime, and I can't get rid of it. This new book is part of my atoning, of clearing my conscience."

The interviewer pressed the point: "You really don't think you'll be able to clear it totally?" Speer shook his head. "I don't think it will be possible."

For thirty-five years Speer has accepted complete responsibility for his crime. His writings were filled with contrition and warnings to others to avoid his moral sin. He desperately sought expiation. All to no avail.

Charles Colson, Who Speaks for God? *(Wheaton, Ill.: Crossway, 1985), 76–77.*

A So-Called Bothered Conscience

The Internal Revenue Service received a letter from a conscience-stricken taxpayer. It said, "Dear Sir: My conscience bothered me. Here is the $175.00 that I owe in back taxes." There was a PS at the bottom that read, "If my conscience still bothers me, I'll send the rest." This taxpayer's response to a red warning light is not only humorous but also illustrates an important truth: Our consciences can become insensitive.

Right and Wrong Matter More than Life
See page 43

CONTENTMENT

A Few Cents and the Smile of God

Years ago Louis Evans served as pastor of the First Presbyterian Church in Hollywood. In his congregation was a gifted surgeon. As a sensitive Christian he was alert to the working of God in his life. Repeatedly he sensed that God was calling him to the mission field. After much inner struggle, he finally surrendered to the voice of God. He went to Korea, little known at that time . . . to set up a medical missionary practice. His pastor, Dr. Evans, stopped off to visit him during a world tour. On the day he arrived, his doctor friend was preparing himself for surgery on an eight-year-old child. Dr. Evans observed through a window in the small hut where the operation took place. The minutes turned into half hours, and the half hours turned into a total of almost three hours. Finally he stepped back from the operating table of the makeshift surgery room and said, "She will be all right now," leaving the child in the care of the national helpers. He went outside and joined his pastor. As they walked along Evans asked, "How much would you have received for that operation back in the States?" "Oh, $500 to $750 is the going rate, I guess." As they talked, his pastor observed that his lips were purple from the strain and his hands were shaking from the exacting labor and tension related to this delicate surgery. He said, "How much for this one?" "Oh, a few cents—a few cents and the smile of God." And then the surgeon put his hand on Pastor Evans's shoulder, shook it slightly, and added, "But man, this is living."

J. Daniel Baumann, An Introduction to Contemporary Preaching *(Grand Rapids, Mich.: Baker, 1972), 172–173.*

Truly Happy and Content

A story is told of a king who was suffering from a malady and was advised by his astrologist that he would be cured if the shirt of a contented man was brought for him to wear. People went out to all parts of the kingdom after such a person, and after a long search they found a man who was really happy and content. But he did not even possess a shirt.

CONVERSION

Advice in caring for new believers: "Don't dig up the seed to see if it is growing."

Dr. L. Nelson Bell

No man can be said to be truly converted to Christ who has not bent his will to Christ. He may give intellectual assent to the claims of Christ and may have had emotional religious experiences; however, he is not truly converted until he has surrendered his will to Christ as Lord, Savior, and Master.

Billy Graham

The Law must be laid upon those that are to be justified, that they may be shut up in the prison thereof, until the righteousness of faith come—that, when they are cast down and humbled by the Law, they should fly to Christ. The Lord humbles them, not to their destruction, but to their salvation. For God woundeth that He may heal again. He killeth that He may quicken again.

Martin Luther

But the Master comes, and the foolish crowd
Never quite can understand
The worth of a soul and the change that's wrought
By the touch of the Master's hand.

Myra Brooks Welch

Bogus Conversions

Take a moment to think about the trauma inflicted by parents who insist that their child "accept Christ" before he or she is capable of making such a decision. Joseph Bayly has rightly decried the bogus conversions anxious parents have perpetrated—especially when the child is told, "Now Jesus is in your heart, and don't let anyone tell you differently." Very well, *if* the child has truly accepted Christ. But there can be literal hell to pay if the parent is wrong.

Joseph Bayly, Out of My Mind *(Grand Rapids, Mich.: Zondervan, 1993), 72–73.*

John Wesley's True Conversion

John Wesley's early life suggested that he had everything working toward his becoming a man of God. He was the son of a clergyman named Samuel Wesley and had a godly, dedicated mother, Susanna. After a privileged upbringing, he attended Charterhouse and Oxford and became a professor of Greek and logic at Lincoln College. He also served as his father's assistant and was ordained by the church.

At Oxford he was a member of the Holy Club, a group so nicknamed by the other students because they seriously attempted to cultivate their spiritual lives. Finally, he even accepted an invitation from the Society for the Propagation of the Gospel to become a missionary to the American Indians in Georgia, where he utterly failed. It was a great fiasco. Forced to return to England, he wrote: "I went to America to convert the Indians; but, oh, who shall convert me?"

Not all was lost, however, because in his earlier travels to America he had encountered some Moravians whose living faith deeply impressed him. So upon his return to London, he sought out one of the leaders and, to use Wesley's words, was "clearly convinced of unbelief, of the want of that faith whereby alone we are saved." So it was on the evening of May 24, 1738, that Wesley entered this famous statement in his journal:

"In the evening I went very unwillingly to a society in Aldersgate Street where one was reading Luther's preface to the Epistle to the Romans. After a quarter before nine, while he was describing the change which God works in the heart through faith in Christ, I felt my heart strangely warmed. I felt I did trust in Christ, Christ alone, for salvation; and an assurance was given me, that He had taken away my sins, even mine, and saved me from the law of sin and death."

Billy Sunday's Conversion

One Sunday in Chicago, a group of professional ballplayers were leaving a saloon when they saw a crowd gathered on the sidewalk. A group of people were playing instruments, singing gospel hymns, and testifying of Christ's power to save. Harry Monroe of the Pacific Garden Mission gave a brief message. One of the men was deeply moved as boyhood memories raced through his mind. He thought of his godly mother's praying for him and of the old church he had attended. With tears in his eyes he said, "Boys, I'm through! I'm going to turn from my sin and come to Christ. I guess it's hard for you to understand, but we've come to a parting of the ways." Some mocked him, while others stood in stunned silence. He went to the mission and there called upon God for mercy. Later he testified, "I staggered out of my sins into the outstretched arms of the Savior. I instantly became a new creature in him!" That ballplayer was Billy Sunday. Leaving his high-paying job, he began serving the Lord at the YMCA for seventy-five dollars a month. Later he went into evangelistic work. Unconventional and sometimes sensational in his preaching, he soon attracted huge crowds. Thousands were converted as he urged them to do what he had done—come to Christ and receive his free salvation.

The Most Valuable Discovery

In 1847 Sir James Simpson of Edinburgh discovered the use of chloroform as an anesthetic in surgery. Some have claimed that this was the most significant discovery of modern medicine. In his later years, Sir James was lecturing at Edinburgh University, and a student asked, "What do you consider to be the most valuable discovery of your lifetime?"

Sir James answered quickly: "My most valuable discovery was when I discovered myself a sinner and that Jesus Christ was my Savior."

Radical Shift

Moshe Rosen of Jews for Jesus tells this account of the power of God in changing lives:

Once I preached to a congregation in Southern California where I had conducted an extensive ministry 30 years ago.

Afterwards a man approximately the same age as I approached me. "Do you remember me?" I searched his face, not recognizing him until he told me his name. Then slowly it came back to me. Thirty years earlier, when I had first met him, "Ted" had been one of the "pretty boys," a denizen of Hollywood Boulevard.

At thirty, Ted had been a confirmed homosexual. His father, a rabbi, had done his best, but religion had not kept the young man from his vice. Ted was miserable, but in ten years of psychotherapy he had received no help to change. Finally the therapist had told him, "You are a homosexual, and that is all you ever can be. You may as well come to terms with it."

Even with the benefits of a moral ancestral religion, an excellent education, and the best psychiatric help available, Ted had been helpless to change. Worse yet, despite the best the world could offer him, Ted was at a point of total despair when we first met. Then he prayed with me to receive Christ. For a while he attended our Bible study, but then he suffered a moral lapse and stopped attending. I moved from Southern California to take up a missionary post in New York City and heard no more about him. Yes, now I remembered Ted, and until that moment at the church I had considered my ministry to him a failure.

Ted interrupted my reverie by introducing me to his wife, daughter, son-in-law and two grandchildren. He was not ashamed to say in their hearing that in Christ God had set him straight and had given him the victory over a besetting sin. He said, "Don't let anyone ever tell you that they were born gay, like I used to say about myself. When you're born again, you have the power to be whatever God wants you to be." What a victory!

"The Power of His Coming," The Jews for Jesus Newsletter, *vol. 2, no. 5751 (1990): 1–2.*

The Old Heart

On one occasion, Dr. Christiaan Barnard, the first man in the world to perform a heart transplant operation, was talking to one of his transplant patients, Dr. Philip Blaiberg. Suddenly Barnard asked, "Would you like to see your old heart?" Blaiberg said that he would. At eight o'clock one evening the men stood in a room of the Groote Schuur Hospital, in Johannesburg, South Africa. Dr. Barnard went up to a cupboard, took down a glass container and handed it to Dr. Blaiberg. Inside that container was Blaiberg's old heart. For a moment he stood there stunned into silence—the first man in history ever to hold his own heart in his hands. Finally, he spoke and for ten minutes plied Dr. Barnard with technical questions. . . . Then he turned to take a final look at the contents of the glass container, and said, "So this is my old heart, that caused me so much trouble." He handed it back, turned it away and left it forever.

Now the point of that illustration is this: conversion is not a transplant. Our old heart (or nature) is not taken away and replaced by a new one, so that we can look back and say, "There was a day when I had an old heart, an old nature, but now it has been taken away and can never again cause me any trouble." The fact of the matter is that our old nature remains entrenched within us, incurably antagonistic to the things of God and constantly promoting "envious desires."

John Blanchard, The Truth for Life *(West Sussex, England: H. E. Walter, 1982), 231.*

New Life, New Crest

We are told that the family crest of the great metaphysical poet, John Donne, a crest which he himself sported in his earlier days, was a sheaf of snakes. And this symbolized well the brood of temptations that twisted and turned in his bosom in his youth, and which in some of his poetry he so graphically and almost revoltingly describes. But to him there came a great change. Suddenly the power of the eternal overshadowed him. Suddenly he came to experience the explosive power of a new affection. The mercy and the might of Jesus Christ delivered him from a sin-ridden nature. Then he replaced his old crest with a new one. He canceled the sheaf of snakes, and in its stead he put Christ crucified, Christ crucified against the background of an anchor.

James Hastings, ed., The Speaker's Bible, *vol. 17 (Grand Rapids, Mich.: Baker, 1971), 169.*

Fallen So Low

During the first half of this century, Mel Trotter had a great influence for Christ in the Chicago area as well as the rest of the country. Before his conversion, Trotter had fallen so low as an alcoholic that on the evening he finally stumbled into the Pacific Garden Mission and found Christ, he was under the influence of the alcohol he had purchased with the shoes he had taken from his little girl's feet as she lay in her coffin. So wondrous was the effect of God's abounding grace in his life that eight years later Trotter was ordained to the Presbyterian ministry, became an outstanding evangelist, and founded more than sixty-seven rescue missions coast to coast.

It Takes More than a Rhinoceros-Hide Whip

One of David Livingstone's first converts was an African chief, Sechale, who thought he could make his tribesmen believe by force. So he suggested one day to Livingstone, "I shall call my head man, and with our whips of rhinoceros hide, we will soon make them all believe together." He did not realize that the natural man is dead spiritually and that a rhinoceros-hide whip cannot make a man believe; only the Holy Spirit can do so.

D. L. Moody's Two and a Half Conversions

D. L. Moody is said to have once returned from a meeting with a report of "two and a half conversions."

"Two adults and a child, I suppose?" queried his host.

"No, two children and an adult," said Mr. Moody. "The children gave their whole lives. The adult had only half of his left to give."

CONVICTION

> We like fallen heroes because, when we watch the pay TV channels, we don't have to squirm so much.
> *Alistair Begg*

COURAGE

To the Rescue

A young English aristocrat happened on an inviting pond and found it irresistible. Shedding his clothes, he jumped into the refreshing, cool water for a pleasant swim. Unexpectedly seized by fierce cramps, he was unable to swim back to shore. Desperately he cried for help. Another young man working in a field nearby heard the noise and rushed to the pond as quickly as possible. Seeing the young boy slipping beneath the surface, he jumped in and saved him.

The next day the young fellow who had come to the rescue was approached by the father of the boy he had saved. A rich man, he wanted to show his gratitude. Eventually his conversation coaxed from the rough-hewn young man an expression of his hidden desire to study medicine, so the grateful father promised to pay for him to go to medical school. He went, and he excelled.

According to Peter Marshall, some years later Winston Churchill became gravely ill with pneumonia in Africa and, knowing of the wonder drug penicillin, asked for Dr. Alexander Fleming, the discoverer of penicillin, to come to his aid. So Fleming came by express flight, administered the drug, and saved Churchill's life—for the second time! For it was Fleming who had rescued Churchill from the pond years earlier.

Nothing Can Harm Me

When Chrysostom was brought before the Roman emperor, the emperor threatened him with banishment if he remained a Christian. Chrysostom replied, "Thou canst not banish me, for this world is my father's house." "But I will slay thee," said the emperor. "Nay, thou canst not," said the noble champion of the faith, "for my life is hid with Christ in God." "I will take away thy treasures." "Nay, but thou canst not, for my treasure is in heaven and my heart is there." "But I will drive thee away from man, and thou shalt have no friend left." "Nay, thou canst not, for I have a friend in heaven from whom thou canst not separate me. I defy thee, for there is nothing that thou canst do to hurt me."

Courage under Fire

Lupercio Taba was a fearless pastor in Colombia. One Sunday he was preaching from his pulpit when a man appeared at a side window of the church, aimed a pistol at Lupercio and ordered him to stop preaching. The congregation, seeing the danger, dove to the floor and hid under the pews. Lupercio, however, never flinched. He went right on preaching the gospel. The man fired four shots at him. Two shots went past his head, one on one side, one on the other, and lodged in the wall behind him. Two shots went past his body, one under his arm, one under the other, and also lodged in the wall. The would-be assassin then dropped his gun and fled. Lupercio, still unmoved, continued his sermon.

Dave Howard, By the Power of the Holy Spirit *(Downers Grove, Ill.: InterVarsity), 43–44.*

God Is God

When Henry Martyn had completed his translation of the New Testament, he determined to gain for it the approval of the Persian Court. But first he had to face the ordeal of an interview with the Shah's Vizier, without whose permission he could not gain access to the Shah. He attended the Vizier's levee bearing the precious Book. All eyes were turned on the solitary Frank. In the court, where verbal swordsmanship was the art of arts, a discussion was inevitable, but Martyn knew that an angry discussion would ruin his chance of seeing the face of the Shah.

He could not prevent the very clash that he dreaded. "There was a most intemperate and clamorous controversy kept up for an hour or two; eight or ten on one side and myself on the other." He came unfriended; the Vizier encouraged the attack, and the veneer of polish was broken through as they set upon him.

"Their vulgarity in interrupting me in the middle of a speech; their utter ignorance of the nature of an argument;

their impudent assertions about the law and the gospel, neither of which they had ever seen in their lives, moved my indignation a little."

His indignation, but not his fear. This Martyn seems to have forgotten how to fear. The Vizier, who had at first set them by the ears, came up at last to the angry group, stilled the hubbub and put to Martyn before them all a crucial question. He challenged the stranger to recite the Moslem creed. "Say God is god and Mohammed is the Prophet of god."

It was an electric moment, the whole court at attention.

"I said, 'God is God' but added, instead of 'Mahomet is the prophet of God,' 'and Jesus is the Son of God.' They all rose up as if they would have torn me in pieces, snarling out one of the classic fighting cries of the Moslem world, 'He is neither begotten nor begets.' 'What will you say when your tongue is burnt out for this blasphemy?'"

He heard them in silence.

"My book, which I had brought expecting to present it to the king, lay before Mirza Shufi, the Vizier. As they all rose up after him to go, some to the king and some away, I was afraid they would trample on the book; so I went in among them to take it up, and wrapped it in a towel before them; while they looked at it and me with supreme contempt."

James Hastings, ed., The Speaker's Bible, vol. 9 *(Grand Rapids, Mich.: Baker, 1974), 394.*

Deflower and Devour
See page 235

Standing Up to Death
See page 101

Tested by Fire
See page 61

The Red-Shirt Challenge
See page 42

A Greater King
See page 210

Turning Out for Fools
See page 74

The Pattern of Suffering
See page 406

COWARDICE

Freud's Departure from Vienna

When invading Nazis broke into Freud's flat in Vienna, Austria, Freud's wife put her housekeeping money on the table: "Won't the gentlemen help themselves?" It required intervention by Roosevelt and Mussolini—and a ransom of 250,000 Austrian shillings—to get the old man permission to leave. He had to sign a statement testifying he had been well-treated, to which he appended the words "I can heartily recommend the Gestapo to anyone." The Germans were delighted. The bitter joke was beyond them. So was pity. Freud's four aged sisters chose not to move: all died in the gas ovens later.

Paul Johnson, Modern Times, *revised ed. (New York: HarperCollins, 1991), 456.*

CREATION

Saint Augustine taught that God created the world out of nothing. Creation was something like the magician pulling a rabbit out of a hat. Except God didn't have a rabbit and He didn't even have a hat.

R. C. Sproul

Before Birth

Canadian psychiatrist Thomas Verny has collected evidence, . . . published in *The Secret Life of the Unborn Child* (Summit Books), that a fetus can feel emotion and respond intellectually months before birth. Item: a test shows that as early as twenty-five weeks a fetus will jump in time to the beat of an orchestra drum. It will grimace when sour liquids are injected into the amniotic sac, and double the rate of sucking when the liquid is sweet. Item: a mother in Oklahoma City discovers her one-year-old daughter reciting breathing instructions for Lamaze childbirth. But the terminology and technique are observably Canadian, not American. The mother had taken Lamaze while living in Toronto more than a year earlier.

This proves nothing; it does warn us to be careful about killing fetuses because they don't feel pain and aren't human.

One other question: could a not-yet-human inherit a sinful nature? Yet David says, "Surely I have been a sinner from birth, sinful from the time my mother conceived me" (Ps. 51:5).

So it seems to me that I fall into the company of Christians who believe a fetus is human, a living soul from the moment of conception.

One theologian suggested recently that for the second group (those who believe that at some point in time in utero the fetus becomes a living soul), abortion is defensible.

My son Tim, who has helped my thinking in this whole area of abortion, has a good answer for that.

"If a hunter is out looking for deer and sees something moving through the trees, he won't think it's either a deer or a human being and shoot. It's up to him to be sure it's a deer before he shoots, or he'll be in court for manslaughter.

"Isn't it logical that if we don't know exactly when a fetus becomes a living soul, a human being, we have no right to terminate its life on the chance that it may not be human yet?"

Joseph Bayly, Out of My Mind *(Grand Rapids, Mich.: Zondervan, 1993), 182–183.*

Do It Again

G. K. Chesterton has made these observations about monotony:

The sun rises every morning. I do not rise every morning; but the variation is due not to my activity, but to my inaction. Now, to put the matter in a popular phrase, it might be true that the sun rises regularly because he never gets tired of rising. His routine might be due, not to a lifelessness, but to a rush of life. The thing I mean can be seen, for instance, in children, when they find some game or joke they specially enjoy. A child kicks his legs rhythmically through excess, not absence, of life. Because children have abounding vitality, because they are in spirit fierce and free, therefore they want things repeated and unchanged. They always say, "Do it again"; and the grown-up person does it again until he is nearly dead. For grown-up people are not strong enough to exult in monotony. But perhaps God is strong enough to exult in monotony. It is possible that God says every morning "Do it again" to the sun; and every evening "Do it again" to the moon. It may not be automatic necessity that makes all daisies alike; it may be that God makes every daisy separately, but has never got tired of making them. It may be that He has the eternal appetite of infancy; for we have sinned and grown old, and our Father is younger than we.

G. K. Chesterton, Orthodoxy *(New York: John Lane, 1914), 60–61.*

Immense Design

Whittaker Chambers dated his initial break with Communism to the time his young daughter smeared porridge on her face. Chambers found himself looking at her "intricate, perfect ears." He saw immense design, not a chance coming together of atoms—and "at that moment, the finger of God was first laid upon my forehead." Millions of Americans, at the moment they see an intricately made unborn child sucking his thumb, may hear not a great and powerful wind nor an earthquake but a gentle whisper.

Marvin Olasky, Abortion Rites *(Wheaton, Ill.: Crossway, 1992), 306.*

The Great Raveled Knot

The "great raveled knot," as the famous English psychologist Sir Charles Sherrington called the brain, is about the size of a grapefruit and weighs approximately three pounds. It is composed of some twelve to fourteen billion cells. . . .

The astronomical number of units is only the starting point of the brain's incredible complexity. Each of these billions of cells sends out branching tentacles to form interconnections with neighboring cells; one cell might be connected to as many as 10,000 of its neighbors, with which it is constantly exchanging data impulses. It is the almost limitless number of cells-plus-interconnections that makes the human brain an intellectual instrument of unparalleled supremacy.

John P. McNeel, The Brain of Man.

Divine "Hand"work

See page 92

The Spider's Design

See page 92

CREATIVITY

It is wrong to think of science as a mechanical record of facts, and it is wrong to think of the arts as remote and private fancies. What makes each human, what makes them universal, is the stamp of the creative mind.

J. Bronowski

Copernicus found that the orbits of the planets would look simpler if they were looked at from the sun and not from the earth. But he did not in the first place find this by routine calculation. His first step was a leap of the imagination—to lift himself from the earth, and put himself wildly, speculatively into the sun.

J. Bronowski

The Creative Mind

Studies at the University of Minnesota have found that teachers smile on children with high IQs and frown upon those with creative minds. Intelligent but uncreative students accept conformity, never rebel, and complete their assignments with dispatch and to perfection. The creative child, on the other hand, is manipulative, imaginative, and intuitive. He is likely to harass the teacher. He is regarded as wild, naughty, silly, undependable, lacking in seriousness or even promise. His behavior is distracting; he doesn't seem to be trying; he gives unique answers to banal questions, touching off laughter among the other children. E. Paul Torrance of Minnesota found that 70 percent of pupils rated high in creativity were rejected by teachers picking a special class for the intellectually gifted. Researchers concluded that a Stanford study of genius, under which teachers selected bright children, would have excluded Churchill, Edison, Picasso, and Mark Twain.

William Manchester, The Last Lion *(Boston: Little Brown and Company, 1983), 159.*

CREATOR

Nobody as Creator

Many years ago, Sir Isaac Newton had an exact replica of the solar system made in miniature. At its center was a large golden ball representing the sun, and revolving around it were smaller spheres attached at the ends of rods of varying lengths. They represented Mercury, Venus, Earth, Mars, and the other planets. These were all geared together by cogs and belts to make them move around the "sun" in perfect harmony.

One day, as Newton was studying the model, a friend who did not believe in the biblical account of Creation stopped by for a visit. Marveling at the device and watching as the scientist made the heavenly bodies move in their orbits, the man exclaimed, "Mr. Newton, what an exquisite thing! Who made it for you?" Without looking up, Sir Isaac replied, "Nobody." "Nobody?" his friend asked. "That's right! I said nobody! All of these balls and cogs and belts and gears just happened to come together, and wonder of wonders, by chance they began revolving in their set orbits and with perfect timing."

His friend got the message.

Divine "Hand"work

Here's Dr. Paul Brand on how the design of the hand proves God:

I could fill a room with volumes of surgical textbooks that describe operations people have devised for the human hand: different ways to rearrange the tendons, muscles, and joints—thousands of operations. But I don't know of a single operation anyone has devised that has succeeded in improving a normal hand. It's beautiful. All the techniques are to correct the deviants, the one hand in a hundred that is not functioning as God designed. There is no way to improve on the hand he gave us. I concur with Isaac Newton, who said, "In the absence of any other proof, the thumb alone would convince me of God's existence."

Gary Vanderet, A Song of Security, Series: Songs for Troubled Hearts, Discovery Papers, *3 July 1988, 3.*

The Spider's Design

The book *Life and Death in Shanghai* by Nien Chaing is her marvelous testimony of courage. After the communists overthrew Chaing Kai Chek in 1949, Nien and her husband decided to stay because her husband was a general manager for Shell Oil Company, which was the only multinational company that chose to remain. When her husband died in 1957, Shell hired her as a special adviser. In 1966, Mao Tse-tung launched the Great Proletarian Revolution, and Nien was arrested, beaten and taken to prison, where she remained in solitary confinement for over six years.

One account in her books parallels what David is saying [in Psalm 139]. One afternoon, while lying in her cell, a spider crawled in and began to climb up one of the iron bars of her window. She said she watched it climb steadily to the top, and it was such a long walk for this tiny creature. When it reached the top, it swung out and descended on a silken thread spun from its body. After it secured its thread to the other end of the bar, it crawled back to where it had started and swung out in a new direction. Nien was fascinated by the fact that this spider knew exactly what to do and where to take the next thread without any hesitation or mistakes. When it had made the frame, it proceeded to make an intricate web that was perfect, with all the strands evenly spaced. As Nien watched this architectural feat, she was flooded with questions: Who had taught the spider to make the web? Could it really have acquired the skill through evolution, or did God make that spider with the ability to make a web for catching food and perpetuating its species? This spider helped her to see that God was in control. From then on, Mao Tse-tung and his revolutionaries seemed much less menacing. She says, "I felt a renewal and a hope surge inside of me."

Gary Vanderet, A Song of Security, Series: Songs for Troubled Hearts, Discovery Papers, *3 July 1988, 3–4.*

CRITICISM

If one person calls you an ass or a donkey, pay no attention to him. But if five people call you one, go out and buy yourself a saddle.

Arabian proverb

They blush on seeing the Church governed by such men as you.
Raphael, in response to cardinals who criticized his portrayal of Peter and Paul as too ruddy

If placed in a situation where you must quote another author always write *[sic]* after words that may be misspelled or look the least bit questionable in any way. If there are no misspellings or curious words, toss in a few *[sic]*s just to break up the flow. By doing this, you will appear to be knowledgeable and "on your toes," while the one quoted will seem suspect and vaguely discredited.
Michael O'Donoghue

If I belittle those whom I am called to serve, talk of their weak points in contrast perhaps with what I think of as my strong points, then I know nothing of Calvary love.
Amy Carmichael

Some people remind me of the inhabitants of Assynt, in the northwest of Scotland, of whom it used to be said that while others went to church to hear the gospel preached, they went to hear if the gospel was preached or not.
F. F. Bruce

Taking Credit

Ray C. Stedman comments on the anonymous letters that pastors sometimes receive:

On occasion I have been on the receiving end of unsigned letters taking me to task or complaining about some matter. My practice through the years has been to throw such letters in the waste basket. If people will not sign their name there is no use in paying attention to what they have to say. Such letters are the work of cowards, or perhaps fools. I heard once of a man who was addressing an audience and someone sent a piece of paper up to him with the word "Fool" written on it. He said to the audience, "I have received many unsigned messages in the past, but this is the first time I have ever received one from a man who signed his name but wrote no message!" Perhaps that is the proper way to respond to something like this.

Ray C. Stedman, Discovery Papers.

Do My Best until the End

Abraham Lincoln talked about criticism in a conversation at the White House reported by Francis B. Carpenter:

If I were to read, much less to answer, all the attacks made on me, this shop might as well be closed for any other business. I do the very best I know how—the very best I can; and I intend to keep doing so until the end. If the end brings me out alright, what is said against me won't amount to anything. If the end brings me out wrong, ten angels swearing I was right would make no difference.

John Wesley's "Cutting" Criticism

Once, while he was preaching, John Wesley noticed a lady in the audience who was known for her critical attitude. All through the service she sat and stared at his new tie. When the meeting ended, she came up to him and said very sharply, "Mr. Wesley, the strings on your bow tie are much too long. It's an offense to me!" He asked if any of the ladies present happened to have a pair of scissors in her purse. When the scissors were handed to him, he gave them to his critic and asked her to trim the streamers to her liking. After she clipped them off near the collar, he said, "Are you sure they're all right now?" "Yes, that's much better." "Then let me have those shears a moment," said Wesley. "I'm sure you wouldn't mind if I also gave you a bit of correction. I don't want to be cruel, but I must tell you, madam, that your tongue is an offense to me—it's too long! Please stick it out; I'd like to take some off!"

The Battle against Criticism

Few preachers have experienced the kind of criticism that Charles H. Spurgeon did when he began his ministry in London. A steady stream of magazine articles and pamphlets examined the young preacher's character, words, works, and motives, and most of them were anything but sympathetic. More than one writer expressed doubts that Spurgeon was even converted! His sermons were called "trashy," and he was compared to a rocket that would climb high and then suddenly drop out of sight! "What is he doing?" one writer asked. "Whose servant is he? What proof does he give that, instrumentally, his is a heart-searching, a Christ-exalting, a truth-unfolding, a sinner-converting, a church-feeding, a soul-saving ministry?" . . . The writer was Rev. Charles Walters Banks. Have you ever heard of him?

At first this criticism deeply hurt Spurgeon, but then the Lord gave him peace and victory. Hearing slanderous reports of his character and ministry week after week could have led him into defeat; but he fell to his knees and prayed, "Master, I will not keep back even my character for Thee. If I must lose that, too, then let it go; it is the dearest thing I have, but it shall go if, like my Master, they shall say I have a devil, and am mad, or like Him, I am a drunken man and a wine-bibber."

Mrs. Spurgeon, knowing the trials her husband was going through, prepared a wall-motto to hang in their room, with Matthew 5:11-12 as the text. The Word of God did its work, and the preacher won the battle. Luther was right when he said that "the love of a woman" is a great help in days of discouragement; and blessed is that pastor's wife who knows when her husband needs that extra touch of love and understanding.

Warren Wiersbe, Walking with the Giants *(Grand Rapids, Mich.: Baker), 267.*

CROSS

Logo Recognition

The trademarks of the fast-food chain McDonald's and of the oil company Shell are better known throughout the world than the Christian cross. Thus reports the marketing magazine *W & V* of Munich, Germany.

In a poll examining the knowledge of trademarks and symbols, commissioned by the International Olympic Committee, 88 percent of the seven thousand people questioned in Germany, Great Britain, Australia, India, Japan, and the United States correctly identified the "golden *M*" of McDonald's, and the Shell Oil sign. In comparison, the symbol of Christ crucified was recognized by a mere 54 percent.

The most well-known noncommercial logo features the five Olympic rings, which were correctly identified by 92 percent of those questioned.

Christ Crucified

Years ago, two prominent men made totally contradictory statements. One was the president of Harvard University. The other was a graduate of Yale University and the president of the Bible Institute of Los Angeles. R. A. Torrey said, "Preach any Christ but a crucified Christ, and you will not draw men for long." At the same time, Charles Eliot, in a lecture entitled "The Future of Religion," said that while it was OK for ancient man to believe in a divine atoning Christ, modern man had outgrown that idea. He said, "Let no man fear that reverence and love for Jesus will diminish as time goes on. The pathos and heroism of his life and death will be vastly heightened when he is relieved of all supernatural attributes and power."

Take Me to the Cross

It has been said that the geographical center of the city of London is Charing Cross. It is in the form of a cross; you can find your way anywhere in London if you are at Charing Cross. The story is told of a little boy who was lost. A bobby came along and wiped away his tears. When he had gotten him settled, he said, "Can I take you home, son?" The boy replied, "Oh, no, sir, take me to the cross, and I'll find my way home." That is true for us. When we orient ourselves to the cross, look to the cross, we begin to see the I AM, the eternity and magnificence of God.

CRUCIFIXION

God Was There

A boy was turning the pages in a book on religious art. When he came to a picture of the crucifixion, he looked at it for a long time, and there came a sad look on his face. Then he said, "If God had been there, he wouldn't have let them do it."

The amazing thing that we read in Scripture is that God was there! He was there at the manger; he was there on the Galilean road; he was there at the cross of Calvary. "God was in Christ reconciling the world to Himself" (2 Corinthians 5:19, NASB).

Christ Crucified

See page 97

Jesus on the Wheel of the World

See page 394

D

DEATH

I am ready to meet my Maker, but whether my Maker is prepared for the great ordeal of meeting me is another matter.

Winston Churchill

If it weren't for death, life would be unbearable.

Malcolm Muggeridge

The radiance of a thousand suns . . . I am become as death, the destroyer of worlds.

Robert Oppenheimer, quoting from the Bhagavad Gita as his plutonium bomb was exploded on the Almogordo bombing range in New Mexico

It is a great mercy that I have no manner of fear or dread of death. I could, if God please, lay my head back and die without terror this afternoon.

Isaac Watts

You may say the world is nothing but the resultant of bodily powers. But why, then, is my soul more luminous when my body begins to fail? Why, when winter is on my head, is eternal spring in my heart? The nearer I approach death, the clearer I hear around me the immor-

tal symphonies of the world about me. My work is only beginning. My thirst for the infinite proves infinity.
Victor Hugo

The Resurrection proves that life is stronger than death. If Jesus had died, never to rise again, it would have proved that death could take the loveliest and the best life that ever lived and finally break it.
William Barclay

Left with Nothing

David Hume, the philosopher and skeptic, not only lost all his early Christian faith but led his mother into skepticism too. The story is told that at her deathbed, she called her noted son to her bedside and said: "You have taken away my faith, and now you have nothing to give me in its stead."

The Two Domenico Taleses

In 1937, Domenico Talese, uncle to author Gay Talese, had been drafted by the Italian army; and because Mussolini was supporting General Franco's cause in the Spanish Civil War, Domenico was dispatched along with many Italian troops to Cádiz, where during the next year he was assigned to battle units and twice was hospitalized with bullet wounds. But the most frightening moment that he wrote about from Spain occurred on a day when he was unscathed in battle.

Crouched in the trenches, Domenico overheard a conversation between two Italian soldiers nearby in which one was saying: "I was born and raised in a time of war, and I'm *still* in a war!" The other soldier asked, "When were you born?" To which the first soldier moaned, as if the day carried a curse: "April 16, 1914." On hearing this, Gay's uncle's interest perked up, for he *too* had been born on that day, in the same year!

"Hey," Domenico yelled over the trench, "what's your name?" "Domenico Talese," came the reply. *"Domenico*

Talese!" the uncle exclaimed. "That's *my* name!" Domenico immediately poked his head up, and, seeing that his namesake had also risen above the trench, he examined a dark-eyed helmeted man with similar facial features—who, smiling and holding up a flask, said: "I'm Domenico Talese of Naples! Come over; let's drink!"

"Yes," Gay's uncle said. "I'll tell the lieutenant." Edging his way toward the lieutenant, who stood yards away in the other direction, Domenico was requesting permission for the visit, when suddenly he was jolted by an explosion behind him. Moments after the dirt had settled and the smoke had cleared, Domenico turned to see that the trench in which his namesake and the other soldier had stood was now completely gone. It had been eliminated by a direct hit from an artillery shell. Domenico Talese of Naples had been blown out of sight, plucked from the earth and carried into oblivion before Gay's uncle could learn exactly where in Naples he had lived, or how they were related.

Gay Talese, Unto the Sons *(New York: Alfred A. Knopf, 1992), 89–90.*

Standing Up to Death

Murat, Napoleon's brother-in-law and French commander, had been captured by his enemies and was to be executed. On the day of his death he had a shock of his hair cut and asked one of the officers to enclose it with a letter he had written to his wife, Napoleon's sister, and his children, who were then all living in Trieste. Then Murat took off his watch and gave it to the officer as a gift. But before he parted with the watch, he removed from its lid a tiny carnelian on which was carved a portrait of his wife. He held this carnelian tightly in the palm of his hand as he followed the soldiers out to the courtyard, where they were preparing to kill him.

The sergeant of the firing squad offered Murat a chair, but Murat said he wanted to die standing up. The sergeant offered to cover up his eyes with a cloth, but Murat said he wanted to die with his eyes open. "I do have one request," Murat then said. "I have commanded in many battles, and now I would like to give the word of command for the last time."

The sergeant granted his wish. Murat then stood against the wall of the castle and called out in a loud voice: "Soldiers, form line." Six soldiers drew themselves up to within about ten feet of him. "Prepare arms—present." The soldiers pointed their muskets at him. "Aim at the heart; save the face," Murat said, with a little smile. And then, after he had held up his hand to look for the final time at the carnelian showing the portrait of his wife, he issued his final command—"Fire!"

The muskets exploded, and six bullets struck him in the chest. Murat fell to the ground without even a groan.

Gay Talese, Unto the Sons *(New York: Alfred A. Knopf, 1992), 179–180.*

Stalin's Wolves

In his later years, Josef Stalin had completely lost touch with the normal world. His daughter said he talked in terms of 1917 prices, and his salary envelopes piled up unopened on his desk (from which they mysteriously vanished at his death). When she visited him on 21 December 1952, she found him sick, refusing to let any doctor near him, and dosing himself with iodine. Even his personal physician for the last twenty years, Stalin believed, had been a British spy all the time. Stalin had always doodled drawings of wolves during meetings. Now the brutes obsessed him. On 17 February 1953, he told the last non-Communist visitor, K. P. S. Menon, how he dealt with his enemies: "A Russian peasant who sees a wolf doesn't need to be told what the wolf intends to do—he knows!—so he doesn't try to tame the wolf, or argue or waste time—he kills it!" The stroke came a fortnight later on 2 March, leaving Stalin speechless. His daughter said that his death on 5 March was "difficult and terrible," his last gesture being to lift his left hand as if to curse, or to ward off something. As Lenin went to eternity raving of electricity, so Stalin departed to the howling of imaginary wolves.

Paul Johnson, Modern Times, *revised ed. (New York: HarperCollins, 1991), 456.*

All for Nothing

The film *Out of Africa* captures for Roger Thompson the meaninglessness Solomon talks about in the book of Ecclesiastes. The film is a nostalgic reflection of a young Danish woman named Karen Blixen. At an early age she goes to Kenya. There she marries a man she hardly knows; she plants a coffee plantation; and for a while, paradise belongs to Karen Blixen. Then, after about fifteen years of hard labor, within the span of a few months she loses it all. She loses her health, she loses her lover, she loses her friends, she loses her coffee crop and her farm, and finally she loses her identity. Everything she lived for has been taken away from her. As she is reflecting in that movie . . . she writes with burning, utterly answerless nostalgia and fatigue about how meaningless it all was. She says, "If I know a song for Africa, of the giraffe and the African new moon lying on her back, of the plows in the fields and the sweaty faces of the coffee pickers, does Africa know a song of me? Would the air over the plain quiver with a color that I had had on? Or the children invent a game in which my name was? Or the full moon throw a shadow over the gravel of the drive that was like me? Or would the eagles of the hills look out for me?" She gives her life to Africa, but when she's gone, Africa doesn't remember. There's nothing there that remembers *her,* though she remembers it.

Roger Thompson, "The Good News Is: The Bad News Is Wrong," Preaching Today, *tape no. 55, Ecclesiastes 3:1-14, 1 Corinthians 15:17-20.*

Nothing to Say about Death

During the Second World War Sir John Lawrence attended what he describes as a "sort of communist memorial" to Stanislavsky in the Moscow Arts Theater. He says:

There was a closed coffin on the stage, draped in a red flag, and the dead man's colleagues came and said good-bye to him in set speeches. One heard some of the world's greatest actors and actresses speaking of their teacher and leader on what should have been a moving occasion, but the experience was empty. I was not at that time a Christian believer, but even so it struck me that Communism has nothing to say about death. There was no development of a theme such as one gets in the prayer book service for the Burial of the Dead. In the same way, to visit the Mausoleum where Lenin lies, and where Stalin lay for a few years beside him, is for me a disturbing experience precisely because it has no content.

J. Lawrence, Russians Observed *(London: Hodder & Stoughton, 1969), 118.*

The Darkest Hour

After one of his great evangelistic campaigns in Britain, Mr. Moody sailed for America. A few days at sea, and the ship's shaft had broken and it was sinking. "I was passing," he says, "through a new experience. I had thought myself superior to the fear of death. I had often preached on the subject, and urged Christians to realize this victory of faith. During the Civil War, I had been under fire without fear. I was in Chicago during the great cholera epidemic, and went round with the doctors visiting the sick and dying; where they could go to look after the bodies of men, I said I could go to look after their souls. I remember a case of smallpox where the sufferer's condition was beyond description; yet I went to the bedside of that poor sufferer again and again, with Bible and prayer, for Jesus' sake. In all this I had no fear. But on the sinking ship it was different. There was no cloud between my soul and my Saviour. I knew my sins had been put away, and if I died there it would only be to wake up in heaven. That was all settled long ago. But as my thoughts went out to my beloved ones at home—my wife, my children, my friends on both sides of the sea, the schools and all the interests so dear to me—and as I realized that perhaps the next hour would separate me forever from all these, so far as this world was concerned, I confess it almost broke me down. It was the darkest hour of my life."

W. R. Moody, The Life of D. L. Moody *(London: Morgan and Scott), 351.*

Life Is a Disappointment

Malcolm Muggeridge saw Western civilization as doomed, the inevitability of death as the most interesting aspect of life, and life itself as an adventure, mystery, and—"for anyone of sensitivity"—a disappointment.

"Human life, I have come to feel, in all its public or collective manifestations is only theater, and mostly cheap melodrama at that," Muggeridge concluded.

"There is nothing serious under the sun except love; of fellow mortals and of God."

The Unfolding Murder Mystery

Mike Mason says that living is like an unfolding murder mystery in which we are the victim:

Death is something which, like odds or like suspense, builds throughout our life. It builds by slow degrees of awareness like the unfolding of a murder mystery in which we ourselves turn out to be the victim. The tension of death mounts in our very cells until, in a way, it explodes inside of us, spewing every one of our precious atoms back to wherever it was they all came from.

Mike Mason, The Mystery of Marriage *(Portland, Oreg.: Multnomah, 1978), 170.*

A Heart after All

Bertolt Brecht expressed the wish to be buried in a gray steel coffin, to keep out worms, and to have a steel stiletto put through his heart as soon as he was dead. This was done and published: The news being the first indication to many who knew him that he had a heart at all.

Paul Johnson, Intellectuals *(New York: Harper & Row, 1988), 195–196.*

The Tombstone Epitaph: Vacant

A man had a very serious automobile accident that involved a long-term recovery. Contemplating his death—a real possibility for a while—he told his wife that he wanted one word on his tombstone. That was *Vacant.* What an epitaph for a tombstone. It would have been precisely accurate. If he had died, he would not have occupied the grave. His body would have, but not he. Paul declared in 2 Corinthians 5:8, "Absent from the body . . . and . . . present with the Lord" (KJV).

Adapted from Perspective, *by Richard Halverson.*

The Death of the Saints

John Wesley died full of praise, counsel, and exhortations. His final words were, "The best of all is, God is with us. The best of all is, God is with us. The best of all is, God is with us. Farewell!"

Adoniram Judson, the great American missionary to Burma, suffering immensely at death, said to those around, "I go with the gladness of a boy bounding away from school. I feel so strong in Christ."

Jonathan Edwards, dying from smallpox, gave some final directions, bid his daughter good-bye, and expired saying, "Where is Jesus, my never-failing friend?" Death often reveals what we are, and certainly it ultimately will when we stand before our Maker and Judge.

Why, God? Why?

The weather was bright and cheerful. The New Guinea sun burned down on a village usually occupied by the Tifalmin natives, but they were out working on their farms and gathering firewood. It was a lazy Sunday afternoon. No one dreamed that disaster was about to strike. On that afternoon, Walt and Vonnie Steinkraus, a dedicated Wycliffe missionary couple, were at home with their daughters Kerry and Kathy.

At precisely 3:00 P.M., a freak of nature occurred. A huge section of the three-hundred-foot mountain across the river from the Steinkraus home suddenly broke loose. With a deafening roar and incredible force, a half-mile-wide, hundred-foot-deep section plunged downward, scooping out sandbanks and crossing the river with lightning speed. It drove through the opposite bank and covered the village with rock, mud, and debris ten feet deep. The missionary family was buried in the landslide. Death was instantaneous. It is possible that they never heard a sound. The news, when it reached outside, stung deep like a shark bite. A numbing disbelief gripped relatives and friends. The Wycliffe family was stunned. How wrong it seemed, how unfair. With a world full of reprobates and rebels, why a missionary family? With a thousand other vacant hillsides miles from any living soul, why that mountain? With pockets of people all over the island not half as strategic as the Steinkraus couple, why them? Engaged in the painstaking process of translating the Bible into the primitive language of that people, Walt and Vonnie were taken before the project was complete.

Thomas Paine's Dying Regrets

Thomas Paine was one of the great intellectuals among the founders of America. He was also an infamous unbeliever. He was a man who led many away from the Scriptures and belief in God. On the day Tom Paine died, these were his final words:

I would give worlds, if I had them, that *The Age of Reason* had not been published. O Lord, help me! Christ, help me! O God, what have I done to suffer so much? But there is no God! But if there should be, what will become of me hereafter? Stay with me, for God's sake! Send even a child to stay with me, for it is hell to be alone. If ever the devil had an agent, I have been that one.

Dr. Herbert Lockyer, Last Words of Saints and Sinners *(Grand Rapids, Mich.: Kregel), 132.*

An Appointment with Death

From Peter Marshall: An old legend tells of a merchant in Baghdad who one day sent his servant to the market. Before very long the servant came back, white and trembling, and in great agitation said to his master: "Down in the marketplace I was jostled by a woman in the crowd, and when I turned around I saw it was Death that jostled me. She looked at me and made a threatening gesture. Master, please lend me your horse, for I must hasten away to avoid her. I will ride to Samarra and there I will hide, and Death will not find me."

The merchant lent him his horse and the servant galloped away in great haste. Later the merchant went down to the marketplace and saw Death standing in the crowd. He went over to her and asked, "Why did you frighten my servant this morning? Why did you make a threatening gesture?"

"That was not a threatening gesture," Death said. "It was only a start of surprise. I was astonished to see him in Baghdad, for I have an appointment with him tonight in Samarra."

Each of us has an appointment in Samarra. But that is cause for rejoicing—not for fear, provided we have put our trust in Him who alone holds the keys of life and death.

Catherine Marshall, ed., John Doe, Disciple *(New York: McGraw-Hill, 1963), 219–220.*

Shanghai Is Burning

This haunting poem was written by a man who had just escaped mainland China as the Communists burned Shanghai:

Tonight Shanghai is burning
And I am dying too
But there's no death more certain
Than death inside of you
Some men die of shrapnel
But most men die inch by inch
While playing at little games

A Cloud of Witnesses

On Friday, December 7, 1979, Biola University junior John Nuskiewicz collapsed while doing his morning exercises. Within minutes he was unconscious, partially paralyzed and in a coma. His strokelike condition was later diagnosed as a congenital rupture of a vein in the left section of his brain. John was placed in intensive care at the University of Southern California Medical Center.

His father came out from Wisconsin, stayed in John's room, and daily visited his son at the hospital. Neither of John's parents were Christians, and he had spent the previous summer attempting to win them to Christ. Having returned to Biola the previous fall thinking he had dismally failed to reach them, John shared with some other students that he would give his own life for their salvation. When Mr. Nuskiewicz experienced the love and compassion of the Biola family and learned of John's burden for his soul, he prayed to receive Christ. He shared his testimony in chapel the morning following his conversion (Wednesday), and the students responded with a long and jubilant standing ovation! . . .

Three days later, John entered the courts of heaven just moments before his father would have been required to decide whether or not to disconnect the life-support systems. Mr. Nuskiewicz then returned home to his grief-stricken wife and four remaining children. At the funeral service, in which some of John's Christian friends participated, Mrs. Nuskiewicz also committed her life to Christ. Christians in their local community nurtured them in the Lord.

The full impact of this story will be assessed by eternity alone. John died that his parents might live! But more than that, God used him—in life and in death—to ignite a renewed sense of spiritual priorities on Biola's campus.

Rich Thune, alumni director for Biola University at the time of this story.

What Does It Profit a Man?

In 1965 Somerset Maugham was ninety-one years old and fabulously wealthy. Royalties were continuing to pour in from all over the world, despite the fact that he had not written a word in years. His fame seemingly was on the upsurge; he received an average of three hundred letters a week from his fans. He was experiencing incredible success, but how did Maugham respond to his success? What had it brought to his life? We gain an insight from the April 9, 1978, edition of the *London Times.* In it was a story by Maugham's nephew, Robin Maugham, after he visited Maugham before his death at his fabulous villa on the Mediterranean. Here's what Robin Maugham wrote:

I looked round the drawing room at the immensely valuable furniture and pictures and objects that Willie's success had enabled him to acquire. I remembered that the villa itself and the wonderful garden I could see through the windows—a fabulous setting on the edge of the Mediterranean—were worth £600,000. . . . Willie had 11 servants, including his cook, Annette, who was the envy of all the other millionaires on the Riviera. He dined on silver plates, waited on by

Marius, his butler, and Henri, his footman. But it no longer meant anything to him. The following afternoon, I found Willie reclining on a sofa, peering through his spectacles at a Bible which had very large print. He looked horribly wizened, and his face was grim. "I've been reading the Bible you gave me . . . and I've come across the quotation: 'What shall it profit a man if he gain the whole world and lose his own soul?' I must tell you, my dear Robin, that the text used to hang opposite my bed when I was a child. . . . Of course, it's all a lot of bunk. But the thought is quite interesting all the same." That evening, in the drawing room, after dinner, Willie flung himself down onto the sofa. "Oh, Robin, I'm so tired. . . ." He gave a gulp and buried his head in his hands. "I've been a failure the whole way through my life," he said. "I've made mistake after mistake. I've made a hash of everything." I tried to comfort him. "You're the most famous writer alive. Surely that means something?" "I wish I'd never written a single word," he answered. "It's brought me nothing but misery. . . . Everyone who's got to know me well has ended up hating me. . . . My whole life has been a failure. . . . And now it's too late to change. It's too late. . . ." Willie looked up, and his grip tightened on my hands. He was staring towards the floor. His face was contorted with fear, and he was trembling violently. Willie's face was ashen as he stared in horror ahead of him. Suddenly, he began to shriek. "Go away!" he cried. "I'm not ready. . . . I'm not dead yet. . . . I'm not dead yet. . . . I'm not dead yet, I tell you. . . ." His high-pitched, terror-stricken voice seemed to echo from wall to wall. I looked round, but the room was empty as before.

London Times, *9 April 1978.*

Death, Heaven, Eternal Life

Dr. R. A. Torrey was one of the great Bible teachers of the past generation. He pastored Moody Church (Chicago, Ill.) and founded the Bible Institute of Los Angeles. This is his story: When the Torreys' twelve-year-old daughter died of diphtheria, Dr. Torrey and his wife went through a great time of heartache. The funeral was held on a miserable rainy day. As they stood around her little grave and watched her body being buried, Mrs. Torrey said, "I'm so glad Elizabeth is with the Lord and not in that box." Yet, despite this knowledge, their hearts were broken. As Dr. Torrey told it, the next day as he was walking down the street, the misery came to him anew. He felt the loneliness that lay ahead, the heartbreak of an empty house. In his misery he cried aloud, "Oh, Elizabeth! Elizabeth!" Here's what happened next, in Dr. Torrey's own words:

And just then this fountain, the Holy Spirit, that I had in my heart, broke forth with such power as I think I had never experienced before, and it was the most joyful moment I had ever known in my life. Oh, how wonderful is the joy of the Holy Ghost! It is an unspeakably glorious thing to have your joy not in things about you, not even in your most dearly loved friends, but to have within you a fountain ever springing up, springing up, springing up, always springing up, springing up under all circumstances into everlasting life.

R. A. Torrey, The Holy Spirit *(Old Tappan, N.J.: Fleming H. Revell, 1983), 95.*

It Is Over!

Elizabeth I, Queen of England, the idol of society and the leader of European fashion, when on her deathbed, turned to her lady-in-waiting and said, "O my God! It is over. I have come to the end of it—the end, the end. To have only one life, and to have done with it! To have lived and loved and triumphed; and now to know it is over! One may defy everything but this."

And as the listener sat watching, in a few moments more the face whose slightest smile had brought her courtiers to her feet, turned into a mask of lifeless clay, and returned the anxious gaze of her servant with nothing more than a vacant stare. . . . How different with the end of the Saviour—"I have glorified Thee on earth; I have finished the work which Thou gavest Me to do."

A. W. Pink

Choosing Death
See page 140

Final Communion
See page 152

The Full Circle of Comfort
See page 58

Ernest Hemingway's Deep Despair
See page 124

Holy Burning
See page 126

A Savior for Me
See page 365

DECEPTION

Stalin Tyranny

In the outside world, the magnitude of the Stalin Tyranny—or indeed its very existence—was scarcely grasped at all. Most of those who traveled to Russia were either businessmen, anxious to trade and with no desire to probe or criticize what did not concern them, or intellectuals who came to admire and, still more, to believe. If the decline of Christianity created the modern political zealot—and his crimes—so the evaporation of religious faith among the educated left a vacuum in the minds of Western intellectuals easily filled by secular superstition. There is no other explanation for the credulity with which scientists, accustomed to evaluating evidence, and writers, whose whole function was to study and criticize society, accepted the crudest Stalinist propaganda at its face value. They needed to believe; they wanted to be duped.

George Bernard Shaw pointed out that in Britain, a man enters prison a human being and emerges a criminal type, in Russia he entered the Soviet prisons and labor camps "as a criminal type and would come out an ordinary man but for the difficulty of inducing him to come out at all. As far as I could make out they would stay as long as they liked."

Paul Johnson, Modern Times, *revised ed. (New York: HarperCollins, 1991), 456.*

Shortchanged

A baker suspected that the farmer who was supplying his butter was giving him short-weight. He carefully checked the weight for several days, and his suspicions were confirmed. Highly indignant, he had the farmer arrested. At the trial the judge was satisfied and the baker chagrined at the farmer's explanation. He (the farmer) had no scales, so he used balances; and for a weight he used a one-pound loaf of bread bought daily from the baker.

Zig Ziglar, See You at the Top [*formerly entitled* Biscuits, Fleas, and Pump Handles] *(Pelican, 1982).*

Master Deceivers

See page 272

Kidnapping of the Brainchild

See page 133

DEDICATION

If I had three hundred men who feared nothing but God, and hated nothing but sin, and were determined to know nothing among men but Jesus Christ and Him crucified, I would set the world on fire.

John Wesley

Be a Real Writer

In an article in the *New York Daily News,* Robert Maynard told a heartwarming story from his childhood. As a boy, Maynard was walking to school one day when he came upon an irresistible temptation. In front of him was a fresh piece of gray cement—a piece that had replaced a broken piece of sidewalk. He immediately stopped and began to scratch his name in it. Suddenly, he became aware that standing over him with a garbage-can lid was the biggest mason he had ever seen, holding his choice of weapons for little boys that day!

Maynard tried to run, but the big man grabbed him and shouted: "Why are you trying to spoil my work?" Maynard remembers babbling something about just wanting to put his name on the ground. A remarkable thing happened. The mason released his arms, his voice softened and his eyes lost their fire. Instead there was now a touch of warmth about the man. "What's your name, son?" "Robert Maynard."

"Well, Robert Maynard, the sidewalk is no place for your name. If you want your name on something, you go in that school. You work hard and you become a lawyer and you hang your shingle out for all the world to see." Tears came to Maynard's eyes, but the mason was not finished yet. "What do you want to be when you grow up?"

"A writer, I think."

This time his voice burst forth in tones that could be heard all over the school yard. "A writer! A writer! Be a writer! Be a real writer! Have your name on books, not on this sidewalk." Robert Maynard continued to cross the street, paused and looked back. The mason was on his knees repairing the damage which Maynard's scratching had done. He looked up and saw the young boy watching and repeated: "Be a writer."

Dynamic Preaching, *vol. 5, no. 2 (February 1990): 8.*

William Booth's Fight to the Finish

These are the last public words of William Booth, at age eighty-two and almost blind, before an audience of ten thousand at Royal Albert Hall in London:

While women weep as they do now, I'll fight
While children go hungry as they do now, I'll fight
When men go to prison, in and out, I'll fight
While there is a drunkard left, I'll fight
While there is a poor girl left on the streets, I'll fight
While there remains one dark soul without the light of God, I'll fight
I'll fight—I'll fight to the very end.

All-Out Commitment

Several years ago Billy Graham published this letter written by a young Communist to his fiancée, breaking off their engagement. The young woman's pastor had sent the letter to Billy Graham. The young man wrote: "We Communists have a high casualty rate. We are the ones who get shot and hung and ridiculed and fired from our jobs and in every other way made as uncomfortable as possible. A certain percentage of us get killed or imprisoned. We live in virtual poverty. We turn back to the party every penny we make above what is absolutely necessary to keep us alive. We Communists do not have the time or the money for many movies or concerts or T-bone steaks or decent homes or new cars. We have been described as fanatics. We are fanatics. Our lives are dominated by one great overshadowing factor: the struggle for world Communism. We Communists have a philosophy of life which no amount of money can buy. We have a cause to fight for, a definite purpose in life. We subordinate our petty personal selves into a great movement of humanity; and if our personal lives seem hard and our egos appear to suffer through subordination to the party, then we are adequately compensated by the thought that each of us in his small way is contributing to something new and true and better for mankind. There is one thing which I am dead earnest about, and this is the Communist cause. It is my life, my business, my religion, my hobby, my sweetheart, my wife and my mistress, my bread and meat. I work at it in the daytime and dream of it at night. Its hold on me grows, not lessens, as time goes on; therefore, I cannot carry on a friendship, a love affair, or even a conversation without relating it to this force which both drives and guides my life. I evaluate people, looks, ideas, and actions according to how they affect the Communist cause, and by their attitudes toward it. I've already been in jail because of my ideals, and if necessary, I'm ready to go before a firing squad." That is total dedication!

No Reserve, No Retreat, No Regrets
See page 62

The Resolve to Return
See page 310

DELUSION

> If you meet with difficulties in your work, or suddenly doubt your abilities, think of him—of Stalin—and you will find the confidence you need. If you feel tired in an hour when you should not, think of him—of Stalin—and your work will go well. If you are seeking a correct decision, think of him—of Stalin—and you will find that decision.
>
> Pravda, *1950.*

Imaginary Worlds

[In medieval periods,] poetry, folklore, and romance repeated old tales of *Anthropophagi* ("man-eaters"), the warlike *Ama-*

zons ("without breast," women who lived without men and received their name because they had removed the right breast in order to draw the bow more powerfully), *Cyclopes* ("round-eyes," the one-eyed giants of Homer and Virgil), *Cynocephali* ("dog-heads," who communicated by barking, had huge teeth and breathed flames), *Pygmies* (who braided their long hair into clothing, and warred with the cranes who stole their crops). Then there were *Amyctryae* ("unsociables," who lived on raw meat and whose protruding lip served them as an umbrella), *Antipodes* ("opposite-footed," who lived at the bottom of the world and had to walk upside down), *Astomi* ("mouthless" apple-smellers, who could neither eat nor drink, and could be killed by a bad odor, but lived by smelling, mostly apples), *Blemmyae* (celebrated by Shakespeare as "men whose heads / Do grow beneath their shoulders"), *Panotii* ("all-ears," whose long ears served for blankets, and, like Dumbo's, could be unfurled for wings), *Sciopods* ("shadow-foot," who had only one great foot, which served as a parasol to protect them from the sun as they lay on their backs).

Daniel J. Boorstin, The Discoverers *(New York: Vintage, 1993), 627.*

Stalin Tyranny
See page 113

The Bigger the Butterfly, the Better
See page 271

DEPRAVITY

We are all like the moon, we have a dark side we don't want anyone to see.

Mark Twain

The true problem lies in the hearts and thoughts of men. It is not a physical but an ethical one. What terrifies us is

not the explosive force of the atomic bomb but the power of the wickedness of the human heart.
Albert Einstein

I have never been able to find in any man's book or any man's talk anything convincing enough to stand up for a moment against my deep-seated sense of fatality governing this man-inhabited world. . . . The only remedy for the Chinamen and for the rest of us is the change of hearts. But looking at the history of the last 2,000 years there is not much reason to expect that thing, even if man has taken to flying. . . . Man doesn't fly like an eagle, he flies like a beetle.
Joseph Conrad

Decadence is the decay that hollows out the forms of life, leaving them devoid of meaning and, even more fatally, flaunting such hollowness as virtue.
Richard John Neuhaus

If I steal money from any person, there may be no harm done by the mere transfer of possession; he may not feel the loss, or it may even prevent him from using the money badly. But I cannot help doing this great wrong towards Man, that I make myself dishonest. What hurts society is not that it should lose its property, but that it should become a den of thieves; for then it must cease to be society. This is why we ought not to do evil that good may come; for at any rate this great evil has come, that we may have done evil and are made wicked thereby.
W. K. Clifford

I used to think the text in James that "he who offended in one point, offends in all" was very harsh; but I now feel the awful, the tremendous truth of it. In the one crime of opium, what crime have I not made myself guilty of!—Ingratitude to my Maker! and to my benefac-

tors injustice! and unnatural cruelty to my poor children!—self-contempt for my repeated promise-breach, nay, too often, actual falsehood.
S. T. Coleridge

The gods have given me almost everything. But I let myself be lured into long spells of senseless and sensual ease. . . . I ceased to be lord over myself. I was no longer the captain of my soul, and did not know it. I allowed pleasure to dominate me. I ended in horrible disgrace.
Oscar Wilde

[In Buchenwald,] I learned that within me, as in others, the murderer and the humanitarian exist side by side; the weak child with the voracious male. That I am not in any way superior, that I am not different from others.
Eugene Heimler

They see only that which is good in me; they see me only at my best. I shudder when I realize how unworthy I am and how ignorant they are of the dark and hidden recesses of my soul where all that is devilish and hideous reigns supreme, at times breaking through onto the surface and causing a turmoil that God and I alone know of.
Dr. Martyn Lloyd-Jones

I do not know what the heart of a bad man is like. But I do know what the heart of a good man is like. And it is terrible.
Ivan Turgenev

Tangle of Vipers

The protagonist in Francois Mauriac's novel *Viper's Tangle* described himself in this way:

Oh, above all don't imagine that I have any very high idea of myself! I know this heart of mine—this heart; this tangle of vipers. Stifled under them, steeped in their venom, it goes on beating under the swarming of them: this tangle of vipers that it is impossible to separate, that needs to be cut loose with a slash of a knife, with the stroke of a sword. "I am not come to bring peace, but a sword."

François Mauriac, Viper's Tangle *(Garden City, N.Y.: Image Books [a division of Doubleday], 1957), 104.*

You Don't Have to Swallow Depravity

A great preacher was preaching on depravity. At the end of his sermon one of his listeners came up and said, "I can't swallow what you say about depravity." The preacher responded, "That's all right. It's in you already."

Community Standards of Sin

See page 71

Symposium on Theft

See page 388

Adam's Fall

See page 388

What's Wrong? I Am.

See page 388

Phil Donahue Doesn't Get It

See page 416

DEPRESSION

Before any great achievement, some measure of depression is very usual. Such was my experience when I first became a pastor in London. My success appalled me, and the thought of the career which seemed to open up, so far from elating me, cast me into the lowest depths. It was just then that the curtain was rising on my life work and I dreaded what it might reveal. This depression comes over me whenever the Lord is preparing a large blessing for my ministry.

Charles H. Spurgeon

When I survey my past life, I discover nothing but a barren waste of time, with some disorders of body, and dis-

turbances of the mind, very near to madness, which I hope He that made me will suffer to extenuate many faults, and excuse many deficiencies.
Samuel Johnson

Martin Luther's Bouts with Depression
Martin Luther had markedly severe periods of depression that were not abated by anything he tried. Even spiritual success like translating the Bible into German did not cause these attacks to end. Luther describes the extremity of his emotional state:

"For more than a week I was close to the gates of death and hell. I trembled in all my members. Christ was wholly lost. I was shaken by desperation and blasphemy of God."

Luther even saw these moods as beneficial to his understanding of the Christian life. "For without them," he wrote, "no man can understand Scripture, faith, the fear or the love of God."

Who Died?
Martin Luther was experiencing a time in his life when he was suffering from deep despair and depression. He couldn't seem to come out of it. Frustrated by it all, his wife came to breakfast one morning wearing a black armband. "Who died?" Luther asked. His wife answered, "Well, with the way you've been carrying on around here, I thought God did."

DESENSITIZATION

Martin Luther's Parable or Dream of Satan
Martin Luther had a parable or dream of an occasion when the devil sat on his throne listening to the reports of his agents and ambassadors and what progress they had made in opposing the truth of Christ and destroying the souls of men. One spirit said there had been a company of Christians crossing

the desert. "I loosed the lions upon them, and soon the sands of the desert were strewn with their mangled corpses."

"What of that?" answered Satan. "The lions destroyed their bodies, but their souls were saved. It is their souls I am after."

Then another made his report. He said: "There was a company of Christian pilgrims sailing through the sea on a vessel. I sent a great wind against the ship which drove the ship on the rocks, and every Christian aboard the ship was drowned."

"What of that?" said Satan. "Their bodies were drowned in the sea, but their souls were saved. It is their souls I am after."

Then a third came forward to give his report, and he said: "For ten years I have been trying to cast a Christian into a deep sleep, and at last I have succeeded." And with that the corridors of hell rang with shouts of malignant triumph.

Clarence E. Macartney, Chariots of Fire *(Nashville: Abingdon, 1951), 50–51.*

DESIGN

Immense Design

See page 89

Divine "Hand"work

See page 92

The Spider's Design

See page 92

DESPAIR

I see clearly that I have achieved practically nothing. The world today and the history of the human anthill during the past 5–7 years would be exactly the same as it is if I had played Ping-Pong instead of sitting on committees and writing books and memoranda. I have therefore to make a rather ignominious confession that I must have in a long life ground through between 150,000 and 200,000 hours of perfectly useless work.

Leonard Woolf

People do not know what old age means. You cannot imagine such a torture as this: to have had nothing out of life, and to await nothing but death—and to feel that there may be nothing beyond this world, that no explanation exists, that the word of the enigma will never be given us.

François Mauriac

Ernest Hemingway's Deep Despair

Like the newlyweds in the story of the wedding at Cana (John 2), the universal experience of humanity—apart from Christ—is that there comes a time when the wine runs out, when the joy and exhilaration of life are gone. There probably has never been a more public example of this in our time than the life of Ernest Hemingway. From the time of his boyhood in Oak Park, Illinois, to those teenage summers in northern Michigan, he went after everything that life offered. He became a reporter for the *Kansas City Star,* served as an ambulance driver in World War I, spent years in Europe, and was intimately involved in the Spanish civil war. His famous friendships ran all the way from the bullfighter Monolete to F. Scott Fitzgerald. In whatever Hemingway did—sports, warfare, romance—he went for all of it. And, of course, he was brilliant. . . . He was a man who did it all.

In Hemingway's biography by Carlos Baker, we read these final words:

Sunday morning dawned bright and cloudless. Ernest awoke early as always. He put on the red "Emperor's robe" and padded softly down the carpeted stairway. The early sunlight lay in pools on the living room floor. He had noticed that the guns were locked up in the basement. But the keys, as he well knew, were on the window ledge above the kitchen sink. He tiptoed down the basement stairs and unlocked the storage room. It smelled dank as a grave. He chose a double-barreled shotgun with a tight choke. He had used it for years of pigeon shooting. He took some shells from one of the boxes in the storage room, closed and locked the door, and climbed the basement stairs. If he saw the bright day outside, it did not deter him. He crossed the living room to the front foyer, a shrinelike entryway, five feet by seven, with oak-paneled walls and floor of linoleum tile. . . . He slipped in two shells, lowered the gun butt carefully to the floor, leaned forward, pressed the twin barrels against his forehead just above the eyebrows and tripped both triggers.

Carlos Baker, Ernest Hemingway, A Life Story *(New York: Scribners), 563–564.*

Nothing to Say about Death
See page 104

DETERMINATION

Nothing worthwhile can be accomplished without determination. In the early days of nuclear power, for example, getting approval to build the first nuclear submarine—the *Nautilus*—was almost as difficult as designing and building it. Good ideas are not adopted automatically. They must be driven into practice with courageous patience.

Admiral Rickover

A Bright Idea

One evening, when Thomas Edison came home from work, his wife said to him, "You've worked long enough without a rest. You must go on a vacation."

"But where on earth would I go?" asked Edison.

"Just decide where you would rather be than anywhere else on earth," suggested his wife.

Edison hesitated. "Very well," he said finally. "I'll go tomorrow."

The next morning he was back at work in his laboratory.

Holy Burning

On the last evening of his life George Whitefield started to mount the stairs of the Presbyterian manse at Newburyport, Massachusetts. Though but fifty-five, he was tired and weak, utterly worn out from his lifetime of evangelistic labors, and for days he had been so infirm that he ought not to have left his bed.

But as he ascended the stairs people came pressing in at the door, begging to hear the Gospel from his lips once more. In response he paused on the landing and began to preach. There he stood, candle in hand, and so sure was his zeal that he spoke on, heedless of the passing of time, till the candle finally flickered, burned itself out in its socket and died away.

That candle was strikingly representative of Whitefield's life—a life that in its holy burning had long given forth brilliant light and constant heat, but burned its last that night.

Arnold Dallimore, George Whitefield *(Banner of Truth Trust, 1989), 37.*

The Fighting Spirit

During the 1976 Olympics in Montreal, there was one incident that was particularly impressive. It occurred in the gymnastics events. You may remember that one of the men from the Japanese team broke his leg during one of his routines. As it turned out, the last day brought his team against the Russian team to determine the best overall performers. Despite the fact that his leg was broken, the gymnast mounted the rings for a final performance. His routine was sparkling. It was magnificent, and he had a look of pride on his face as he ran through the exercise. Yet perhaps you can still recall the anguish on his face as he completed his exercise and from ten feet in the air came hurtling to the floor for his dismount, landing on his broken leg. He remained indomitable because of a fighting spirit.

The Steady Plop, Plop, Plop
See page 139

We Shall Fight Them
See page 72

DEVIL

The Devil Is a Great Fool
Jonathan Edwards once said, "Although the devil be exceedingly crafty and subtle, yet he is one of the greatest fools and blockheads in the world, as the subtlest of wicked men are. Sin is of such a nature that it strangely infatuates and stultifies the mind."

> *John Blanchard,* The Truth for Life *(West Sussex, England: H. E. Walter, 1982), 190.*

Possessed by a "Fox Spirit"
Early one morning Amy Carmichael was told that a man nearby was possessed by a "fox spirit." This spirit was worshiped in Japan, shrines were dedicated to him, and stone foxes were often set side by side with Buddhas. What this demon was doing to the poor man sounded very like New Testament stories—"Wherever he is, it gets hold of him, throws him down on the ground and there he foams at the mouth and grinds his teeth." Amy went straight to her room and asked the Lord why she couldn't cast him out. "Because of your unbelief," was His answer. She spent hours on her knees before she asked Misaki San if she believed the Lord Jesus was willing to cast the devil out of the man. Misaki San was startled, but after some thought and prayer, declared that she believed. Amy's impulse was to go at once, but she remembered that the disciples were

told that such a demon required fasting as well as prayer. So she and her friend did both, having sent a message in the meantime to ask if they would be permitted to see the man. Yes, came the answer, but he was very wild. He had six foxes, and was tied up.

After some hours of which Amy said only that they were solemn, the two went to the house. Stretched on the floor, fastened crosswise on two beams, bound and strapped hand and foot, his body covered with burns and wounds, lay the man. Little cones of powdered medicine had been set on his skin and lighted. They burned slowly, with a red glow. Nothing had so far daunted the fox spirits, but Amy called to mind that the power of God had conquered a demon whose name was Legion. She told the crowd in the room that her mighty Lord Jesus could cast out the six spirits. At the name of Christ a fearful paroxysm took hold of the man, hellish power was loosed, and blasphemies which even she could recognize as blasphemies poured from the man's mouth. He struggled, was forcibly held down, the women knelt and prayed, the struggle increased. Satan seemed to be mocking them. "Can you think how I felt then?" Amy wrote. "The Lord's name dishonored among the heathen, and *I had done it!* Far, far better never to have come!" But she heard the Shepherd answer: *My sheep hear My voice and I know them and they follow Me. All power is given unto Me. These signs shall follow them that believe: in My name shall they cast out devils. Fear thou not; for I am with thee.*

Amy assured the wife that God would answer, and the two went home. An hour later a message came—the foxes had gone, the cords were off, the man was himself again. Next morning he asked to see Amy and Misaki San. Unrecognizable except for the burns, he offered them a spray of scarlet pomegranate blossom and sugared ice water. He and his wife gladly knelt with the women as they prayed, joining in with "Hai! Hai!" (yes, yes).

Elisabeth Elliot, A Chance to Die *(Old Tappan, N.J.: Fleming H. Revell, 1987), 89–90.*

DEVOTION

The things that God is most concerned about are our coldness of heart towards Himself and our proud, unbroken natures. Christian service of itself can, and so often does, leave our self-centered nature untouched.

Roy Hession

DIFFICULTY

A Monument to the Boll Weevil

Vance Havner, in his book *It Is Toward Evening,* tells the story of a small town that made its living entirely from growing cotton. It was not a great living; nevertheless, it was a living. Then calamity struck as the boll weevil invaded the community, destroyed the economy, and threatened to ruin everyone. The farmers were forced to switch to peanuts and other crops that eventually brought them greater return than they would ever have made raising cotton. Ultimately, that which had seemed a disaster became the basis for an undreamed prosperity. To register their appreciation, they erected a monument—to the boll weevil. To this very day in that very little southern town, there is a monument to the boll weevil.

A Slightly Opposed Wind

See page 42

DIRECTION

Right Side Up toward God

Corrie ten Boom had a good way of explaining the perspective we need when confronting problems in life that puzzle us: "Picture a piece of embroidery placed between you and God, with the right side up toward God. Man sees the loose, frayed ends; but God sees the pattern."

DISCIPLESHIP / DISCIPLING

Preaching While We Were Walking

"Brother," St. Francis said one day to one of the young monks at the Portiuncula, "let us go down to the town and preach!" The novice, delighted at being singled out to be the companion of Francis, quickly obeyed. They passed through the principal streets; turned down many of the byways and alleys; made their way out to some of the suburbs; and at length returned, by a winding route, to the monastery gate. As they approached it, the younger man reminded Francis of his original intention.

"You have forgotten, Father," he said, "that we went down to the town *to preach!*"

"My son," Francis replied, "we *have* preached. We were preaching while we were walking. We have been seen by man; our behavior has been closely watched; it was thus that we preached our morning sermon. It is of no use, my son, to walk anywhere to preach unless we preach everywhere as we walk."

James Hastings, ed., The Speaker's Bible, *vol. 8 (Grand Rapids, Mich.: Baker, 1971), 92.*

DISCIPLINE

Discipline is a reminder that we are sinful by nature.

David Castle

Treated as Gods

British mystery writer P. D. James wrote this memorable statement in her novel *The Children of Men:*

If from infancy you treat children as gods they are liable to act as devils.

P. D. James, The Children of Men *(New York: Alfred A. Knopf, 1993).*

A Peek of a Mistake

On August 7, 1954, the mile championship of the British Empire Games in Vancouver, Canada, became the "Miracle Mile" when Roger Bannister and John Landy, the only two sub-four-minute milers, ran against each other in top condition. Bannister had a cold during the week before the race. Landy had cut his foot while strolling barefoot the day before. But both qualified easily: Bannister in 4:08.4; Landy in 4:11.4.

Bannister had plans to relax during his third lap and save everything for his finishing drive; however, Landy was not slowing down, and his lead was too great. Bannister changed his plan of action. He increased his pace and began to gain. He cut the lead in half, then closed the gap as they reached the bell.

Landy ran faster. Bannister followed. He doubted he would win unless Landy slowed down. In the last stride before home stretch, the crowds roared. Landy could not hear Bannister behind him. He peeked over his shoulder. At that moment, Bannister launched his attack. Landy did not see him until he had inched ahead. Bannister shortened his stride and won by five yards. . . .

John Landy, the great miler from Australia, ran a very strong race through the last stretch. He darted out into an early lead, and applied pressure to his opponents as he grew stronger during the race. In the end, however, he took his eyes off his goal and lost the race. In short, Landy, whose intentions may have been to run a good race, ended up running to beat Bannister, rather than to win the race.

Roger Bannister, the famous British miler who was the

first man to break the 4:00 barrier in the mile run, moved warily at first, but after determining the direction of his course, finished well and won the race. Though Bannister's game plan had called for a period of rest, he quickly realized that if he did not make a change, the race would be lost.

Discipline and commitment to the sport enabled one man to keep his focus, while another wavered. The determining factor in the race was Landy's peek, a fundamental mistake. Perhaps he had grown accustomed to doing it in previous races, afforded to him because of his speed. What should be noted is that although Landy's mistake was a small one, it proved costly.

David Castle

DISCOVERY

Sacred Frenzy

Kepler's ecstasy at discovering the third law of planetary motion recalls other great religious prophets:

Now, since the dawn eight months ago, since the broad daylight three months ago, and since a few days ago, when the full sun illuminated my wonderful speculations, nothing holds me back. I yield freely to the sacred frenzy; I dare frankly confess that I have stolen the golden vessels of the Egyptians to build a tabernacle for my God far from the bounds of Egypt. If you pardon me, I shall rejoice; if you reproach me, I shall endure.

Daniel J. Boorstin, The Discoverers *(New York: Vintage, 1993), 311–312.*

DISHONESTY

You mustn't forget that art's a swindle. Life's a swindle. To survive you have to engage in swindles yourself, cautiously, successfully.

Bertolt Brecht

Kidnapping of the Brainchild

In an essay for *Time* magazine, Lance Morrow writes about "kidnapping the brainchild":

[A] book critic for a newspaper plagiarized an old essay of mine. Someone sent the thing to me. There on the page, under another man's name, my words had taken up a new life—clause upon clause, whole paragraphs transplanted. My phrases ambled along dressed in the same meanings. The language gesticulated as before. It argued and whistled and waved to friends. It acted very much at home. My sentences had gone over into a parallel universe, which was another writer's work. The words mocked me across the distance, like an ex-wife who shows up years later looking much the same but married to a gangster. The thoughts were mine, all right. But they were tricked up as another man's inner life, a stranger's. . . .

The Commandments warn against stealing, against bearing false witness, against coveting. *Plagiarius* is kidnapper in Latin. The plagiarist snatches the writer's brainchildren, pieces of his soul. . . .

The only charming plagiarism belongs to the young. Schoolchildren shovel information out of an encyclopedia. Gradually they complicate the burglary, taking from two or three reference books instead of one. The mind (still on the wrong side of the law) then deviously begins to intermingle passages, reshuffle sentences, disguise raw chunks from the Britannica, find synonyms, reshape information until it becomes something like the student's own. A writer, as Saul Bellow has said, "is a reader moved to emulation." Knowledge transforms theft. An autonomous mind emerges from the sloughed skin of the plagiarist.

Lance Morrow, "Kidnapping the Brainchild," Time, *3 December 1990, 126.*

DISSATISFACTION

There have been a few moments in my life when I have known complete satisfaction, but only a few. I have rarely been free from the disturbing realization that my playing might have been better.
Paderewski

DIVORCE

When you're divorced from a woman, the friendship can then start because one's sexual vanity is not in it any longer.
Norman Mailer

It is ridiculous to think that you can spend your entire life with just one person. Three is about the right number. Yes, I imagine three husbands would do it.
Clare Booth Luce

Therapeutic Marriage

Tom Wolfe, the innovative journalist, labeled the 1980s the "Me Generation."

Writes Joe Bayly in *Out of My Mind:* "We are obsessed with ourselves, our bodies, our gratification, our pleasure. We judge every situation by its effect on us."

Writing in the *Yale Review,* Dr. Fred Bloom, a psychiatrist, tells about one woman, a social worker, who divorced her husband because he wasn't helping her grow as a person. "A therapeutic conception of marriage that would have surprised Freud."

If my wife does not help me grow, I dissolve our marriage. If I think I would find greater pleasure, perhaps the fountain of youth, in young flesh, I dissolve our marriage. If my wife has fallen behind me in intellectual growth and ability to relate to the business and social groups I aspire to—regardless of the fact that her faithfulness in providing a home and raising our children caused the gap—I dissolve our marriage.

Or an extreme example: I heard of a man whose wife was diagnosed as having cancer. His first reaction? "I'll divorce her."

The Me Generation.

Joseph Bayly, Out of My Mind *(Grand Rapids, Mich.: Zondervan, 1993).*

More Important than Staying Married

See page 278

Marriage among the Clergy

See page 276

DOUBT

Doubt is natural within faith. It comes because of our human weakness and frailty. . . . Unbelief is the decision to live your life as if there is no God. It is a deliberate decision to reject Jesus Christ and all that he stands for. But doubt is something quite different. Doubt arises within the context of faith. It is a wistful longing to be sure of the things in which we trust. But it is not and need not be a problem.

Alister McGrath

DRIVING

An average American male became a man at the age of sixteen, with his possession of a driver's license, and every seventeen years thereafter he drove the distance to the moon. Not just the robust but the timid and the crippled and the myopic and the senile and the certifiably insane daily hurtled about on the highways, only inches and a flick of the wrist removed from murderous collision. Every pair of hands resting on the steering wheel held the power of death; the wonder is not that accidents occurred but that most of us daily lived through that siege of rushing miles.

John Updike

EDUCATION

Education is a method whereby one acquires a higher grade of prejudices.

Laurence J. Peter

EGO

I Must Be God

Master pets dog, and the dog thinks: *He must be God.* Master pets cat, and the cat thinks: *I must be God.* This shows the contrast between the regenerate and unregenerate mind. The unregenerate thinks lightly at the goodness of God.

As Good as I

In his diary Tolstoy wrote: "I have not yet met a single man who was morally as good as I."

Paul Johnson, Intellectuals *(New York: Harper & Row, 1988), 107.*

A Heart after All

See page 106

EGOTISM

The person who can love me as I can love is still to be born. No one ever had more talent for loving. I was born to be the best friend that ever existed.

Jean Jacques Rousseau

ELITISM

Clothes Made the Man

In Victorian England gentlemen, no less than ladies, could be identified by their clothing. They wore top hats, indoors and out, except in homes or churches. Cuffs and collars were starched, cravats were affixed with jeweled pins, waistcoats were white, wide tubular trousers swept the ground at the heel but rose in front over the instep, black frock coats were somber and exquisitely cut. Swinging their elegant, gold-headed canes, gentlemen swaggered when crossing the street, dispensing coins to fawning men who swept the dung from their paths. . . . Bowlers were worn by clerks and shopkeepers and caps by those below them. Switching hats wouldn't have occurred to them, and it wouldn't have fooled anyone anyway. Despite advances in the mass production of menswear, dry cleaning was unknown in the London of the time. Suits had to be picked apart at the seams, washed, and sewn back together. Patricians wore new clothes or had tailors who could repair the garments they had made in the first place. The men in bowlers and caps couldn't do it; their wives tried but were unskillful, which accounts for their curiously wrinkled Sabbath-suit appearance in old photographs.

William Manchester, The Last Lion *(Boston: Little Brown and Company, 1983), 63.*

ENCOURAGEMENT

This ministry of consolation and encouragement is not to be regarded as inferior and of secondary importance. . . . Did we but discern it, we are daily surrounded by lonely, aching and sometimes broken hearts.

J. Oswald Sanders

Don't Stop; Don't Quit

Paderewski, the famous composer-pianist, was scheduled to perform at a great concert hall in America. . . . Present in the audience that evening was a mother with her fidgety nine-year-old son. Weary of waiting, he squirmed constantly in his seat. His mother was in hopes that her boy would be encouraged to practice the piano if he could just hear the immortal Paderewski at the keyboard. So—against his wishes—he had come.

As she turned to talk with friends, her son could stay seated no longer. He slipped away from her side, strangely drawn to the ebony concert-grand Steinway and its leather-tufted stool on the huge stage floored with blinding lights. Without much notice from the sophisticated audience, the boy sat down at the stool, staring wide-eyed at the black and white keys. He placed his small, trembling fingers in the right location and began to play "Chopsticks." The roar of the crowd was hushed as hundreds of frowning faces turned in his direction. Irritated and embarrassed, they began to shout: "Get that boy away from there." "Who'd bring a kid that young in here?" "Where's his mother?" "Somebody stop him!"

Backstage, the master overheard the sounds out front and quickly put together in his mind what was happening. Hurriedly, he grabbed his coat and rushed toward the stage. Without one word of announcement, he stepped over behind the boy, reached around both sides, and began to improvise a countermelody to harmonize and enhance "Chopsticks." As the two of them played together, Paderewski kept whispering in the boy's ear: "Keep going. Don't quit, son. Keep on playing. . . . Don't stop. . . . Don't quit."

ENDURANCE

Dear God, let me soar in the face of the wind: up, up, like the lark—so poised and so sure, through the cold on the storm with wings to endure. Let the silver rain wash all the dust from my wings. Let me soar as he soars, let me sing as he sings; let it lift me, all joyous and carefree and swift. Let it buffet and drive me, but God, let it lift.

Ruth Graham

The Steady Plop, Plop, Plop

The Christian race is not a competitive event to see who comes in first but an endurance run to see who finishes faithfully. It's like the experience of Bill Broadhurst, who entered the Pepsi Challenge 10,000-meter road race in Omaha, Nebraska. Ten years earlier, surgery for an aneurysm in his brain had left him paralyzed on his left side. Now, on a misty July morning in 1981, he stands with 1,200 lithe-looking men and women at the starting line. The gun cracks! The crowd surges forward. Bill throws his still left leg forward and pivots on it as his right foot hits the ground. His slow *plop-plop-plop* rhythm seems to mock him as the pack fades into the distance. Sweat rolls down his face, pain pierces his ankle, but he keeps going. Six miles and two hours and twenty-nine minutes later, Bill reaches the finish line. A man approaches from a small group of bystanders. Bill recognizes him from pictures in the newspaper. He's Bill Rodgers, the famous marathon runner. "Here," says Rodgers, putting his newly won medal around Bill's neck. "You've worked harder for this than I have." Broadhurst is a winner too.

Running to the Limit

The famous runner Jim Ryun, who set a mile record when he was eighteen years old, talked about his training: "I would run until I felt I couldn't take another step; then I would run until I felt my lungs were going to burst. When I came to that state, then I would run until I thought I was going to pass out. When I did this, I was making progress."

ENVY

Envy shooteth at others and woundeth herself.
Thomas Fuller

ETERNAL LIFE

The stars shine over the mountains,
The stars shine over the sea,
The stars look up to the mighty God,
The stars look down on me;

The stars shall last for a million years
A million and a day,
But God and I will live and love
When the stars have passed away.
Robert Louis Stevenson

ETERNITY

The eternally gathered church will finally hear the triune God singing over the eternal creation.
Harold Best

EUTHANASIA

Choosing Death

The ABC program *Prime Time* featured on December 8, 1994, covered the story of a man in Holland who was suffering from an illness and was pursuing euthanasia, which is legal in Holland.

This hour-long program focused on the kind doctor who continued to give the man other options. The day came when the man was examined to see if he met the criteria that the state had set up for euthanasia. As he passed the test, a smile broke out on his face and on the face of his wife of thirty-two years. Then the process began.

As the day of his death drew closer, the wife remarked to her husband that she was disappointed that he was going on a journey without her. He replied, "You know where to find me. Look for me at the Milky Way and the Big Dipper. That's where you can find me." The wife responded, "Funny, isn't it?"

As the injections were given to the man, first the sedative and then the strong dose of muscle relaxant that would shut down his heart, the wife looked over her dying husband and said to the doctor, "It's best this way, isn't it?" The doctor said, "It's best. I *think* so."

A few moments later, the doctor said to the wife, "Is this wrong, what you've seen?" Her response was, "No. It is beautiful."

The show was serene and peaceful on the surface, but it wasn't really. It was horrible enough to make a person shout out, "No, no!"

EVANGELISM

> There is no excuse for a Christian to be boring or one-dimensional or to come to life in a conversation with a non-Christian only when the topic is about the Bible.
> *Rebecca Manley Pippert*

Making Good on a Pledge

Coach Sam looked like Alley Oop, a bulky, hairy guy who spoke as if his mouth were full of marbles, but he had an effective ministry with teens in a Young Life club in Denver, Colorado.

Before he came to Christ, Sam was a high school teacher and coach. He had a foul temper and mouth and was well-known for his cursing. One of the students in his school, a quiet junior-varsity cheerleader, made a pledge to God to begin witnessing aggressively. Following the final football game of a losing season, the cheerleader approached Coach Sam.

"Coach, when you say the Lord's name, it hurts me because I am a Christian."

He yelled at the girl, and she began to cry and walked away. But from then on, every day in history class, Coach Sam watched the girl closely. At the end of the year, following final exams, Coach Sam asked her to remain after the exam. He sat down next to her and asked, "Do you remember when you spoke with me about my swearing?"

"Yes, sir."

"You said you're a Christian. Isn't everyone in America?"

"No, sir."

As the two talked, the coach noticed his voice getting softer and this young woman becoming more bold and aggressive. Finally, Coach Sam asked, "What would I do to become a Christian?"

The girl turned to face him directly and put her finger in his face. "Coach, you need to get down on your knees right now, confess your sins, and ask the Lord to forgive you for taking his name in vain!"

Coach Sam did just that. Eventually Coach Sam went into ministry and served the Lord for at least twenty years with Young Life. He lost track of the girl because her father was in the military and the family moved a lot. But what would have happened if that girl had not been bold in witnessing?

The Staying Power of Christ

In an Albanian church, among the approximately 120 people who meet every week, there is a group of elderly men. For more than 55 years these men have been committed Christians, and during all these years they have met regularly to pray and read the Bible. Under Enver Hoxha they risked their lives. All of the men found their faith in childhood due to the missionary work of Art Konrad and his colleagues. Before World War II, they had a missionary center in Korce with a Sunday school where 150–500 children heard the Gospel every week. That's where that group of elderly men first heard the good news of Christ and responded.

From a newsletter, Konrad Klippings, *August 1992.*

Thomas Huxley Convicted by Genuine Faith

As far as we know, Thomas Huxley never put his faith in Christ, but he did experience some degree of conviction. Toward the end of the century, this great agnostic was a guest at a house party in a country home. Sunday came around, and most of the guests prepared to go to church, but, very naturally, Huxley did not propose to go. Yet he approached a man known to have a simple and radiant Christian faith. Huxley said to him, "Suppose you don't go to church today. Suppose you stay at home and you tell me quite simply what your Christian faith means to you and why you are a Christian." "But," said the man, "you could demolish my arguments in an instant. I'm not clever enough to argue with you." Huxley said gently, "I don't want to argue with you; I just want you to tell me simply what this Christ means to you." The man stayed and told Huxley most simply of his faith. When he had finished, there were tears in the great agnostic's eyes. "I would give my right hand," Huxley said, "if only I could believe that." Huxley had seen something of the spiritual realities through the life of a humble, spirit-filled believer.

William Barclay, The Gospel of John, *vol. 1 (Philadelphia, Penn.: Westminster, 1975), 76.*

A Stranger's Gentle Witness

A traveling man came into a hotel to secure a room for the night. Upon being informed that every room in the building had been taken, he was naturally quite perturbed, until a portly gentleman standing nearby kindly offered to share his room with him. The offer was thankfully accepted.

Upon retiring, the portly man knelt and prayed, tenderly mentioning his guest for the night in his petition. In the morning he informed his guest that it was his custom to read a portion of the Word of God and pray before taking up the responsibilities of the day.

The effect upon the guest was moving; a strange feeling came over him; something had been working in his heart all night. When gently pressed by this stranger to accept the Lord Jesus as his personal Savior, his resistance went down in a heap. A soul had been won for Christ.

But who was this humble ambassador of Christ, who so strikingly resembled a member of President Wilson's cabinet? When business cards were exchanged before parting, to the guest's amazement, he read, "William Jennings Bryan, Secretary of State."

The Risks in Evangelism

In about the first three years of L'Abri all our wedding presents were wiped out. Our sheets were torn. Holes were burned in our rugs. . . . Drugs came into our place. People vomited on our rugs. . . . How many times have you had a drug-taker come into your home? Sure it is a danger to your family, and you must be careful. But have you ever risked it? . . . If you have never done any of these things or things of this nature, if you have been married for years and years and had a home (or even a room) and none of this has ever occurred, if you have been quiet especially as our culture is crumbling about us, if this is true—do you really believe that people are going to hell?

Francis A. Schaeffer, The Church at the End of the Twentieth Century *(Downers Grove, Ill.: InterVarsity).*

EVIL

Exceptional Depravity

Saddam Hussein was well-known to Western governments

as a man of exceptional depravity, from a clan of professional brigands. He had acquired his first gun at the age of ten (and committed his first murder, it was claimed, two years later). As the head of the secret police from 1968, and as president from 1979, his career had been punctuated both by the slaughter of his colleagues and rivals, often by his own hand, and by atrocities on the largest possible scale, not least mass public hangings of Jews.

Paul Johnson, Modern Times, *revised ed. (New York: HarperCollins, 1991), 456.*

The Sin Forecast for Today Is . . .

Here is Lance Morrow's imaginary sin "forecaster" as he reports on sin around the world:

I think there should be a Dark Willard.

In the network's studio in New York City, Dark Willard would recite the morning's evil report. The map of the world behind him would be a multicolored Mercator projection. Some parts of the earth, where the overnight good prevailed, would glow with a bright transparency. But much of the map would be speckled and blotched. Over Third World and First World, over cities and plains and miserable islands would be smudges of evil, ragged blights, storm systems of massacre or famine, murders, black snows. Here and there, a genocide, a true abyss.

"Homo homini lupus," Dark Willard would remark. "That's Latin, guys. Man is a wolf to man."

Dark Willard . . . would add up the moral evils—the horrors accomplished overnight by man and woman. Anything new among the suffering Kurds? Among the Central American death squads? New hackings in South Africa? Updating on the father who set fire to his eight-year-old son? . . .

The only depravity uncharted might be cannibalism, a

last frontier that fastidious man has mostly declined to explore. Evil is a different sort of gourmet.

Lance Morrow, "Evil," Time, *10 June 1991, 48.*

God Took His Own Medicine

Whatever the answer to the problem of evil, this much is true: God took His own medicine.

Dorothy Sayers

EVOLUTION

Nobody can imagine how nothing could turn into something. Nobody can get an inch nearer to [evolution] by explaining how something could turn into something else. It is really far more logical to start by saying, "In the beginning God created heaven and earth," even if you only mean, "In the beginning some unthinkable power began some unthinkable process."

G. K. Chesterton

EXCELLENCE

The society which scorns excellence in plumbing because plumbing is a humble activity, and tolerates shoddiness in philosophy because philosophy is an exalted activity, will have neither good plumbing nor good philosophy. Neither its pipes nor its theories will hold water.

John W. Gardner

EXPERIENCE

You can talk about religious experiences all you wish, but, if it does not have doctrinal roots, it is like cut flowers stuck into the ground. They will soon wither and die.

Bishop J. C. Ryle

F

FAILURE

Christianity, from Golgotha onwards, has been the sanctification of failure.

Malcolm Muggeridge

There is no loneliness greater than the loneliness of a failure. The failure is a stranger in his own house.

Eric Hoffer

I have revised some folk wisdom lately; one of my edited proverbs is—Nothing fails like success because you do not learn anything from it. The only thing we ever learn from is failure. Success only confirms our superstitions.

Dr. Wayne Dyer

Failure after Failure

Some years ago, a young man ran for the legislature in a large state and was badly swamped. He next entered business, failed, and spent seventeen years of his life paying off the debts of a worthless partner. He was in love with a beautiful woman to whom he became engaged, and then she died. Reentering politics, he ran for Congress and was badly defeated. He then tried to get an appointment to the United States Land Office but failed. He became a candidate for the United States Senate and was badly defeated. Two years later, he was defeated again. One failure after another, bad failures, great setbacks. His name was Abraham Lincoln, one of our greatest and most original presidents.

Flops and Flubs

These flops, flubs, failures, and fiascoes are condensed from *The Incomplete Book of Failures* by Stephen Pile:

- In 1969, a Portland, Ore., bank robber wrote instructions on a piece of paper and held it up for the cashier to read: "This is a holdup and I've got a gun." The bemused bank clerk waited while the robber wrote another note: "Put all the money in a paper bag." When this message was pushed through the grille, the cashier wrote on the bottom, "I don't have a paper bag," and passed it back. The robber fled.
- During a strike by British firemen in January 1978, the British army assumed firefighting duties. Thus, when the cat of an elderly lady in South London became trapped up a tree, she summoned an army unit. So grateful was the lady when they discharged their duty that she invited them all in for tea. Driving off later, they ran over the cat and killed it.
- A homing pigeon was released in Dyfed, Wales, in June 1953, and was expected to reach its base that evening. It was mailed home, dead, in a cardboard box, eleven years later, from Brazil. ("We had given it up for lost," its owners said.)

Stephen Pile, The Incomplete Book of Failures *(New York: E. P. Dutton).*

At the Bottom of the Heap

See page 348

The Response to Failure

See page 18

FAITH

Note now the order: first God gives me light to see the goodness and righteousness of the law, and mine own sin and unrighteousness. Out of which knowledge springeth repentance. . . . Then the same Spirit worketh in mine heart, trust and confidence to believe the mercy of God and his truth, that he will do as he hath promised, which belief saveth me.

William Tyndale

Faith is that attitude in which, acknowledging our complete insufficiency for any of the high ends of life, we rely utterly on the sufficiency of God. . . . It is an act which is the negation of all activity, a moment of passivity out of which the strength for action comes, because in it God acts.

C. H. Dodd

Most of us would live by faith if we knew that the rewards would be forthcoming inside of two weeks.

Vance Havner

I desire . . . that you exercise your minds, your faith, your spiritual powers and vividly believe that Jesus is here; so believe it, so that your inner eye beholds what you believe.

Charles H. Spurgeon

Hook Up

Just before World War II, there was a school fire in Itasca, Texas, that took the lives of 263 children. It was a horrifying tragedy. After the war, the town built a new school with the finest sprinkler system in the world. Never again would the citizens of Itasca experience another tragedy like that. Honor students were selected to take the community on tours through the new school and show them the sprinkler system. The town grew, and seven years later, the school needed an addition. As the construction began, workers discovered that the sprinkler system had never been hooked up.

Faith in Faith

A Unitarian Universalist student once remarked to Frederick Buechner that what he believed in was faith. When Buechner asked him faith in what, his answer was faith in faith. Writes Buechner: "I don't mean to disparage him—he was doing the best he could—but it struck me that having faith in faith was as barren as being in love with love or having money that you spend only on the accumulation of more money. It struck me too that to attend a divinity school [Harvard] when you did not believe in divinity involved a peculiarly depressing form of bankruptcy, and there were times as I wandered through those corridors that I felt a little like Alice on the far side of the looking glass."

Frederick Buechner, Telling Secrets *(San Francisco, Calif.: Harper San Francisco, 1991), 62.*

The Absolute Demand and Final Succor

A few years ago, Bryan Green (Church of England preacher) was invited to speak at an outstanding women's college in the Eastern United States. While he acknowledged his respect for other religions in his sermon, Canon Green nonetheless gave a clear explanation of Christianity's doctrinal content. He used a definition of Christianity suggested by Dr. Herbert Farmer: "Belief in Jesus Christ as the absolute demand and final succor."

Joseph Bayly, Out of My Mind *(Grand Rapids, Mich.: Zondervan, 1993), 50.*

Faith Is Good for You

The Associated Press reports that pollster George H. Gallup Jr. has found striking evidence that faith is good for you—and for others with whom you deal. But the benefits, he said, seem to show up clearly only when faith is strong. "We now have empirical evidence of it," he said.

For a half century, the Gallup organization has been taking measurements of people's religious beliefs and practices, providing a kind of running graph of overt religious leanings and activity in America. But only lately has Gallup delved into the more complex ramifications of faith—the impact on lives.

In two recent studies, one on effects of prayer and another on conduct and attitudes in relation to strength of belief, findings were that the most genuinely devout were the happiest and most helpful people. "The evidence overwhelmingly points to their being truly better and happier," Gallup said in an interview. He added that there has been little investigation of effects of religion on individual outlook and behavior. "This area has been mostly neglected by the social sciences," he said.

The Gallup study, whose full results were published in book form as *The Saints among Us,* used factors on a one-to-twelve scale to gauge levels of religious commitment. By those measurements, developed by the Gallup Institute's expanding Religion Research Center in Princeton, N.J., only 13 percent of believers were found in the category of the most religiously committed.

Those with this strong, transforming faith were found, through further extensive, indirect, yet revealing responses, to be set apart from others by the following characteristics: They were more ethical in personal dealings, more tolerant of persons with different backgrounds, more apt to perform charitable acts, more concerned about the betterment of society, and far happier.

"We've all heard stories of people of deep faith rising above circumstances to heroic altruism," Gallup said. "Here we have full-scale statistical evidence of it."

On the other hand, he said, the study showed that the further people are down the scale of religious commitment, the less happy they are.

In contrast to the distinguishing qualities of the highly committed, he said, comparisons between ordinary religion members and nonmembers showed little ethical difference in such matters as lying, tax evasion, and pilfering.

However, the research showed that those who are members of religions have a brighter outlook and are more active in civic-charitable work and in volunteering time.

Gallup said another recent study showed powerful personal effects of a certain kind of prayer—meditative or "listening-to-God" prayer, in which a sense of closeness to the divine is most likely.

Final Communion

At his final communion before his death, Samuel Johnson wrote and fervently prayed this prayer:

Almighty, and most merciful Father, I am now, as to human eyes, it seems, about to commemorate, for the last time, the death of thy Son Jesus Christ, our Saviour and Redeemer. Grant, O Lord, that my whole hope and confidence may be in his merits, and thy mercy; enforce and accept my imperfect repentance; make this commemoration available to the confirmation of my faith, the establishment of my hope, and the enlargement of my charity; and make the death of thy Son Jesus Christ effectual to my redemption. Have mercy upon me, and pardon the multitude of my offenses. Bless my friends; have mercy upon all men. Support me, by thy Holy Spirit, in the days of weakness, and at the hour of death; and receive me, at my death, to everlasting happiness, for the sake of Jesus Christ. Amen.

James Boswell, The Life of Johnson *(London: Penguin, 1979), 340.*

The Same As

Have faith that whatsoever you ask for in prayer is already granted you, and you will find that it will be.

When my little son was about ten years of age, his grandmother promised him a stamp album for Christmas. Christmas came, but no stamp album and no word from Grandmother. The matter, however, was not mentioned; but when his playmates came to see his Christmas presents, I was astonished, after he had named over this and that as gifts received, to hear him add, "And a stamp album from Grandmother."

I had heard it several times, when I called him to me, and said, "But, Georgie, you did not get an album from your grandmother. Why do you say so?"

There was a wondering look on his face, as if he thought it strange that I should ask such a question, and he replied, "Well, Mama, Grandma said, so it is the same as." I could not say a word to check his faith.

A month went by, and nothing was heard from the album. Finally, one day, I said, to test his faith, and really wondering in my heart why the album had not been sent, "Well, Georgie, I think Grandma has forgotten her promise."

"Oh, no, Mama," he quickly and firmly said, "she hasn't."

I watched the dear, trusting face, which for a while, looked very sober, as if debating the possibilities I had suggested. Finally a bright light passed over it, and he said, "Mama, do you think it would do any good if I should write to her thanking her for the album?"

"I do not know," I said, "but you might try."

A rich spiritual truth began to dawn upon me. In a few minutes a letter was prepared and committed to the mail, and he went off whistling his confidence in his grandma. In just a short time a letter came, saying:

"My dear Georgie: I have not forgotten my promise to you, of an album. I tried to get such a book as you desired, but could not get the sort you wanted; so I sent on to New York. It did not get here till after Christmas, and it was still not right, so I sent for another, and as it has not come as yet, I'm sending you three dollars to get one in Chicago. Your loving grandma."

As he read the letter, his face was the face of a victor. "Now, Mama, didn't I tell you?" came from the depths of a heart that never doubted, that "against hope, believed in hope" that the stamp album would come. While he was trusting, Grandma was working, and in due season faith became sight.

Attributed to Mrs. Rounds in Mrs. Charles E. Cowman, Streams in the Desert *(Grand Rapids, Mich.: Zondervan, 1996).*

Good Mental Health

When David Larson was training for a career in psychiatry, faculty advisers warned him, "You'll harm your patients if you try to combine your Christian faith with the practice of psychiatry." Instructors insisted that religion usually hurts a person's mental health.

Does research confirm that notion? Larson wondered. Or is it a myth passed around in academic circles? His curiosity led him on a quest he has followed for 15 years. He spends his time poring over academic journals and obscure research reports, pondering "negative curvilinear variables" and seeking clues into how religion affects mental and physical health.

At once Larson noticed that most research studies ignored the subject of religion altogether. This seemed odd, since 90 percent of Americans believe in God, 40 percent attend religious services weekly, and a large minority claim religion is "very important" in their lives. Could the omission reflect the antireligious bias of the field? Studies reveal that fewer than half of psychiatrists and psychologists believe in God, and one survey found that 40 percent regard organized religion as "always, or usually, psychologically harmful."

. . . In short, Larson found that religious commitment, far from causing health problems, has a pronounced effect on reducing them. "In essence the studies empirically verify the wisdom of the book of Proverbs," he says. "Those who follow biblical values live longer, enjoy life more, and are less diseased. The facts are in; we need to get the word out." As a consultant to the National Institute of Mental Health and a fellow of the newly formed Paul Tournier Institute (sponsored by the Christian Medical and Dental Society), he seeks to do just that.

Philip Yancey, "Health and the God Factor," Christianity Today, *7 October 1991, 88.*

An Embarrassing Lesson in Faith

Dr. Bruce Waltke told once of a man who was attempting to cross the frozen St. Lawrence River in Canada. Unsure of whether the ice would hold, the man first tested it by laying one hand on it. Then he got down on his knees, and gingerly began making his way across. When he got to the middle of the frozen river, where he trembled with fear, he heard a noise behind him. Looking back, he saw a team of horses pulling a carriage coming down the road toward the river. And upon reaching the river, it didn't stop, but bolted right onto the ice, and past him, while he sat there on all fours, turning a deep crimson.

The Eyes of Faith

In the middle of the night in a small Midwest farming community, the two-story house of a young family caught fire. Quickly everyone made their way through the smoke-filled house out into the front yard. Everyone except a five-year-old boy. The father looked up to the boy's room and saw his son crying at the window, rubbing his eyes.

The father knew better than to reenter the house to rescue his son, so he yelled, "Son, jump! I'll catch you." Between sobs, the boy responded to the voice he knew so well. "But I can't see you."

The father answered with great assurance. "No, Son, you can't, but I can see you!" The boy jumped and was safe in his father's arms.

The boy had faith in his father, but when he jumped he made a commitment.

Undisturbed Faith

A young Chinese was traveling from China to America to study at one of the universities. A fellow passenger noticed him reading his Bible on the deck of the ship. He engaged the Chinese in conversation. He spoke disparagingly of the Bible, endeavoring to create doubt in it, adding, "I would not like to disturb your faith in Christ, however." The Chinese replied, "Sir, if you could disturb my faith in Christ, He would not be a big enough Savior for me!"

J. Stuart Holden

Remembering the Fundamentals of Faith

I wish they'd remember that the charge to Peter was feed my sheep; not try experiments on my rats, or even, teach my performing dogs new tricks.

C. S. Lewis, Letters to Malcolm *(New York: Harcourt Brace, 1983), 5.*

God and Three Shillings

When St. Theresa was laughed at because she wanted to build a great orphanage and had but three shillings to begin with, she answered: "With three shillings Theresa can do nothing; but with God and three shillings there is nothing that Theresa cannot do."

A Great Debt, Who Can Pay?
See page 15

William Booth's Fight to the Finish
See page 116

FAME

Celebrity has become the product of a cult of personality, no longer a mark of accomplishment but an end in itself.

Harry S. Ashmore

The Broadcaster from Omaha

Success can sometimes dazzle you in the achieving, but there's usually someone around to help you keep a proper perspective. TV anchorman Tom Brokaw has a story about that:

Brokaw was wandering through Bloomingdale's in New York one day, shortly after he was promoted to co-host on the *Today Show*. The *Today Show* was a pinnacle of sorts for Brokaw after years of work, first in Omaha, then for NBC in Los Angeles and Washington, and he was feeling good about himself. He noticed a man watching him closely. The man kept staring at him and finally, when the man approached him, Brokaw was sure he was about to reap the firstfruits of being a New York television celebrity.

The man pointed his finger and said, "Tom Brokaw, right?"

"Right," said Brokaw.

"You used to do the morning news on KMTV in Omaha, right?"

"That's right," said Brokaw, getting set for the accolades to follow.

"I knew it the minute I spotted you," the fellow said. Then he paused and added, "Whatever happened to you?"

James S. Hewett, ed., Parables, Etc., *vol. 6, no. 4 (Saratoga Press: June 1986): 1.*

FAMILY

Out of ego needs, we put our best foot forward for the people we care the least about, and our worst foot forward for the people who mean the most to us.
Lane Adams

Dogs and cats should be brought up together. . . . It broadens their minds so.
C. S. Lewis

Lord, I find the genealogy of my Savior strangely checkered with four remarkable changes in four immediate generations.

1. Rehoboam begat Abia; that is, a bad father begat a bad son.
2. Abia begat Asa; that is, a bad father a good son.
3. Asa begat Jehoshaphat; that is, a good father a good son.
4. Jehoshaphat begat Joram; that is, a good father a bad son.

I see, Lord, from hence, that my father's piety cannot be handed on; that is bad news for me. But I see also that actual impiety is not always hereditary; that is good news for my son.
Thomas Fuller

Flawed Families

All our heritages are flawed—of course some far more than others. Modern men and women are so sensitized to this that many have come to use the sins of their parents as a cloak for their own sins and parental deficiencies. This has brought about, as Robert Hughes writes, "the rise of cult therapies teaching that we are all the victims of our parents, that whatever our folly, venality, or outright thuggishness, we are not to be blamed for it, since we come from 'dysfunctional families.'"
Robert Hughes, "The Fraying of America," Time, *3 February 1992, 45–46.*

Happy Families

Happy families . . . own a surface similarity of good cheer. For one thing, they like each other, which is quite a different thing from loving. For another, they have, almost always, one entirely personal treasure—a sort of purseful of domestic humor which they have accumulated against rainy days. This humor is not necessarily witty. The jokes may be incomprehensible to outsiders, and the laughter springs from the most trivial of sources. But the jokes and the laughter belong entirely to the family.

Phyllis McGinley, The Province of the Heart *(New York: Dell, 1959), 72.*

Wow! Wow!

[Winston Churchill's] feelings about his family were laced with sentimentality. His home was an independent kingdom, with its own laws, its own customs, even its own language. "Wow!" one of them would say in greeting another. When Churchill entered the front door he would cry: "Wow! Wow!" and his wife would call back an answering "Wow!" Then the children would rush into his arms and his eyes would mist over.

William Manchester, The Last Lion *(Boston: Little Brown and Company, 1983), 36–37.*

The Pull of Grandparents

A pastor and his wife in southern California tell how their little grandson, who is a missionary's kid living in Taiwan, kept asking his parents if he could go over and visit another of his little friends. Finally they asked him why, and he said, "Because they say that they have grandparents over there."

Pajama Ride

We owe this idea to Dr. Bob Smith, retired college professor and grand family man. This is how it worked one summer night. Shortly after the children were tucked into bed, we went to their bedrooms and shouted, "Pajama ride!" Robes and slippers back on, and pillows in hand, we drove to the local Dairy Queen and had a round of ice cream. Then, to doubly surprise them, we drove across town to the other Dairy Queen and announced, "Seconds!" The variations of a pajama ride are endless—a trip to the drive-in movie, a visit to Grandma and Grandpa's, a nocturnal dip in the lake—you name it.

Kent and Barbara Hughes, Common Sense Parenting *(Wheaton, Ill.: Tyndale, 1995), 38.*

Honor Your Father

Once upon a time, there was a young family—a father, mother, and their young son. Living with them was the father's dad. Grandpa was old and shaky and very feeble. He dripped everything, especially when he ate. He slobbered everything and made a terrible mess. It was embarrassing to the family, especially when company came over. So they put the old man off to one side, away from the table. They gave him an earthen bowl to eat out of. But he broke that. In fact, he continued to slobber and make a mess. Finally, his daughter-in-law spoke out harshly to him and moved him to a far corner of the room, far from the dinner table. He was given a wooden trough to eat out of. At mealtime he would look wistfully at the family, wishing that he could eat with them. But that was not to be.

One day the daughter-in-law found her son fiddling with some pieces of wood as he tried to put them together. She asked him what he was doing. His answer: "I'm making a trough for you and Daddy that I can give you when I grow up." With these words, judgment was brought to the daughter-in-law, and she shared it with her husband. They brought their dad back to the table. He didn't stop slobbering or shaking, but it didn't matter anymore. They were finally honoring their father.

Just like Mom

Every time a young man brought home a prospective wife, his mother criticized her terribly. Finally, the young man received some advice: Find someone like his mother. So he found someone just like her—a clone, in fact—and took her home. His friend wanted to know how it went with his mother. "It was great," the young man replied. "My mother loved her—but my father couldn't stand her!"

All-Consuming Choice
See page 429

We Are Men
See page 46

A Mother's Love
See page 290

Elizabeth Barrett Browning's Love Letters
See page 66

Wearing of the Green
See page 265

FATE

Fate is, that all events are fixed by an immanent, physical necessity in the series of causes and effects themselves; a necessity as blind and unreasoning as the tendency of the stone towards the earth, when unsupported from beneath; a necessity as much controlling the intelligence and will of God as of creatures; a necessity which admits no modification of results through the agency of second causes, but renders them inoperative and non-essential, save as the mere, passive stepping stones in the inevitable progression. The doctrine of a Providence teaches that the regular, natural agency of second causes is sustained, preserved and regulated by the power and intelligence of God; and that in and through that agency, every event is directed by his most wise and holy will, according to his plan, and the laws of nature which he has ordained. Fatalism tends to apathy, to absolute inaction: a belief in the providence of the Scriptures, to intelligent and hopeful effort.

Robert L. Dabney

FATHERHOOD

[A child] needs to know that his father and his mother are lovers, quite and apart from their relationship to him. It is the father's responsibility to make the child know that he is deeply in love with the child's mother.

Elton Trueblood

Thou hast been faithful to my highest need:
And I, thy debtor, ever, evermore,
Shall never feel the grateful burden sore.
Yet most I thank thee, not for any deed,
But for the sense thy living self did breed
That fatherhood is at the world's great core.

George Macdonald, a dedication to his father in the first volume of Poems *(1857).*

The Best View of Life

In a Father's Day essay contest, Christopher Shelton, ten years old at the time, wrote this essay on why his father had the best view of life:

The man that I call dad is really my stepdad. My real dad died when I was very young. My stepdad is very large. When he stands in the door he blocks the sunlight. One day he said: "Once I climbed a mountain when I was in the army in Europe and I saw God." I do not think that he really saw God. I think he felt God there and found peace in the mountains, because he told me that he found out what was really important in life and what was not. . . .

When I say my prayers, sometimes I see my real father smile at me. I do not really see him, but I can feel him smile. He is smiling because my stepdad is making me become the gentleman that my dad would want me to be.

Chicago Tribune, *21 June 1993, 1, 10.*

What a Dad

A dad really loved his family and wanted them to enjoy a summer vacation, but because of business commitments he couldn't go with them. But, being dedicated to their happiness, he assured them of his desire that they take the trip and enjoy themselves. "You go on without me. You'll have a great time. I'll make sure of that. I'm so sorry that I have to work." So Dad helped them plan every day of the camping trip. He even planned the route they would drive in the family station wagon. They would drive to California, camp up and down the coast, and then travel back home. Each day was carefully arranged—even the highways they would travel and the places they would stop. Their dad knew the route, the time they would arrive at each place; it was planned almost to the hour. But there was something Dad had planned that he didn't tell his family. The father took off work and flew to an airport near where his family would be on that day of the trip. He had arranged to have someone pick him up and drive him to a place where every car on that route had to pass. Then he sat down and waited, grinning from ear-to-ear as he waited for the sight of that familiar station wagon, packed full of camping gear and kids. When he spotted the car, he stood up, stepped out onto the shoulder of the road, and stuck out his thumb to hitchhike a ride with his family—who thought he was thousands of miles away. It's a wonder they didn't drive off the road or collapse from heart failure. But can you imagine the fun they had for the rest of the vacation? And the memories they stored away in their mental scrapbooks were never to be forgotten. When later asked by a friend why he went to all that trouble, this unusually creative father answered: "Well, someday I'm going to be dead, and when that happens, I want my kids and my wife to say, 'You know, Dad was a lot of fun.'"

I Want You!

He would appear at meals, pay allowances, and give advice, often without really listening to the problems of his family before he spoke. One afternoon as he was preparing an article for a respected journal of medicine, his little son crept into the forbidden sanctuary of his study.

"Daddy," he appealed. Without speaking, the doctor opened his desk drawer and handed the boy a box of candy. "Daddy," the boy persisted. To this the doctor responded with a grunt, indicating that he knew the boy was there but didn't really acknowledge his presence personally. "Daddy!" the boy called out again. With this the busy doctor swung around in his chair and said, "What on earth is so important that you insist on interrupting me? Can't you see I'm busy? I have given you candy and a pencil. Now what do you want?" "Daddy, I don't want any of those things. I want you! I just want to be with you!"

FATHERHOOD OF GOD

Into His Father's Lap

John Huffman told of a little child crawling through all the wonders of Revelation chapter 4: across the sea of glass, past the twenty-four elders, up the throne, and into his Father's lap, and crying "Daddy." This reflects what every believer gets to do.

Christianity Explained

If you want to judge how well a person understands Christianity, find out how much he makes of the thought of being God's child and having God as his Father. If this is not the thought that prompts and controls his worship and prayers and his whole outlook on life, it means that he does not understand Christianity very well. For everything that Christ taught, everything that makes the New Testament new and better than the Old, everything that is distinctively Christian, is summed up in the knowledge of the Fatherhood of God the Father.

J. I. Packer, Knowing God *(Downers Grove, Ill.: InterVarsity, 1973), 19–20.*

FEAR

Fear, in and of itself, is not morally evil or wrong; fear is neutral.

Robert E. Morosco

What Does It Profit a Man?
See page 110

The Darkest Hour
See page 104

FELLOWSHIP WITH CHRIST

A soul habitually in contact with Jesus will imbibe sweetness from him, just as garments laid away in a drawer with some . . . perfume absorb fragrance from that beside which they lie.

Alexander Maclaren

FLATTERY

Flattery, provided that it be disguised as something other than flattery, is infinitely sweet. So Decius Brutus says of Caesar: "But when I tell him he hates flatterers, he says he does, being then most flattered."

Richard John Neuhaus

FOOTBALL

Any man who watches more than three football games a year—his wife should have him declared legally dead and his estate in probate.

Erma Bombeck

FORGIVENESS

A Bitter Buildup

John R. Claypool, in *The Preaching Event,* tells this story about identical twin boys. The boys' lives became inseparably intertwined. From the first they dressed alike, went to the same schools, did all the same things. In fact, they were so close that neither ever married, but they returned home and took over the family business when their father died. Their relationship was pointed to as a model of creative collaboration.

One morning a customer came into the store and made a small purchase. The brother who waited on him put the dollar bill on top of the cash register and walked to the front door with the man. Sometime later he remembered what he had done, but when he went to the cash register, the dollar was gone. He asked his brother if he had seen the money and put it in the register, and the brother replied that he knew nothing of the money in question.

"That's funny," said the other, "I distinctly remember placing the bill here on the register, and no one else has been in the store since then."

Had the matter been dropped at that point—a mystery involving a tiny amount of money—nothing would have come of it. However, an hour later, this time with a noticeable hint of suspicion in his voice, the brother asked again, "Are you sure you didn't see that dollar bill and put it into the register?" The other brother was quick to catch the note of accusation, and flared back in defensive anger.

This was the beginning of the first serious breach of trust that had ever come between these two. It grew wider and wider. Every time they tried to discuss the issue, new charges and countercharges got mixed into the brew, until finally things got so bad that they were forced to dissolve their partnership. They ran a partition down the middle of the store and turned what had once been a harmonious partnership into an angry competition. In fact, that business became a source of division in the whole community, each twin trying to enlist allies for himself against the other. This warfare went on for more than twenty years.

Then one day a car with an out-of-state license plate parked in front of the store. A well-dressed man got out, went into one of the sides, and inquired how long the merchant had been in business in that location. When the man learned it was more than twenty years, the stranger said, "Then you are the one with whom I must settle an old score.

"Some twenty years ago," he said, "I was out of work, drifting from place to place, and I happened to get off a boxcar in your town. I had absolutely no money and had not eaten for three days. As I was walking down the alley behind your store, I looked in and saw a dollar bill on the top of the cash register. Everyone else was in the front of the store. I had been raised in a Christian home and I had never before in all my life stolen anything, but that morning I was so hungry, I gave in to the temptation, slipped through the door, and took that dollar bill. That act has weighed on my conscience ever since, and I finally decided that I would never be at peace until I came back and faced up to that old sin and made amends. Would you let me now replace that money and pay you whatever is appropriate for the damage?"

The stranger was surprised to see the old man shaking his head in dismay and beginning to weep. When that brother had gotten control of himself, he took the stranger by the arm and said, "I want you to go next door and repeat the same story you have just told me." The stranger did, only this time there were two old men, who looked remarkably alike, both weeping uncontrollably.

John R. Claypool, The Preaching Event *(Waco, Tex.: Word, 1980), 39.*

By God's Grace

My wife, Barbara, learned some important lessons about forgiveness through difficult experiences with her father. She recalls:

I was just fourteen years old that warm June day as I readied myself for graduation from Stephens Junior High School. I was about to receive the Daughters of the American Revolution Award for citizenship, scholarship, and service to one's school, and I was to address the graduates. Nervously, I scanned my notes and straightened the hem of my new blue organdy dress, which Grandma Barnes had lovingly made for me.

As I began to ascend the platform, one of my girlfriends ran to me giggling, "There's a drunk man over there!" Dad's noisy arrival was unavoidably conspicuous. His clothes were a mess, and he was so intoxicated that he had difficulty staying on his feet as he walked to his place. Dad's struggle with alcohol had always been a source of fear and pain in our family, but now it was the cause of my personal humiliation.

I began to pray. And that prayer helped me to get through the painful situation. My trembling legs nearly gave way as I rose to speak, but inside something solid and good was taking place. I wasn't experienced enough to fully comprehend it. But I did understand that my father, my daddy, was causing me pain and that my heavenly Father had taught me to forgive: "And forgive us our sins, just as we have forgiven those who have sinned against us" (Matt. 6:12, TLB). So as the principal presented the award, tarnished now of its anticipated glory, I made a decision. *By the grace of God* I would not hate my father. I would *forgive* him. Then I began my speech.

Kent and Barbara Hughes, Common Sense Parenting *(Wheaton, Ill.: Tyndale, 1995), 5–7.*

Forgive as Christ Has Forgiven You

In his book *Let Justice Roll Down,* John Perkins told how the example of Christ's forgiveness enabled him to forgive. Here is his account:

The spirit of God worked on me as I lay in that bed. An image formed in my mind. The image of the cross—Christ on the cross. It blotted out everything else in my mind.

This Jesus knew what I had suffered. He understood. And He cared. Because He had experienced it all Himself.

This Jesus, this One who has brought good news directly from God in heaven, had lived what He preached. Yet He was arrested and falsely accused. Like me, He went through an unjust trial. He also faced a lynch mob and got beaten. But even more than that, He was nailed to rough wooden planks and killed. Killed like a common criminal . . .

But when He looked at that mob who had lynched Him, He didn't hate them. He loved them. He forgave them. And He prayed to God to forgive them. "Father, forgive these people, for they don't know what they are doing."

His enemies hated. Jesus forgave. I couldn't get away from that.

The Spirit of God kept working on me and in me until I could say with Jesus, "I forgive them, too." I promised Him that I would "return good for evil," not evil for evil. And

He gave me the love I knew I needed to fulfill His command to me of "love your enemy." . . .

It's a profound, mysterious truth—Jesus' concept of love overpowering hate. I may not see its victory in my lifetime. But I know it's true.

I know it's true, because it happened to me. On that bed, full of bruises and stitches—God made it true in me. He washed my hatred away and replaced it with a love for the white man in rural Mississippi.

I felt strong again. Stronger than ever. What doesn't destroy me makes me stronger.

I know it's true.

Because it happened to me.

John Perkins, Let Justice Roll Down *(Glendale, Calif.: Regal Books Division, G/L Publications, 1976).*

Unbearable Silence

Two unmarried sisters lived together. Because of a slight disagreement over an insignificant issue, they stopped speaking to each other. Unable and unwilling to move out of their small house, the sisters continued to use the same rooms, eat at the same table (separately), and sleep in the same bedroom. Without one word. A chalk line divided the sleeping area into two halves, separating a doorway and a fireplace. Each would come and go, cook and eat, sew and read without crossing over into the other's domain. Through the night, each could hear the breathing of the foe, but because neither was willing to take the first step toward reconciliation and forgiveness, they coexisted for years in grinding silence.

Too Poor to Pay

In a rural village lived a doctor who was noted both for his professional skill and his devotion to Christ. After his death, his books were examined. Several entries had writing across them in red ink: "Forgiven—too poor to pay." Unfortunately, his wife was of a different disposition. Insisting that these debts be settled, she filed a suit before the proper court. When the case was being heard, the judge asked her, "Is this your husband's handwriting in red?" She replied that it was. "Then," said the judge, "not a court in the land can obtain the money from those whom he has forgiven."

The Past Is Blotted Out

Years ago, in Winchester, Virginia, there was a boy by the name of Charles Broadway Rousse. He was the son of a poor widowed working woman. Charles went to Sunday school, sang in the choir, and was a useful member in that little church of poor and inconspicuous people. By and by, the boy fell in with evil associates, was implicated in a crime, and was sent to the penitentiary. But the members of the church got up a petition to the governor and had the boy pardoned. They sent a delegation and brought him home. On their arrival home they went directly to the little church where all the congregation had gathered and there, in the presence of all the people, exercised the divine function that has been committed to the church: They forgave his sins. They said to him, "We want you to come right back into the church and take your place in the Sunday school and the choir. The past is blotted out, forgiven and forgotten, and is as though it had never been." Then, one by one, all the members of the church took him by the hand, personally ratifying the action of the church.

The Old Heart

See page 81

Guilt That Could Never Be Forgiven

See page 74

Transformed Life

See page 346

On My Enemy's Behalf
See page 266

Heavy Laden in Body and Soul
See page 261

The Soup a Spider Swills
See page 198

FREEDOM

Our freedom, Son of God, arose
When Thou wast cast in prison,
And from the durance Thou didst choose
Our liberty is risen.
Didst Thou not choose a slave to be,
We all were slaves eternally.
J. S. Bach

All other freedoms, once won, soon turn into a new servitude. Christ is the only liberator whose liberation lasts forever.
Malcolm Muggeridge

Any persuasive effort which restricts another's freedom to choose for or against Christ is wrong.
Em Griffin

The Captivity of Ideology
Philosopher Hannah Arendt described totalitarianism as a process in which lonely, rootless individuals, deprived of meaning and community, become the captives of ideology.

A Matter of History
See page 248

FREE WILL

The most extraordinary thing about human beings [is the fact] that they pursue ends which they know to be disas-

trous and turn their backs on ways which they know to be joyous.
Malcolm Muggeridge

FRIENDS

If I had to choose between betraying my country and betraying my *friend,* I hope I should have the guts to betray my country.
E. M. Forster

Friends are an expensive luxury, and when one invests one's capital in a calling or mission in this life, one cannot afford to have friends. The expensive thing about friends is not what one does for them, but what, out of consideration for them, one leaves undone.
Henrik Ibsen

FRUSTRATION

Where the Monkey Drops It

At the Calcutta Country Club and Golf Course in Calcutta, India, ground rule number ten on the golf course is simply "Play the ball where the monkey drops it." This ground rule may also provide special insight for families.

India itself is a country of contrasts. Though surrounded by slums of abject poverty, the Calcutta Country Club is one of the most posh and refined golf facilities in the world, reserved for the privileged few of wealth and influence. This beautifully laid-out and maintained course is cut directly out of a magnolia jungle. Thus, the course is surrounded by thick groves of huge, lush magnolias. These magnolias are also home to large monkey populations. In the trees, the monkeys find not only shelter from the sweltering Indian sun but also a superb view of the fairways.

For reasons as yet undiscovered, these same monkeys have developed a special affinity for golf balls, especially as the balls bounce and roll down the fairways. As you might imagine, this affinity poses quite a problem for golfers. At the Calcutta Country Club, they have developed a unique solution to a unique problem.

As the golfer connects with the golf ball, a rustling can be heard among the magnolia trees. The ever vigilant monkeys spring from the trees in pursuit of the bouncing projectile. At that time, the caddie launches forth in his task: intimidating the monkeys. The caddie, madly waving a golf club, races down the fairway toward the ball. Usually these tactics succeed in preventing the monkey from capturing the ball. On occasion, however, it is the monkey who is successful. As the monkey grasps the ball and flees, the caddie intensifies his efforts at intimidation. Invariably, at the approach of the human, the monkey will drop the golf ball. And there's the rub. The monkey may or may not drop the ball in the fairway, in a good lie, or even within the boundary. The golfer is not allowed the prerogative of returning the ball to its original spot, regardless of whether its position has worsened or improved. Thus, we are left with the Calcutta Country Club rule number ten: *Play the ball where the monkey drops it!*

In families, especially in stepfamilies, we often discover that the courts or prior relationships have left us with "unfavorable lies." At the discovery, we are left with the choice: either we expend our lives trying to change the unchangeable and bemoaning our lot or we deal with the reality. The first option leads only to frustration; the second opens our lives to divine intervention that can make something meaningful and worthwhile out of that which has been broken.

G

GENEROSITY

Check Out the Motive

Lining Miami's Flagler Street are beautiful royal palm trees. One night vandals cut down six of the magnificent trees, and the city did not have the money to replace them. Then, at last, a donor came forward and offered to replace the lost trees. But while the former trees had been 15 feet tall and formed a perfect foreground for a big Delta Air Lines billboard, the new trees were 35 feet tall and completely hid the billboard. The donor? Eastern Airlines.

There are many motives for giving.

The Anglican Digest, *8.*

Faith and Spending Habits

Does faith influence spending?

Most Americans believe God cares what they do with their money, says Princeton professor Robert Wuthnow. But that has little effect on how they actually spend their money.

Wuthnow bases this indictment on the results of a three-year study of religion and economic values that included a survey of over 2,000 people in the U.S. labor force.

Faith provided earlier generations "with a moral language that helped curb the pursuit of money," and it continues to do so to some extent now, Wuthnow explains in a recent discussion of his findings in *The Christian Century*. "Nevertheless, faith makes little difference to the ways in which people actually conduct their financial affairs."

Here is why he says that:

While 71 percent of those surveyed agreed that "being greedy is a sin against God," only 12 percent said they had been taught that it is wrong to want a lot of money. Among those who attend church every week, the proportion was only 16 percent.

Wuthnow's survey finds that many want a lot of money; 84 percent said they wish they had more money than they do. Any statistical analysis of the survey results reveals that there is no conflict for religious people between valuing one's relationship with God and valuing making a lot of money. "Taking other differences into account, people who highly value their relationship with God were no less likely to value making a lot of money."

Other findings include:

- 92 percent believe that the condition of the poor is a serious social problem;
- 74 percent reject the view that "it is morally wrong to have a lot of nice things when others are starving";
- 53 percent believe "people who work hard are more pleasing to God than people who are lazy."

His findings also provide some signs of hope. Three out of four surveyed say they would like churches and synagogues to "encourage people to be less materialistic."

Christianity Today, *26 April 1993, 57.*

All the Silver

In his book, *The Life of Johnson,* James Boswell describes how Johnson would frequently give all the silver in his pocket to the poor, who watched him, between his house and the tavern where he dined. Johnson would walk the streets at all hours and said he was never robbed, for the rogues knew he had little money, nor the appearance of having much.

James Boswell, The Life of Johnson *(London: Penguin, 1979).*

Plow Work

Dr. Roy L. Laurin tells of a Christian businessman who was traveling in Korea. In a field by the side of the road was a young man pulling a crude plow while an old man held the handles. The businessman was amused and took a snapshot of the scene. "That is curious! I suppose these people are very poor," he said to the missionary who was interpreter and guide to the party. "Yes," was the quiet reply, "these two men happen to be Christians. When their church was being built, they were so eager to give something toward it, but they had no money. So they decided to sell their one and only ox and give the proceeds to the church. This spring they are pulling the plow themselves." The businessman was silent for some moments. Then he said, "That must have been a real sacrifice." "They did not call it that," said the missionary. "They thought themselves fortunate that they had an ox to sell!" When the businessman reached home, he took the picture to his pastor and told him about it. Then he added, "I want to double my giving to the church and do some *plow* work. Up until now I have never given God anything that involved real sacrifice."

Adapted from Roy L. Laurin, II Corinthians: Where Life Endures *(Findlay, Ohio: Dunham, 1946), 158.*

God Is Always Ahead

One of the fundamental lessons for Christians is that we cannot outgive God. He is no man's debtor. Henry Parsons Crowell, builder of the great Quaker Oats cereal enterprise, when asked for his average rate of giving, said, "For over forty years I have given sixty to seventy percent of my income to God. But I have never gotten ahead of Him! He has always been ahead of me!"

Stephen Olford, The Grace of Giving *(Memphis, Tenn.: Encounter Ministries, 1972), 10.*

Gold for Iron

Early in the nineteenth century the king of Prussia, Frederick William III, found himself in great trouble. He was carrying on expensive wars; he was endeavoring to strengthen his country and make a great nation of the Prussian people. But he did not have enough money to accomplish his plans. He could not disappoint the people, and to capitulate to the enemy would be unthinkable.

After careful reflection he decided to approach the women of Prussia and ask them to bring their gold and silver jewelry to be melted down and made into money for their country. He resolved, moreover, that for each gold or silver ornament he would give in exchange a bronze or iron decoration as a token of his gratitude. Each decoration would bear the inscription, "I gave gold for iron, 1813."

The response was overwhelming. And what was even more important was that these women prized their gifts from the king more highly than their former possessions. The reason, of course, is clear. The decorations were proof that they had sacrificed for their king. Indeed, it is a matter of history that it became unfashionable for women to wear jewelry. So the Order of the Iron Cross was established. Members of this order wore no ornaments, save a cross of iron for all to see.

The church today needs an army of people who are so committed to the King of Kings that sacrifice becomes a way of life! . . . Recruits for this army should be known as members of the Order of the Cross of Christ because they have experienced the grace of giving.

Stephen Olford, The Grace of Giving *(Memphis, Tenn.: Encounter Ministries, 1972), 18–19.*

The Church Costs Too Much

A certain Christian once said to a friend, "Our church costs too much. They are always asking for money." [Her friend replied in this fashion:] "Sometime ago a little boy was born in our home. He cost [us] a lot of money from the very beginning: he had a big appetite; he needed clothes, medicine, toys and even a puppy. Then he went to school, and that cost a lot more; later he went to college; then he began dating, and that cost a small fortune! But in his senior year at college he died, and since the funeral he hasn't cost [us] a penny. Now which situation do you think [we] would rather have?" After a significant pause, the friend continued, "As long as this church lives it will cost. When it dies for want of support it won't cost us anything. A living church has the most vital message for all the world today; therefore, I am going to give and pray with everything I have to keep our church alive."

Alan Redpath, The Royal Route to Heaven *(Westwood, N.J.: Revell, 1960), 226–227.*

Bismarck's Cigar

Bismarck is reported to have said that the cigar he enjoyed most in life was a cigar he never smoked. It was after one of the big battles of the Franco-German war. It had been a grim struggle, but at last the issue had been decided and victory won. And Bismarck—the tension over—took out a cigar, the last he had, happy in the thought of a smoke. But just as he was about to apply the match to it, he saw a wounded soldier looking at his cigar with longing eyes. Bismarck understood the appeal. He lit the cigar and gave it to the wounded soldier, and saw him in the enjoyment of his smoke almost forget the pain of his wound. "It was the best cigar I ever had," said the old warrior.

James Hastings, ed., The Speaker's Bible, *vol. 17 (Grand Rapids, Mich.: Baker, 1971), 118.*

A Generous Solution

A man was having a lot of trouble with his eyes. His doctor examined him carefully and then shook his head. "My friend," he said, "you are in trouble. There is only one doctor anywhere near here who can help you. It is going to take a very difficult and expensive operation to fix them up." The doctor wrote down a name and address on a piece of paper and gave it to the man. "Here is the name of the doctor who can help you," he said. "I would advise you to go at once and take plenty of money with you, for it's going to cost a lot."

The man had eighty dollars in the bank, so he got his money and went to see the other doctor. After examining his eyes very carefully, he said, "Yes, you need the operation, and in a hurry. And I am not sure you can pay what it will cost. I never accept less than five hundred dollars for this particular operation."

"Well, then," said the man in sad despair, "I guess I'll just have to go blind, because I have only eighty dollars."

But the good doctor said, "There is one other way to solve our trouble. You don't have enough to pay for the bill, and I can't charge you as little as eighty dollars, but there is another way open to us—I will do the operation for nothing." And that is just what he did.

Kenneth N. Taylor, Romans for the Family Hour *(Chicago: Moody, 1959), 55–56.*

Heavy Laden in Body and Soul

See page 261

GENIUS

If people knew how hard I worked to get my mastery, it wouldn't seem so wonderful after all.
Michelangelo

A genius? Perhaps, but before I was a genius I was a drudge.
Paderewski

All the genius I may have is merely the fruit of labor and thought.
Alexander Hamilton

Genius: an infinite capacity for taking pains.
Thomas Carlyle

The Creative Mind
See page 91

GIVING

Sold for a Silver Coin

D. James Kennedy told of a peasant woman in West Africa who had been wonderfully saved about fifty years ago. She had always longed to do something for Jesus. People were bringing gifts of corn to an evangelistic crusade, but this woman was so poor that she had nothing to offer. Yet later in the week, she went forward and placed a silver coin on the altar. Although it was worth only a dollar, at that time it represented a large sum. Thinking she might have gotten it dishonestly, the missionary hesitated to receive it. But he didn't want to make a scene, so he said nothing.

Following the service, he found the woman and questioned her about the money. She said that because the Lord Jesus had freed her from the bondage of her sins and had given her eternal life, she wanted to serve him and help make him known to others. So she had gone to a nearby plantation and sold herself as a slave for life for one dollar. That was the gift she laid on the altar that night.

A Generous Solution
See page 180

A Passion for Prisoners
See page 67

GLORY

A White Tunnel of Light

John Piper recalls a thunderstorm he experienced while flying at night from Chicago to Minneapolis:

I was . . . almost alone on the plane. The pilot announced that there was a thunderstorm over Lake Michigan and into Wisconsin. He would skirt it to the west to avoid turbulence. As I sat there staring out into the total blackness, suddenly the whole sky was brilliant with light and a cavern of white clouds fell away four miles beneath the plane and then vanished. A second later, a mammoth white tunnel of light exploded from north to south across the horizon, and again vanished into blackness. Soon the lightning was almost constant and volcanoes of light burst up out of cloud ravines and from behind distant white mountains. I sat there shaking my head almost in unbelief. "O Lord, if these are but the sparks from the sharpening of your sword, what will be the day of your appearing!" And I remembered the words of Christ,

As the lightning comes from the east,
and shines as far as the west,
so will be the coming of the Son of man.

Even now as I recollect that sight, the word *glory* is full of feeling for me. I thank God that again and again he has awakened my heart to desire him, to see him, and to sit down to the feast of Christian Hedonism and worship the King of Glory. The banquet hall is very large.

John Piper, Desiring God *(Portland, Oreg.: Multnomah, 1986), 84.*

Christ Is Everything
See page 49

Sacred Frenzy
See page 132

GOD

We want, in fact, not so much a Father in heaven as a grandfather in heaven—a senile benevolence who, as they say, "liked to see young people enjoying themselves" and whose plan for the universe was simply that it might be truly said at the end of each day, "a good time was had by all."
J. B. Phillips

Whatever God is He is infinitely. In Him lies all the power there is; any power at work anywhere is His. Even the power to do evil must first have come from Him since there is no other source from which it could come.
A. W. Tozer

You sum up the whole of New Testament teaching in a single phrase, if you speak of it as a revelation of the Fatherhood of the holy Creator. . . . "Father" is the Christian name for God.
J. I. Packer

In the absence of any other proof, the thumb alone would convince me of God's existence.
Isaac Newton

I change
He changes not,
The Christ cannot die.
His love, not mine
The resting place;
His love, not mine
The tie.
Anonymous

A Big-Godder

Robert Dick Wilson was one of the great professors at Princeton Theological Seminary. One of his students was once invited back to preach in Miller Chapel twelve years after he had graduated. Old Dr. Wilson came in and sat down near the front. At the close of the meeting, the old professor came up to his former student, cocked his head to one side in his characteristic way, extended his hand, and said, "If you come back again, I will not come to hear you preach. I only come once. I am glad that you are a big-Godder. When my boys come back, I come to see if they are big-Godders or little-Godders, and then I know what their ministry will be." His former student asked him to explain, and he replied. "Well, some men have a little God, and they are always in trouble with him. He can't do any miracles. He can't take care of the inspiration and transmission of the Scripture to us. He doesn't intervene on behalf of his people. They have a little God and I call them little-Godders. Then there are those who have a great God. He speaks and it is done. He commands and it stands fast. He knows how to show himself strong on behalf of them that fear him. You have a great God, and he will bless your ministry." He paused a moment, smiled, and said, "God bless you," and turned and walked out.

Drawing God

Teacher: What are you doing?

Boy: I'm drawing God.

Teacher: You can't do that. No one knows what God looks like.

Boy: They will when I'm through.

The Good Shepherd

A party of tourists was on its way to Palestine, and its guide was describing some of the quaint customs of the East.

"Now," he said, "you are accustomed to seeing the shepherd following his sheep through the English lanes and byways. Out in the East, however, things are different, for the shepherd always leads the way, going on before the flock. And the sheep follow him, for they know his voice."

The party reached Palestine, and to the amusement of the tourists, almost the first sight to meet their eyes was that of a flock of sheep being driven along by a man. The guide was astonished and immediately made it his business to accost the shepherd.

"How is it that you are driving these sheep?" he asked. "I have always been told that the Eastern shepherd leads his sheep."

"You are quite right, sir," replied the man. "The shepherd does lead his sheep. But you see, I'm not the shepherd; I'm the butcher."

God Is Cold
See page 13

The Modest Fool
See page 14

Nobody as Creator
See page 91

GOD'S WILL

To experience the glory of God's will for us means absolute trust. It means the will to do his will, and it means joy.

Elisabeth Elliot

If you should find yourself in the sight of God and one said to you: "Look thither" and God on the other hand, should say: "It is not my will that you should look"; ask your own heart what there is in all existing things which would make it right for you to give that look contrary to the will of God?

I must confess that I ought not to oppose the will of God even to preserve the whole creation.
St. Anselm

The Arbitrariness of the Spirit
J. B. Phillips suggested that "there is an apparent capriciousness and arbitrariness about the working of the Spirit of God which is singularly exasperating to the tidy-minded."

Lord, What Thou Wilt
The last words of Richard Baxter say it all: "Lord, what thou wilt, where thou wilt, and when thou wilt."

The Mueller Method
See page 328

GOODNESS

Not until I went into the churches of America and heard her pulpits flame with righteousness did I understand the secret of her genius and power. America is great because America is good, and if America ever ceases to be good, America will cease to be great.
de Tocqueville

Nothing is so beautiful, nothing so continually fresh and surprising, so full of sweet and perpetual ecstasy, as the good; no desert is so dreary, monotonous, and boring as evil.
Simone Weil

GOOD WORKS

Thought without action is a disease.
Goethe

It is sheer profanity to speak of the merit of works, especially in the presence of God. . . . Let us be silent about the merit of our works, which amounts to very little or rather nothing at all, and let us magnify the grace of God, which is everything.
Lefevre d'Etaples

We have even our good works from God, from whom likewise our faith and our love come.
St. Augustine

When God rewards our good works he is rewarding his works and gifts in us, rather than our own works.
Martin Buber

The Points System

A man appeared at heaven's gate and was met there by an angel, who told him, "It will take one thousand points to get in. Tell me about yourself so that I will know how many points to give you."

The man smiled and said, "Well, I've been going to church almost every Sunday all my life."

"Excellent," the angel said. "That will give you three points. What else?"

The man was shocked. "Only three points?" he gasped. "Well, I was Sunday school superintendent for a while, and I tithed, and I tried to be a good neighbor."

"Very good," the angel said. "That will give you ten points."

The man gasped again. "At this rate," he said, "I'll never get in except by the grace of God."

"Exactly," the angel said. "Come on in."

GOSSIP

The longer I live, the more I feel the importance of adhering to the rules which I have laid down for myself in relation to such matter [as gossip].

- 1st To hear as little as possible what is to the prejudice of others.
- 2nd To believe nothing of the kind till I am absolutely forced to it.

- 3rd Never to drink in the spirit of one who circulates an ill report.
- 4th Always to moderate, as far as I can, the unkindness which is expressed toward others.
- 5th Always to believe that if the other side were heard, a very different account would be given of the matter.

Charles Simeon

Tales Remembered

Here are Samuel Johnson's comments on telling tales:

A man should be careful never to tell tales of himself to his own disadvantage. People may be amused and laugh at the time, but they will be remembered, and brought out against him upon some subsequent occasion.

Murdered by the Church

A marble slab in a New Hampshire cemetery gives a wife's name, followed by this bitter, almost unbelievable epitaph: "Murdered by the Baptist Ministry and Churches." Then it proceeds to sketch the story. Apparently a pastor and a deacon had accused the woman of lying in a church meeting. She was condemned unheard and reduced to poverty. When an exparte council was asked of the church, the latter voted not to receive any communication on the matter. The malicious assassination of the woman's character helped bring an early death. Her last words were, "Tell the truth and this iniquity will out."

Leslie B. Flynn, Great Church Fighters *(Wheaton, Ill.: Victor, 1976), 29.*

Feathers on the Doorsteps

The story is told of a young man during the Middle Ages who went to a monk, saying, "I've sinned by telling slanderous statements about someone. What should I do now?" The monk replied, "Put a feather on every doorstep in town." The young man did just that. He then came back to the monk wondering if there was anything else he should do. The monk said, "Go back and pick up all those feathers." The young man replied excitedly, "That's impossible! By now the wind will have blown them all over town!" The monk said, "So has your slanderous word become impossible to retrieve."

Taking Credit
See page 94

GRACE

Gentlemen, for half my life I have been teaching the grace of God, but I am just beginning to understand it. And gentlemen, it is magnificent. It is magnificent!
Lewis Sperry Chafer

Christ, our Lord [is] an infinite source of all grace, so that if the whole world would draw enough grace and truth from it to make the world all angels, yet it would not lose one drop; the fountain always runs over, full of grace.
Martin Luther

Cheap grace is the preaching of forgiveness without requiring repentance, baptism without church discipline, Communion without confession, absolution without personal confession. Cheap grace is grace without discipleship, grace without the cross, grace without Jesus Christ.
Dietrich Bonhoeffer

God's grace is not infinite. God is infinite and God is gracious. We experience the grace of an infinite God, but grace is not infinite. God sets limits to His patience and forbearance. He warns us over and over again that someday the ax will fall and His judgment will be poured out.
R. C. Sproul

Believers who are the most desperate about themselves are the ones who express most forcefully their confidence in grace. . . . Those who are the most pessimistic about man are the most optimistic about God; those who are the most severe with themselves are the ones who have the most serene confidence in divine forgiveness. . . . By degrees the awareness of our guilt and of God's grace increase side by side.

Paul Tournier

Man is born broken. He lives by mending. The grace of God is glue.

Eugene O'Neill

Grace is getting what we don't deserve. Mercy is not getting what we do deserve.

Anonymous

If I ever reach heaven I expect to find three wonders there: first, to meet some I had not thought to see there; second, to miss some I had thought to meet there; and third, the greatest wonder of all, to find myself there.

John Newton

No Condemnation

Martin Luther once said, "Once upon a time the devil came to me and said, 'Martin, you are a great sinner, and you will be damned!' 'Stop! Stop!' said I. 'One thing at a time. I am a sinner, it is true, though you have no right to tell me of it. I confess it. What next?' 'Therefore you will be damned.' 'That is not good reasoning. It is true I am a great sinner, but it is written, "Christ Jesus came into the world to save sinners, of whom I am chief," therefore I shall be saved. Now go your way.'" Martin Luther could say, like Paul, "Who is he that condemneth? It is Christ that died, yea, rather, that is risen again!" (Romans 8:34, KJV).

John Wesley White, The Devil *(Wheaton, Ill.: Tyndale, 1971), 146.*

Tribute to God's Grace

In heaven there was once a great debate as to who was the greatest monument of God's grace. All breasts were bared and all secrets were told as the redeemed sought to pay tribute to the grace of God. One after another related the sin or transgression out of which Christ had delivered him. At length the choice seemed to be settling down upon one man who apparently had committed all sins. Iniquity after iniquity he related as he turned over the ghastly pages of his autobiography. And then he related how on his deathbed Christ came and saved him as he had saved the thief on the cross.

But just before the vote was taken another of the redeemed stepped forward and asked to tell his story. It was this: He had come to know and love Christ as a child and had followed him all the days of his life, and by his grace he had been kept from the sins and transgressions of which the others had spoken. Then the vote was taken; and it was not the drunkard, the thief, the adulterer, the perjurer, the murderer, or the blasphemer, but the man who had followed Christ all his days and had been kept by his grace who was selected as the greatest monument to the grace of God.

Clarence Edward Macartney, Macartney's Illustrations *(New York: Abingdon), 148.*

Amazing Grace

Back in the eighteenth century, a young boy was born into a Christian home. For the first six years of his life, he heard the truths of the gospel and he was loved. Sadly, though, his parents died. The orphaned boy went to live with his relatives. There he was mistreated and abused and ridiculed for his faith in Christ.

The boy couldn't tolerate that situation, and he fled and joined the Royal Navy. In the navy, the boy's life went downhill. He became known as a brawler, was whipped many times, and participated in some of his comrades' being keel-hauled. Finally, while he was still young, he deserted the Royal Navy and fled to Africa, where he attached himself to a Portuguese slave trader. There, his life reached its lowest point. There were times when he actually ate off the floor on his hands and knees. He escaped, then became attached to another slave trader as the first mate on his ship. But the young man's pattern of life had become so depraved, he couldn't stay out of trouble. As the story goes, he stole the ship's whiskey and got so drunk that he fell overboard. He was close to drowning when one of his shipmates harpooned him and brought him back on board. As a result, the young man had a huge scar in his side for the rest of his life. After that escapade, he couldn't get much lower. In the midst of a great storm off the coast of Scotland, when days and days were filled with pumping water out of the boat, the young man began to reflect on the Scripture verses he had heard as a child. He was marvelously converted. The new life John Newton found is reflected in these familiar words:

> Amazing grace! how sweet the sound—
> That saved a wretch like me!
> I once was lost but now am found,
> Was blind but now I see.

It's Magnificent

It was a hot afternoon in Dallas, Texas, in May 1951. A small class of graduating seminarians sat around the school's president, Lewis Sperry Chafer, who was delivering his lecture from a wheelchair. The students who sat and listened were about to graduate from Dallas Theological Seminary. At the end of the class, the old gentleman, very near to death, reached into his pocket, pulled out his handkerchief, and wiped the perspiration from his face. He had just finished his final lecture on his favorite subject—the grace of

God. Chafer closed his eyes as tears came, and his last words to that graduating class were these: "Gentlemen, for half my life I have been teaching the grace of God, but I am just beginning to understand it. And gentlemen, it is magnificent. It is magnificent!"

Fallen So Low
See page 82

Heavy Laden in Body and Soul
See page 261

The Points System
See page 187

GRIEF

Should it be ours to drain the cup of grieving,
even to the dregs of pain, at thy command,
we will not falter, thankfully receiving
all that is given by thy loving hand.
Joseph Bayly

If the only thing you have to offer is a broken heart, you offer a broken heart. So in a time of grief, the recognition that this is material for sacrifice has been a very great strength for me. Realizing that nothing I have, nothing I am will be refused on the part of Christ.
Elisabeth Elliot

Carry On with Christian Dignity
On Sunday, March 18, 1979, in Aspen, Colorado, a twin-engine light plane crashed shortly after takeoff. At that moment, Mrs. Stephanie Ambrose May, a fine Christian woman, lost her husband, John Edward, her son David Edward, her daughter Karla Emily, and her son-in-law Richard Owen Snyder. Mrs. May kept a diary for the next

two months in which she recorded her feelings, her emotions. Here are her entries for May 7 and 8:

My burden is heavy, but I don't walk alone. My pain is unrelenting, but I thank God for every moment that He blessed me with. I pray that my life will be used for His glory, that I might carry my burden with Christian dignity, and that out of my devastation, may His kingdom become apparent to someone lost and in pain. I close this diary, and with it goes all my known ability and capacity for love. I must climb to a different plane and search for a different life. I cannot replace or compare my loss. It is my loss. I am not strong. I am not brave. I am a Christian with a burden to carry and a message to share. I have been severely tested, but my faith has survived, and I have been strengthened in my love and devotion to the Lord. Oh, God, my life is Yours—comfort me in Your arms and direct my life. I have walked in hell, but now I walk with God in peace. John Edward, David, Karla, and Richard are in God's hands. I am in God's arms and His love surrounds me. This rose will bloom again.

GROWTH

More Beyond

It is said that, before the discovery of America, Spanish coins that bore the imprint of the Pillars of Hercules had a motto: *Ne plus ultra,* "Nothing else beyond"; but after the success of Columbus, the motto was changed to *Plus ultra,* "More beyond." So it is with the Christian life; whatever may be the heights to which the believer attains, "Still there is more to follow."

A Monument to the Boll Weevil

See page 129

GUILT

You have to look people in the eye and make them feel guilty.

A thirteen-year-old Girl Scout, on how she sold 11,200 boxes of cookies.

I have come to the conclusion that none of us in our generation feels as guilty about sin as we should or as our forefathers did. I think this basically is the problem of living in a psychologically oriented age.

Francis A. Schaeffer

Painful Pride

Samuel Johnson never considered himself an "undutiful son," but he recalls a time he was disobedient. "I refused to attend my father to Uttoxeter-market [where Johnson's father had a stall]. Pride was the source of that refusal, and the remembrance of it was painful. A few years ago, I desired to atone for this fault; I went to Uttoxeter in very bad weather, and stood for a considerable time bareheaded in the rain, on the spot where my father's stall used to stand. In contrition I stood, and I hope the penance was expiatory."

James Boswell, The Life of Johnson *(London: Penguin, 1979), 333–334.*

The Culture of Victimhood

In a comic by cartoonist Bill Watterson featuring Calvin and Hobbes, the two are walking and Calvin remarks: "Nothing I do is my fault. My family is dysfunctional, and my parents don't empower me! Consequently, I'm not self-actualized! My behavior is addictive, functioning in a diseased process of toxic codependency! I need holistic healing and wellness before I'll accept any responsibility for my actions! I love the culture of victimhood."

Hobbes's observation: "One of us needs to stick his head in a bucket of ice water."

HABITS

Relaxation, communication, and a measure of beauty and pleasure should be part of even the shortest of meal breaks.
Edith Schaeffer

Could the young but realize how soon they will become mere walking bundles of habits, they would give more heed to their conduct while in the plastic state.
William James

Habit is a cable; we weave a thread of it every day, and at last we cannot break it.
Horace Mann

The chains of habit are too small to be felt until they are too strong to be broken.
Benjamin R. Dejung

Choose Your Rut Carefully

Sign on the Alaskan Highway: "Choose your rut carefully because you'll be in it for the next 300 miles."

HAPPINESS

There are only three kinds of persons: those who serve God, having found Him; others who are occupied in seeking Him, not having found Him; while the remainder live without seeking Him, and without having found Him.

The first are reasonable and happy, the last are foolish and unhappy; those between are unhappy and reasonable.
Blaise Pascal

All men seek happiness. This is without exception. Whatever different means they employ, they all tend to this end. The cause of some going to war, and of others avoiding it, is the same desire in both, attended with different views. The will never takes the least step but to this object. This is the motive of every action of every man, even of those who hang themselves.
Blaise Pascal

Happiness . . . you cannot command it. When you expect to be happy you are not; when you don't expect to be happy there is suddenly Easter in your soul, though it be midwinter.
Elizabeth Goudge

The greatest happiness you can have is knowing that you do not necessarily require happiness.
William Saroyan

Happiness Is Overrated

Is he happy? No. Why should he be? We weren't put here to be happy. But the knowledge of his unhappiness does not gnaw. Everyone is unhappy, or rather everyone has a boring job, a marriage that's turned to disinterest, a life that's turned to sameness. And because he does not expect to be happy the knowledge of his unhappiness does not weigh on him. He looks perhaps to other more eternal forms of comfort.

Somewhere in the Seventies, or the Sixties, we started expecting to be happy, and changed our lives (left town, left families, switched jobs) if we were not. And society strained and cracked in the storm.

I think we have lost the old knowledge that happiness is overrated—that, in a way, life is overrated. We have lost, somehow, a sense of mystery—about us, our purpose, our meaning, our role. Our ancestors believed in two worlds, and understood this to be the solitary, poor, nasty, brutish and short one. We are the first generations of man that actually expected to find happiness here on earth, and our search for it has caused such—unhappiness. The reason: If you do not believe in another higher world, if you believe only in the flat material world around you, if you believe that this is your only chance at happiness—if that is what you believe, then you are not disappointed when the world does not give you a good measure of its riches. You are despairing.

Peggy Noonan, "You'd Cry Too If It Happened to You," Forbes, *14 September 1992, 65.*

HATRED

The Soup a Spider Swills

Walter Wangerin, Jr., is a poet in nonfiction. His accounts of his experience as a pastor in an inner-city parish are achingly moving. He too plays with language, for its sound, for its effect, and for its power. In one short essay, he begins with what seems to be a biology lesson. Spiders, he tells us, have no stomachs. They inject their digestive juices into their prey. In Wangerin's words:

"Through tiny punctures she injects into a bounded fly digestive juices; inside *his* body his organs and nerves and tissues are broken down, dissolved, and turned to warm soup. This soup she swills—even as the most of us swill souls of one another after having cooked them in various enzymes: guilt, humiliations, subjectivities, cruel love—there are a number of fine, acidic mixes. And some among us are so skilled with the hypodermic word that our dear ones continue to sit up and to smile, quite as though they were still alive. But the evidence of eating is in our own fatness."

Gene Edward Veith, Reading between the Lines *(Wheaton, Ill.: Crossway, 1990).*

The Appropriate Title

In a controversy with the great Baptist preacher Robert Hall on some religious point, the Reverend Newman Smith wrote a bitter pamphlet, denouncing Hall and his doctrine. Unable to select what he thought was just the appropriate title, he sent the pamphlet to a friend upon whose judgment he relied, and asked him to suggest a suitable title. Some time before, Newman Smith had written a widely read and very helpful pamphlet, "Come to Jesus." When his friend read this bitter tirade against Hall, he sent the pamphlet back to Smith and wrote to him, "The title which I suggest for your pamphlet is this, 'Go to Hell' by the author of 'Come to Jesus.'"

Clarence Edward Macartney, The Woman of Tekoah *(New York, Nashville: Abingdon), 128–129.*

HEART

O dearest Jesus, holy child,
Prepare a bed, soft, undefiled,
A holy shrine, within my heart,
That you and I need never part.

Martin Luther

HEAVEN

At present we are on the outside of the world, the wrong side of the door. We discern the freshness and purity of morning, but they do not make us fresh and pure. We cannot mingle with the splendors we see. But all of the leaves of the New Testament are rustling with the rumor that it will not always be so. Someday, God willing, we shall get in.

C. S. Lewis

There have been times when I think we do not desire heaven, but more often I find myself wondering whether in our heart of hearts, we have ever desired anything else.

C. S. Lewis

I shall be so like God that the devil himself shall not know me from God. He will not be able to tempt me any more than he can tempt God. Nor will there be any more chance of my falling out of the kingdom than of God being driven out of it.
John Donne

I cannot pretend to be impartial about the colours. I rejoice with the brilliant ones, and am genuinely sorry for the poor browns. [When I reach heaven I would] require a still gayer palette than I get here below. I expect orange and vermilion will be the darkest, dullest colours upon it, and beyond them there will be a whole range of wonderful new colours which will delight the celestial eye.
Winston Churchill

A Better Likeness

Andrew Bonar sent Charles Spurgeon a copy of his commentary on Leviticus. Spurgeon was so blessed by the exposition that he returned the book with this notation: "Dr. Bonar, please place herein your autograph and photograph."

Soon the book was returned with this message from the saintly Bonar: "Dear Spurgeon: Here is the book with my autograph and photograph. If you had been willing to wait a short season, you could have had a better likeness; for *I shall be like Him. I shall see Him as He is.*"
Paul R. Van Gorder, In the Family.

People without a Country

Might it be said of us what was described in the *Epistle to Diognetus, V,* written in the second century?

"The distinction between Christians and other men is neither in country nor language nor customs. For they do not dwell in cities in some places of their own, nor do they use any strange variety of dialect . . . yet while living in Greek and barbarian cities, according as each obtained his lot, and following local customs, both in clothing and food and the rest of life, they show forth the wonderful and confessedly strange character of the constitution of their own citizenship. Though they are residents at home in their own countries, their behavior there is more like that of transients; they take their full part as citizens, but they also submit to anything and everything as if they were aliens. For them, any foreign country is a homeland, and any homeland a foreign country."

Michael Cromartie, "Resident Aliens," Tabletalk *18.3 (March 1994): 10.*

To Hear the King Say, "Excellent"

A friend of Bernie May's (U.S. division director of Wycliffe) had the opportunity to meet a king and queen. This man worked in a tiny nation, doing community-development work. Struggling to encourage tribal people living in the high mountain valleys was difficult, and he often wondered if he was doing any good. It was easy to get discouraged.

He was invited to a stand-up dinner party on the castle lawn, hosted by the queen. He felt deeply honored to be invited. In the crowd of about four hundred local people, he stood out as an obvious Westerner.

The king and queen spent an hour and a half going through the crowd, greeting each guest. When the royal couple came to May's friend, he told them his name and the work he was doing. The king hesitated. He was not familiar with the mountain village where the man worked. The queen, who had met him earlier, gave a brief explanation to the king. The king then asked him how long he had been there.

He replied, "Sixteen years."

The king seemed touched. Looking him in the eye, he said meaningfully, "Excellent." He then moved on to the next person.

Bernie May's friend admitted it was a short conversation,

but that was all he needed to hear. He had heard the king say, "Excellent."

Not Home Yet

Henry C. Morrison, after serving for forty years on the African mission field, headed home by boat. Theodore Roosevelt was also aboard that same boat. Morrison was quite dejected when, upon entering New York harbor, the president received a great fanfare as he arrived home. Morrison thought he should get some recognition for his forty years in the Lord's service. Then a small voice came to Morrison: *Henry, you're not home yet.*

Ed Young, The Minister's Manual *(New York: Harper & Row, 1978).*

John 14—Comfort for Generations

It is very possible that more tears have fallen on John 14 than on any other passage in the New Testament. Dr. A. L. Gabelein used to say that among his family treasures was a German Bible that went back many generations. He said that one could open that Bible to some pages and it would look as if it had come right off the press, but if opened to John 14, the pages were spotted, soiled, and worn from the tears of many generations.

It was John Watson, the great preacher, who said that when someone in his flock was dying, going through deep waters, sometimes he would kneel down next to that person and whisper, "In my Father's house are many mansions," and he said that three-quarters of the way through the river, they would almost turn around and come back, and he would hear them repeating, " . . . Father's house . . . many mansions . . ."

One old Puritan preacher by the name of Henry Ven was dying, and his biography says this: "The prospect made him so high-spirited and jubilant that his doctor said that his joy at dying kept him alive a further fortnight." You see, it is wonderfully clear that we are to derive comfort from the fact that Jesus is coming to take us to be with him.

HEDONISM

Exhausted from Pleasure

A psychologist tells the story of a despairing young woman, spent in an endless round of parties, exhausted by the pursuit of pleasure. When told she should simply stop, she responded, "You mean I don't have to do what I want to do?"

Charles Colson, "The Enduring Revolution," Templeton Address, *1993, 7.*

Feel-Good Worship

The sign on the front of a Presbyterian church in Indianapolis reads: "Join Us for Worship. You Will Feel Better for It!" It is far from obvious that worship will make one feel better. To be sure, in a very ultimate sense, surrendering oneself to God in thankful trust will make one *be* better. But along the way to being better the Christian is sure to go through times of *feeling* worse. Repentance, after all, involves a painful loss of self, an abandonment of false securities, and the travail of new birth. It is also true with respect to what happens on Sunday mornings: Woe to you when they say it feels so good.

Richard John Neuhaus, Freedom for Ministry *(Grand Rapids, Mich.: Eerdmans, 1979), 139.*

HELL

I am bound to admit that I have seen a far larger number surrender to Christ when I have been preaching on the terrible results of neglecting salvation than when dwelling on any other theme.

G. Campbell Morgan

Almost every natural man that hears of hell, flatters himself that he shall escape it.
Jonathan Edwards

Hell is truth seen too late.
Thomas Hobbes

Heaven for climate, hell for company.
James M. Barrie

One fears that some will inherit hell and be content. Large and ample opportunity is given to us; but if that be deliberately and finally rejected, it is "impossible" to renew us to repentance.
John Watson

Lost Forever

Billy Graham said this at Amsterdam '86: "Unless we believe in a future judgment or that people are lost forever without Christ, the cutting edge of evangelism is blunted."

HELP

A Helping Hand

French painter Emile Ranouf had depicted in one of his paintings an old man dressed in fisherman's garb, seated in a boat with a little girl next to him. Both the elderly gentleman and the child have their hands on a huge oar. The old man is looking down fondly at the little girl and has apparently told the girl that she may assist him in rowing the boat. The child feels as if she is doing a great share of the task. It's easy to see, however, that it is the old man's strong, muscular arms that are actually propelling the boat through the water. The painting is called *A Helping Hand*.

Christ has granted us the privilege of sharing his work here on earth, but we must never forget that it is only as God works in and through us that we are able to perform our task. While he directs us to put our hand upon the oar, we must always be aware of the source of our power. He is the strength of our lives!

HOLINESS

> Hence that dream and amazement with which Scripture uniformly relates [that] holy men were struck and overwhelmed whenever they beheld the presence of God. . . . Men are never duly touched and impressed with a conviction of their insignificance, until they have contrasted themselves with the majesty of God.
> *John Calvin*

A Round of Golf with Billy Graham

A few years ago one of the leading golfers on the professional tour was invited to play in a foursome with Gerald Ford, then president of the United States, Jack Nicklaus, and Billy Graham. The golfer was especially in awe of playing with Ford and Billy Graham (he had played frequently with Nicklaus before).

After the round of golf was finished, one of the other pros came up to the golfer and asked, "Hey, what was it like playing with the President and with Billy Graham?"

The pro unleashed a torrent of cursing, and in a disgusted manner said, "I don't need Billy Graham stuffing religion down my throat." With that he turned on his heel and stormed off, heading for the practice tee.

His friend followed the angry pro to the practice tee. The pro took out his driver and started to beat out balls in fury. His neck was crimson and it looked like steam was coming from his ears. His friend said nothing. He sat on a bench and watched. After a few minutes the anger of the pro was spent. He settled down. His friend said quietly, "Was Billy a little rough on you out there?" The pro heaved an embarrassed sigh and said, "No, he didn't even mention religion. I just had a bad round."

Astonishing. Billy Graham had said not a word about God, Jesus, or religion, yet the pro had stormed away after the game accusing Billy of trying to ram religion down his throat. How can we explain this? It's really not difficult. Billy Graham didn't have to say a word; he didn't have to give a single sideward glance to make the pro feel uncomfortable. Billy Graham is so identified with religion, so associated with the things of God, that his very presence is enough to smother the wicked man who flees when no man pursues. Luther was right, the pagan does tremble at the rustling of a leaf. He feels the hound of heaven breathing down his neck. He feels crowded by holiness even if it is only made present by an imperfect, partially sanctified human vessel.

R. C. Sproul, The Holiness of God *(Wheaton, Ill.: Tyndale, 1985), 91–93.*

The Most Honored Guest

When Queen Victoria reigned in England, she would occasionally visit some of the humble cottages of her subjects. One time she entered the home of a widow and stayed to enjoy a brief period of Christian fellowship. Later on, the poor woman was taunted by her worldly neighbors. "Granny," they said, "who's the most honored guest you've ever entertained in your home?" They expected her to say it was Jesus, for despite their constant ridicule of her Christian witness, they recognized her deep spirituality. But to their surprise she answered, "The most honored guest I've entertained is Her Majesty, the queen." "Did you say the queen? Ah, we caught you this time! How about this Jesus you're always talking about? Isn't he your most honored guest?" Her answer was definite and scriptural: "No, indeed! He's not a guest. He lives here!" Her hecklers were put to silence.

Explosive Power

See page 358

HOLY SPIRIT

A man full of the Spirit is one who is living a normal Christian life. Fullness of the Spirit is not the state of spiritual aristocracy, to which only a few can attain.

G. Campbell Morgan

Where the Spirit reigns, believers relate to the Word—teaching.
Where the Spirit reigns, believers relate to each other—koinonia.
Where the Spirit reigns, believers relate to God—worship.
Where the Spirit reigns, believers relate to the world—evangelism.

R. Kent Hughes

The Spirit's Timing

In his book *By the Power of the Holy Spirit,* Dave Howard recalls this incident that occurred while he was a missionary in Colombia:

Some years ago my colleague Ernest Fowler and I determined to visit an Indian tribe in Colombia where we had reason to believe the gospel had not yet gone. We laid plans carefully for our trip. We packed our knapsacks, had our hammocks and other equipment in good order, had maps of the river and surrounding jungle area where these Indians lived, and had our travel plans checked out. On the morning of departure I rose early, for my accustomed quiet time with the Lord. For some strange reason, as I went to prayer, I became obsessed with an overwhelming sense of restraint about the trip. I could not pray with any freedom about it. I opened the Word, but nothing I read seemed to fit my need at the moment. For nearly an hour I struggled with this problem, wondering what God was trying to say to me. All I could sense was an intangible feeling that we should not go.

I went to Ernest (who had spent that night in our home so we could leave together at an early hour) and asked how he felt about the trip. He had not experienced the same sense of restraint that seemed to bear down on me. But when I explained my feelings he said, "Well, let's pray about this together and see what God says." After breakfast and some further discussion and prayer, Ernest said with a quiet settled conviction, "I don't think we should go. If God has placed this restraint in your heart, whatever may be the reason, I don't think we should violate it. We won't go."

Three years later he and I received an invitation from two Indian brothers of that tribe to spend a week with them to teach them the Scriptures. They had become Christians through the witness of Colombian believers, but they needed instruction in the Word. They were our point of contact to enter this tribe with the Word of God. Three years earlier, when we had planned our trip, these two men were not yet Christians, nor was anyone else in the tribe. We would have had no bridge, no entering wedge, to commend us to the people had we gone at that time.

HONESTY

Honest History

Vàclav Havel, Czech playwright and president, made a pointed address in the presence of Kurt Waldheim of Austria. "He who fears facing his own past," Havel said, "must necessarily fear what lies before him. . . . Lying can never save us from the lie. Falsifiers of history do not safeguard freedom but imperil it. . . . Truth liberates man from fear." Honest history is the weapon of freedom.

Arthur M. Schlesinger Jr., The Disuniting of America *(New York: W. W. Norton & Company, 1992), 52.*

Small Notes

See page 231

Do the Right Thing

See page 229

Two Exams
See page 228

HONOR
My Reputation Is in Your Hands
A Boston pastor who was President of the Lord's Day League and well known as a speaker on temperance and for his gifted humor, used to tell a story of a clerk employed by the governor whose son had received an invitation to dinner at the governor's mansion. The boy's mother prepared him for the great occasion, and just before he left for the dinner, his father took him aside and said, "Son, you are now going to the governor's mansion. Remember, my reputation is in your hands." After telling this story, the temperance speaker would often emphasize the fact that God's reputation is in our hands as His children.

Then came a day when the papers were filled with the story of how this minister's son brought disgrace to the family name. Driving the family car one Sunday while he was drunk, he killed a man, much to the agonized shame of his father, who had preached against drunkenness and Sabbath breaking all these years. Shortly after that, the ministers were giving a dinner to which they wanted to invite this minister, but because of the tragedy were doubtful what to do. They felt, however, that they ought to invite him, anyway, and did. This time he told no jokes, indulged in no humor. He simply repeated his story of the son going to the governor's mansion and those final words, "My reputation is in your hands." Everybody understood. It was like a message from heaven. True it is, that with the privilege goes also the duty to uphold God's honor. His reputation is in our hands.

Harold J. Ockenga, Ph.D., Faithful in Christ Jesus; Preaching in Ephesians *(New York: Fleming H. Revell, 1958), 43.*

A Greater King

Frederick the Great at one time called all his generals together. One of them, Hans Von Zieten, refused to come. He had duties to perform at his church that night, and a Communion to participate in, so he refused. Later he was again invited to dinner with all the generals and Frederick the Great. Von Zieten came, and the others made light of him, joking about his religious duties and about the Lord's Supper. Von Zieten stood and said to Frederick the Great, "My lord, there is a greater king than you, a king to whom I have sworn allegiance, even unto death. I am a Christian, and I cannot sit quietly as the Lord's name is dishonored, his character belittled, and his cause subjected to ridicule. With your permission I shall withdraw." There was silence because the generals knew this could mean death. But Frederick the Great was smitten, begged him to stay at the dinner, and promised him that he would never again demean those sacred things.

The Tragic End of a Traitor

Benedict Arnold's name is synonymous with treachery and treason because he sold the fortification plans of West Point to the British for gold and rank. His last years were tragic ones, lived out in London in financial distress and mental anguish. Here are the last entries from his diary:

April 19th. I have been very ill again—at death's door, they tell me, and out of my mind. . . . I have called for these memoirs again, to dedicate them to the American people. . . . But I cannot change them much. . . .

June 12th. I have made a private memorandum for my personal belongings—the sword-knots, etc.,—and I have called Sage to get them with the Continental uniform. . . .

"The old blue and buff one?" said the stupid English fool. . . . I said, Yes, and I looked at it a long time; it had one rip in the shirt I got at Ridgefield. . . . James, thinking it too shabby, was for getting a smart scarlet one. I told him No. I fell asleep, and he must have put it away. . . .

June 13th. It is the only uniform I have ever worn with honor, and I would be buried in it. . . . Sage has left me. . . .

June 14th, 1801 (Note by an unknown hand, probably Miss Fitch):—General Arnold expired at half past six this morning. His last moments were unconscious, but at dawn he was heard calling to his body-servant, Sage. He lay across the bed, half-dressed, his lame leg in the buff breeches, the other still unclothed, as if he had fainted while drawing it on; on his body an old blue coat they told me had been his American uniform.

Allan Emery, A Turtle on a Fencepost *(Waco, Tex.: Word, 1979), 89.*

Right and Wrong Matter More than Life

See page 43

HOPE

Man Flies like a Beetle

Author Joseph Conrad once wrote the following to philosopher Bertrand Russell: "I have never been able to find in any man's book or any man's talk anything convincing enough to stand up for a moment against my defeated sense of fatality governing this man-inhabited world. . . . The only remedy for Chinamen [Russell was currently offering solutions to *The Problem of China,* in his latest book] and for the rest of us is the change of hearts. But looking at the history of the last 2,000 years there is not much reason to expect that thing, even if man has taken to flying. . . . Man doesn't fly like an eagle, he flies like a beetle."

Paul Johnson, Modern Times, *revised ed. (New York: HarperCollins, 1991), 456.*

Who Died?

See page 122

Nothing Can Harm Me
See page 84

The Exact Day of Salvation
See page 369

HUMANISM

By the year 2000 we will, I hope, raise our children to believe in human potential, not God.
Gloria Steinem

My dream is that the artist class—people who have proven through their work that they are humanists and wish to push for what Aldous Huxley called the desirable human potentialities of intelligence, creativity and friendliness—will seize the instrument of technology and try to take humanity into a period of history in which we can reach for utopia.
Francis Ford Coppola

Men perish, but man shall endure. Lives die, but the life is not dead. Glory to man in the highest for man is the master of things.
Algernon Charles Swinburne

Modern myth makers have revised and condensed the story of Prometheus and tell it not as a tragedy but as a triumph. The bowdlerized version takes the single element of stealing fire from the gods, that is, the inauguration of technology, energy, and tools, and celebrates this as a gateway to utopia. The other parts of the story—amnesia rewarding death, unguided ambition, the daily renewed suffering that is a consequence of living without wisdom in defiance of our human nature—are edited out.
Eugene H. Peterson

God placed man in the middle of the world without a secure place, without a distinctive identity, without a special function, while all these things were granted to the rest of his creatures. Man is created neither earthly nor heavenly; he can degenerate into a beast, he can ascend to heaven; everything depends solely and entirely on his will. It is granted to man to possess what he wishes, to be what he wants.

Pico Della Mirandola

Brief and powerless is man's life; on him and all his race the slow, sure doom falls pitiless and dark.

Bertrand Russell

HUMANITY

When God made man, He gave him five kisses, five fiery kisses, five fiery kisses, which are known as his senses.

Hans Christian Andersen

HUMILITY

I would rather that my posterity, as long as I am remembered at all, should know that I was a minister and disciple of Jesus Christ. If the angel of truth may be commissioned to write this on my tombstone, I should ask no other recognition in the present world.

Samuel Cox

Though long by following multitudes admired,
No party for himself he e'er desired;
His one desire, to make the Saviour known,
To magnify the Name of Christ alone.
If others strove who should the greatest be,
No lover of pre-eminence was he.

Charles Wesley writing of George Whitefield, "the greatest preacher that England has ever produced."

I often think that God must have been looking for someone small enough and weak enough for Him to use, and that He found me.

Hudson Taylor

While humility is the sovereign grace of Christianity, the Greeks had no symbol in their language to denote it. Every word akin to it has in it some element of meanness, feebleness, or contempt.

William Gladstone

The men who are aware of their own essential poverty; not the men who are poor in friends, poor in influence, poor in acquirements, poor in money, but those who are poor in spirit, who feel themselves poor creatures; . . . who know that they need much to make their life worth living, to make their existence a good thing, to make them fit to live; these humble ones are poor whom the Lord calls blessed.

George Macdonald

O Heavenly Father, for Thy dear Son's sake, keep me from climbing. Let me hate preferment. For Thine infinite mercies' sake, let me love a low contemptible life, and never think to compound matters between the happiness of this world and the next.

George Whitefield

The first link between
my soul and Christ is
not my goodness
but my badness;
not my merit
but my misery;
not my standing but my falling.

Charles H. Spurgeon

Humility Is the First, Second, and Third Thing

One of the greatest theologians in the history of Christendom was undoubtedly Aurelious Augustinius, better known as St. Augustine, who was converted in the year 387 and later became Bishop of Hippo in North Africa. One of his memorable sayings was this—"For those who would learn God's ways, humility is the first thing, humility is the second, and humility is the third." That may at first sound like an unwarranted exaggeration, but it is surely an echo of these words in the Old Testament—"[God] has showed you, O man, what is good. And what does the Lord require of you? To act justly and to love mercy and to walk humbly with your God" (Micah 6:8).

John Blanchard, The Truth for Life *(West Sussex, England: H. E. Walter, 1982), 262.*

Money Is a Poor Substitute for Purpose

J. C. Penney was a man of advanced years before he committed his life fully to Jesus Christ. He was a good man, honest, but primarily interested in becoming a success and making money. "When I worked for six dollars a week at Joslin's Dry Goods Store back in Denver," he confessed as he looked back on his life, "it was my ambition, in the sense of wealth in money, to be worth one hundred thousand dollars. When I reached that goal I felt a certain temporary satisfaction, but it soon wore off and my sights were set on becoming worth a million dollars."

Mr. and Mrs. Penney worked hard to expand the business; but one day Mrs. Penney caught cold and pneumonia developed, which claimed her life. It was then that J. C. Penney realized having money was a poor substitute for the real purposes in living. "When she died," he said, "my world crashed about me. To build a business, to make a success in the eyes of men, to accumulate money—what was the purpose of life? What had money meant for my wife? I felt mocked by life, even by God Himself."

After several more fiery trials, J. C. Penney was financially ruined, and naturally, in deep distress. That is when God could deal with his self-righteous nature and his love for money. After his spiritual conversion he could testify of God's working.

"I had to pass through fiery ordeals before reaching glimmerings of conviction that it is not enough for men to be upright and moral men. When I was brought to humility and the knowledge of dependence on God, sincerely and earnestly seeking God's aid, it was forthcoming, and a light illumined my being. I cannot otherwise describe it than to say that it changed me as a man."

James S. Hewett, ed., Parables, Etc., *vol. 6, no. 1 (Saratoga Press: 1986).*

Treated like a Servant

The Navigators are well known for their emphasis on having a servant attitude. A businessman once asked Lorne Sanny, president of the Navigators, how he could know when he had a servant attitude. The reply? "By how you act when you are treated like one."

Tangle of Vipers

See page 120

HUMOR

Sign in a gas station:

Labor:

$10 per hour.

If you watch, $12 per hour.

If you help, $15 per hour.

If you worked on it first and then brought it in, $27.50 per hour.

Paul Harvey

I think one way to tell when something important is going on [in a laboratory] is by laughter.

Dr. Lewis Thomas of Memorial Sloan-Kettering Cancer Center

An English bishop once said, "Everywhere Paul went there was a revolution, while everywhere I go they serve tea."

Steak for Two

A Scotsman . . . took his wife out to dinner. Both ordered steak. The wife started eating hers at top speed, but the man left his untouched.

"Something wrong with the steak, sir?"

"No, no, I'm waiting for my wife's teeth."

Kingsley Amis, Memoirs *(New York: Summit, 1991), 1.*

Winston Churchill's Quips

Here are some famous quips Winston Churchill made:

One day in the White House, according to Harry Hopkins, Churchill stepped naked from his bathroom just as Roosevelt was wheeling his chair into the room. This was always happening to him; the maids in his household and at No. 10 had grown accustomed to his nudity. In this case FDR apologized and turned to go, but Churchill held up a detaining hand. He said solemnly: "The Prime Minister of Great Britain has nothing to hide from the President of the United States."

On his seventy-fifth birthday a photographer said: "I hope, sir, that I will shoot your picture on your hundredth birthday." Churchill answered: "I don't see why not, young man. You look reasonably fit and healthy."

On his eighty-fifth birthday a back-bencher in the House, assuming that Churchill was out of earshot, told the MP beside him: "They say the old man's getting gaga." Without turning, Winston said: "Yes, and they say he's getting deaf, too."

William Manchester, The Last Lion *(Boston: Little Brown and Company, 1983), 34.*

Total Commitment

A hen and a pig approached a church and read the posted sermon topic, "What can we do to help the poor?" Immediately the hen suggested they feed them bacon and eggs.

The pig thought it sounded good, but he told the hen there was one thing wrong with feeding bacon and eggs to the poor. "For you it requires only a contribution, but for me it requires total commitment!"

A So-Called Bothered Conscience
See page 75

Unanswered Prayer
See page 327

Out Together
See page 278

HYPOCRISY

You must act as you believe, for you will eventually believe as you act.
Anonymous

Millions of Christians live in a sentimental haze of vague piety, with soft organ music trembling in the lovely light from stained-glass windows. Their religion is a pleasant thing of emotional quivers, divorced from the will, divorced from the intellect and demanding little except lip service to a few harmless platitudes.
Chad Walsh

No man can for any considerable time wear one face to himself, and another to the multitude, without finally getting bewildered as to which is the true one.
Nathaniel Hawthorne

A young man hears his father say that he believes certain things and because he respects his father he believes that he ought to believe the same things. When he has said this to himself for a sufficient number of times the next step soon follows, and that is, that he says in public that he himself believes in these things.
Martyn Lloyd-Jones

A Double Life

Stuart Briscoe tells the story that when he was in business, he had to deal with a coworker who had embezzled a large sum of money from the bank for which they both worked. The reason for the embezzlement was that he had two wives and families and was trying to run two homes. When he was apprehended and fired, he stunned everyone by saying, "I am very sorry for what I have done, and I need to know whether I should fulfill my preaching commitments on Sunday in our local church!" Briscoe says that in the following weeks he spent much of his time mending the damage done by the man's inconsistency. To Briscoe's chagrin, he found that his fellow workers not only despised the man but also "were quick to dismiss the church he belonged to as a 'bunch of hypocrites,' the gospel he professed to believe as a 'lot of hogwash,' and the God he claimed to serve as 'nonexistent.'"

I

IDENTITY

Today we see millions desperately searching for their own shadows, devouring movies, plays, novels and self-help books, no matter how obscure, that promise to help them locate their missing identities. In the United States, the manifestations of the personality crisis are bizarre. Its victims hurl themselves into group therapy, mysticism, or sexual games. They itch for change but are terrified by it. They urgently wish to leave their present existence and leap, somehow, to a new life—to become what they are not.
Alvin Toffler

IDOLATRY

He loves Thee too little
who loves anything together with Thee,
which he loves not for Thy sake.
St. Augustine

Hollow Idols, Hidden Treasures

When Mahmud of Ghazni invaded India, his conquering forces entered a celebrated temple to destroy it. Mahmud was entreated by a priest to spare a certain idol, but he refused.

Instead, he rained repeated blows upon it. Suddenly the image burst open, and a stream of precious stones cascaded from its hollow interior. In the same way, for each idol the Christian destroys in his life, he gains more than he loses! Every idol that is demolished brings him new treasures of grace and removes another hindrance to a powerful life of prayer.

IGNORANCE

> Many persons might have attained wisdom, had they not assumed that they already possessed it.
> *Seneca*

> Though 500 million Bibles are published in America each year . . . over 100 million [Americans] confess they never open one. . . . If the average churchgoer is uninformed, however, one does not have to look far to understand why. Church leaders have treated us to a smorgasbord of trendy theologies, pop philosophies, and religious variants of egocentric cultural values.
> *Charles Colson*

An Ill-Prepared Expedition

In 1845, Sir John Franklin and 138 officers and men embarked from England to find the northwest passage across the high Canadian Arctic to the Pacific Ocean. They sailed in two three-masted barques. Each sailing vessel carried an auxiliary steam engine and a twelve-day supply of coal for the entire projected two or three years' voyage. Instead of additional coal, according to L. P. Kirwan, each ship made room for a 1,200-volume library, "a hand-organ, playing fifty tunes," china place settings for officers and men, cut-glass wine goblets, and sterling silver flatware. The officers' sterling silver knives, forks, and spoons were particularly interesting. The silver was of ornate Victorian design, very heavy at the handles and richly patterned. Engraved on the handles were the individual officers' initials and family crests. The expedition carried no special clothing for the Arctic, only the uniforms of Her Majesty's Navy.

Annie Dillard, Teaching a Stone to Talk *(New York: Harper & Row, 1982), 24–25.*

Hardheaded Explanation

See page 66

IMMORALITY

A Narrow Definition

Perhaps the bitterest commentary on the way in which Christian doctrine has been taught in the last few centuries is the fact that to the majority of people the word *immorality* has come to mean one thing and one thing only [that is, sexual immorality]. A man may be greedy and selfish; spiteful, cruel, jealous, and unjust; violent and brutal; grasping, unscrupulous, and a liar; stubborn and arrogant; stupid, morose, and dead to every noble instinct—and still we are ready to say of him that he is not an immoral man. I am reminded of a young man who once said to me with perfect simplicity: "I did not know there were seven deadly sins; please tell me the names of the other six."

Dorothy Sayers, The Whimsical Christian.

IMMORTALITY

I do not want to die—no; I neither want to die nor do I want to want to die; I want to live forever and ever and ever. I want this "I" to live—this poor "I" that I am and that I feel myself to be here and now.

Unamuno y Jugo

Nature is mortal. We shall outlive her. When all the suns and nebulae have passed away, each one of you will still be alive.

C. S. Lewis

INCARNATION

For this rose contained was
Heaven and earth in little space.
There Is No Rose

His martial ensigns Cold and Need,
And feeble Flesh his warrior's steed.
This Little Babe

If we could only grasp the significance of the Incarnation, the word *sacrifice* would disappear from our vocabulary.
Nate Saint

My guess is that the whole story—that a Virgin was selected by God to bear His Son as a way of showing His love and concern for man—is not an idea that has been popular with theologians in spite of all the lip service they have given it. It is a somewhat illogical idea, and theologians love logic almost as much as they love God. It is so revolutionary a thought that it probably could only come from a God who is beyond logic and beyond theology.
Harry Reasoner

Contrary to Human Ways

In a radio program called *Man to Man,* Dr. Richard C. Halverson talked about the Incarnation:

God's eternal purpose fulfilled in a baby. Incredible as it sounds, that is the staggering import of Christmas. The total eternal program and purpose of almighty God was all wrapped up in an infant, born in a manger in Bethlehem twenty centuries ago. One of the facts about the Christian way that commends it to thoughtful men, is its uninventibility. This is a big word to say that Christianity, rightly understood, is utterly unlike religion that man invents. It is so completely contrary to the way man does things, that it must have come from God. Take Christmas, for example; only God could have thought of that. When man invents a super being, he comes up with a Superman, or a Captain Marvel. God gives the world a baby. And in that baby is tied up the whole destiny of the world and mankind and history.

Laid Aside Royal Robes

Peter the Great, when czar of Russia, wanted to build a navy. But the Russian people were not a maritime people. As the result of wars he got a seaport for Russia on the Baltic Sea. He said, "I will build a navy." But his people knew nothing about ships. What did Peter do? He laid aside his royal robes, and crown, and invested Katherine, his czarina, with the regent's authority over the Russian dominion. He dressed as a common working-man, and made his way to Holland and England. There he veiled his identity and worked as an apprentice to a ship's carpenter, and learned how to build ships. Then he went back to Russia, laid aside his workman's garb, and arrayed himself once more in his royal robes. He was the same person when he was in Holland and in England as he was in Russia. He had simply emptied himself of the outward dignity of his royal estate. So our Lord, when He came to this earth, laid aside His glory, and came as God clad in robes of flesh.

H. A. Ironside, "Our Lord's High-Priestly Prayer," Address Fifty-Six (II).

INDEPENDENCE

The maturity of modern psychology's autonomous person who is adjusted to "reality" without the aid of religion's props and crutches is the sickness of which the gospel of reconciliation is the cure.

Richard John Neuhaus

INDIFFERENCE

To Care or Not to Care

Here are Martin Marty's thoughts on caring and not caring in an article he wrote back in 1987 for *The Christian Century:*

Caring, like sharing, acquired a good name in the '70s and then a bad name in the '80s. Both qualities acquired good names because they point to good things. They then got bad reputations because (a) they were overused or (b) used unthinkingly or (c) they refer to actions that are not "in" in our grabby decade or (d) the monitors who are the first to tell us that something is "out" decided it was time for them to be out.

On the assumption or in the hope that (a) and (b) are more valid than (c) and (d), I would like to contribute to a rescue mission. It might be useful to find times when "not caring" is more valid than "caring." That could be the first step toward rehabilitating "caring." I have in mind two people about whom I recently read who rather defiantly said or acted out a "don't care" situation. Both are creative.

First: I was reading the Wheaton (Illinois) College alumni magazine and came across a depiction of a 50-year alumna of that evangelical school. She is Sarah Buller Mattson, class of '37. She led a rather typical Wheaton alumna existence. As Sarah Buller she left for Africa "with a mind-set like Abraham's," not knowing where she was going. She was fun-loving, and had enjoyed "dating all these men," including classmate Enoch Mattson. But Africa beckoned more urgently than Mattson.

I read that she took along five dresses that lasted her 38 years. She learned to teach, and while we did our uncaring things for 38 years, unmindful of Miss Buller, she started a school in Benin. In the '70s, she returned to the U.S. to study logopedics, but was mugged and stabbed (six inches deep). She healed and then went back to Africa. Retired in 1976, she became part of the Institute of Logopedics.

Along came a widower named Enoch Mattson, also retired from missionary and pastoral existence. Now for the point of it all, after that humdrum biographical lead-in. Sarah: "We got married in our sunset years. People thought it was such tomfoolery, but we didn't care."

. . . The other case is brief, I saw a *New York Times* story about 100-year-old Rabbi Moses Rosenthal of Far Rockaway, Queens, New York. He graduated from Jewish Theological Seminary in 1914, and retired from his rabbinical work at age 92. At his centennial party they told him to "Keep it short!" This he found difficult to do to his remarks, because he wanted to thank everyone on the staff of the Long Island Hebrew Living Center "by name and title."

Rabbi Rosenthal has trouble getting around. His daughter said they helped him once and he screamed for an hour. "I don't want it," said the rabbi. "I have one hand on my cane, and I wave this arm and I get momentum and I go forward." He doesn't care what anyone things about his method of locomotion. If he does not really, really need help, he really, really does not care what you think if he does not accept. Thinking of when my day comes, I've been practicing waving my arms to get momentum and go forward. You won't like that mode of moving? I don't care.

INSANITY

Sent to Kingston

In his book *Freedom for Ministry,* Richard John Neuhaus recalls a conversation between his parents:

I remember that when I was a very small boy, perhaps no more than age four or five, my parents were talking about an older person I knew and saying that he would likely "have to be sent to Kingston." (Kingston, Ontario, Canada, was the site of the insane asylum, as it was then called.) I was utterly intrigued by this possibility of drawing a line between the sane and the "crazy," and after some reflection on the subject, I proudly declared to my mother that I thought I could be crazy if I really tried. Her reaction was strong and immediate: "Don't you ever say that! Don't you ever decide to be crazy!" The interesting thing, and this made a lasting impression, is that she assumed I was quite capable of it. It was understood that there was a thin line between sanity and insanity, that there was something arbitrary about the distinction itself, and that crossing the line was somehow related to choice and character.

The point of the story is not that the "mentally ill" choose to be that way. Obviously there are compulsions, traumas, and environmental pressures that produce derangements, and it is often impossible to trace their complicated interrelationships to anything that we would recognize as choice. At the same time, however, we live by what the sociologists of knowledge call "constructions of reality," and, for the person whose consciousness is capable of entertaining the possibility of different constructions, there is an inescapable element of choice. Some constructions we call health and others we call sickness. It is toward these labels that we ought to exercise the most robust skepticism.

Richard John Neuhaus, Freedom for Ministry *(Grand Rapids, Mich.: Eerdmans, 1979).*

INSULAR CHRISTIANITY

We have felt that God is not interested in the world, that He wants only us, that we are the favored people of God. We have gathered our robes of self-righteousness about ourselves and drawn into our Christian ghettos and said, "Let the world go to hell! We are going to enjoy God's favor and blessing." And we have resisted the charge to reach out to the lost, fragmented humanity around us.

Ray Stedman

INTEGRITY

We need some men like Margaret Thatcher. What brought her meteoric rise? She was a politician of conviction! What brought her fall? The same thing.
Alistair Begg

The avoidance of one small fib . . . may be a stronger confession of faith than a whole "Christian philosophy" championed in lengthy, forceful discussion.
Helmut Thielicke

Angelic Students

In September 1982, Moody Bible Institute students Kristen and Karen Turner, who are twins, made the newspaper because they returned a wallet containing $350. As they were returning to Moody at about nine o'clock one night, they crossed Rush Street and, in the middle of the street, found a wallet. They picked it up, discovered $350 in it, and took it to the nearby police station. That is an unusual thing in Chicago; so unusual, that it made the front page of the *Chicago Tribune.* The *Trib's* story explained that a man had gone out to test-drive a motorcycle and lost his wallet on Rush Street. When he got back and attempted to pay for the motorcycle, he discovered his loss. He mournfully told his friend that the money was gone and he would never find it unless the angels provided it. And that's exactly what two angels from Moody Bible Institute did!

Two Exams

Dr. George Sweeting, past president of Moody Bible Institute, tells a story of a trigonometry professor who, upon giving an exam, would always share these words with his students:

He would say, "Today I am giving you two exams. The first is in trigonometry; the second is in honesty. I hope you can pass them both. However, if you are going to fail one, fail trigonometry. There are many good people in this world who have failed trigonometry, but there are no good people in the world who have failed the test of honesty."

Do the Right Thing

Rob Mouw isn't a household name, and what he did wasn't of heroic proportions—or was it? This incident happened when Rob was a senior at Wheaton Academy in Wheaton, Illinois. Here's the local newspaper's write-up of Rob Mouw:

Rob Mouw's high-school soccer career ended with a loss to Willowbrook Saturday night, but don't think for a second his career didn't end on a high note.

In Wheaton Christian's [now Wheaton Academy] final regular-season game last Tuesday, the Warriors lost a hard-fought match to Waubonsie Valley 3-2. Behind the box score and a tremendous Wheaton Christian effort to stay close to one of the top teams in the area is a pretty interesting story.

Waubonsie Valley scored the go-ahead goal with about a minute left. With less than 10 seconds left, Mouw got the ball at midfield. Mouw, a senior forward, quickly dribbled upfield and scored to apparently tie the match in an upset.

But the result was far from decided. Because there was just one referee on-hand, official time was being kept on the scoreboard so the referee could concentrate on the action. When Mouw was making his run at the goal, most eyes were focused on him and not the dwindling scoreboard clock. The clock read :00 afterward, but because the referee did not see the clock run out he felt he could not disallow the goal, and let the 3-3 result stand.

"I was personally watching the clock because I like to instruct my players as to what to do," said Waubonsie Valley coach Angelo DiBernardo. "It was easy for us to see, but it always comes down to the referee. Our players stopped and their player scored. That was our mistake."

DiBernardo was a little frustrated about the situation, but accepted the tie and congratulated Wheaton Christian coach Wes Dusek afterward. At first, Dusek thought his team had tied the match because he too was watching Mouw and not the clock.

Dusek, however, informed DiBernardo that the goal had indeed been scored after time expired and Waubonsie Valley should be ruled the winner.

How did Dusek know the goal was scored after time expired if he wasn't watching the clock?

"[Mouw] came up to me and said, 'When I shot the ball, the clock was on :00,'" said Dusek, who was told the same by his assistant coach. "With quality people like that telling me what the truth was, I couldn't doubt it." . . .

A game-tying goal against one of the area's powers would have brought respect to Mouw as a top-notch player. But that is already true. The fact that Mouw declined to accept the goal—even though it would have been easy to do so—should earn Mouw respect as a top-notch person.

"From age five I was taught to play the whistle, so I just figured we had some time left and kept playing," Mouw said. When told the scoreboard was the official clock, he told Dusek the clock did run out before he scored.

"We did the right thing," Mouw added, "I would have loved to have it count, but it was our responsibility to accept the loss."

Perhaps an asterisk should be placed next to Mouw's record of 55 goals in a career at Wheaton Christian in memory of what could have been No. 56.

Score one for sportsmanship, Wheaton Christian, and Rob Mouw.

Small Notes

The piano Jake Thielke bought for $700 at an estate sale rang out with small notes—$140,000 worth—found stashed inside.

Thielke and his wife, Diane, wanted to find out whether the century-old oak upright was worth repairing, so they summoned piano technician Dan Shereda to check it.

Then they watched as Shereda started pulling out neatly wrapped, moldy, smelly bundles of $5, $10, and $20 bills dating from the 1930s from the back of the turn-of-the-century instrument.

"I have never found something hidden in a piano until now," said Shereda, who has been working with pianos for 17 years.

Thielke said he consulted a lawyer immediately after the discovery. The lawyer concluded the money legally still belonged to the estate of the late Harley Stimm, . . . who had stashed money in a mattress and books before his death. . . .

The Thielkes gave the $140,000 to the estate and said they have no regrets about their decision.

"Morally, we believe we did the right thing," Thielke said. "It didn't feel right to keep it."

Chicago Tribune, *28 December 1993, sec. 6, p. 1.*

A Wartime Romance

Lieutenant John Blandford was a fighter pilot in the Second World War. Prior to being shipped overseas, he was in the base library, reading the novel *Of Human Bondage.* Because many of the volumes were donated by civilians, he noticed the name Hollis Meynell and an address on the inside cover. As he read, every so often he found a written response to the text. Blandford thought, *What does a woman know about the feelings of a man?* But the more he read, the more fascinated he became. By the conclusion of the novel, he was determined to know more about Hollis Meynell.

He called New York City information . . . and got a phone number. He called and she answered, but he was too timid and hung up! But Blandford wrote to her, and correspondence began to flow between them. As he saw many die in the war, her letters of encouragement kept him going. John sent her a picture of himself, hoping for one in return. Hollis did not send a picture but continued to encourage him to consider a meeting following the war.

It happened in New York City's Grand Central Station, under the clock. At the arranged time, Blandford was standing under the clock in full-dress military uniform, with the copy of the book under his arm. Hollis was to approach him with a red rose in the lapel of her dress.

A young woman was coming toward him. Her figure was long and slim. Her blonde hair lay back in curls from her delicate ears. Her eyes were blue as flowers; her lips and chin had a gentle firmness. In her pale green suit she was like springtime come alive. He started toward her, entirely forgetting to notice that she was wearing no rose. A small, provocative smile curved her lips:

"Going my way, soldier?" she murmured.

Uncontrollably Blandford took one step closer to her. Then he saw Hollis Meynell. She was standing almost directly behind this girl, a woman well past forty, her graying hair tucked under a worn hat. She was more than plump; her thick-ankled feet were thrust into low-heeled shoes. But she wore a red rose in the rumpled brown lapel of her coat.

The girl in the green suit was walking quietly away. The soldier felt as though he were being split in two, so keen was his desire to follow the young girl, yet so deep was the longing for the woman whose spirit had truly upheld his own; and there she stood. Her pale, plump face was gentle and sensible. Her gray eyes had a warm, kindly twinkle.

Lieutenant Blandford did not hesitate. He squared his shoulders, saluted, and spoke: "I'm Lieutenant John Blandford, and you—you are Miss Meynell. I'm so glad you could meet me. . . . May I take you to dinner?"

The woman's face broadened in a tolerant smile: "I don't know what this is all about, son. That young lady in the green suit, she begged me to wear this rose on my coat. And she said that if you asked me to go out with you, I should tell you that she is waiting for you in that big restaurant across the street. She said it was some kind of a test. I've got two boys with Uncle Sam myself, so I didn't mind to oblige you."

Personal Responsibility Comes Home

The USS *Astoria* (C-34) was the first U.S. cruiser to engage the Japanese during the Battle of Savo Island, a night action fought 8–9 August 1942. Although she scored two hits on the Imperial flagship *Chokai,* the *Astoria* was badly damaged and sank shortly after noon, 9 August.

About 0200 hours a young midwesterner, Signalman 3rd Class Elgin Staples, was swept overboard by the blast when the *Astoria's* number one eight-inch gun turret exploded. Wounded in both legs by shrapnel and in semi-shock, he was kept afloat by a narrow life belt that he managed to activate with a simple trigger mechanism.

At around 0600 hours, Staples was rescued by a passing destroyer and returned to the *Astoria,* whose captain was attempting to save the cruiser by beaching her. The effort failed, and Staples, still wearing the same life belt, found himself back in the water. It was lunchtime. Picked up again, this time by the USS *President Jackson* (AP-37), he was one of 500 survivors of the battle who were evacuated to Noumea.

On board the transport Staples, for the first time, closely examined the life belt that had served him so well. It had been manufactured by Firestone Tire and Rubber Company of Akron, Ohio, and bore a registration number.

Given home leave Staples told his story and asked his mother, who worked for Firestone, about the purpose of the number on the belt. She replied that the company insisted on personal responsibility for the war effort, and that the number was unique and assigned to only one inspector. Staples remembered everything about the life belt, and quoted the number. It was his mother's personal code and affixed to every item she was responsible for approving.

Commander Eric J. Berryman, U.S. Naval Reserve, Proceedings, U.S. Naval Institute, vol. 15/6/1036 (June 1989): 48.

A Self-Checkup

The pharmacist of the town drugstore overheard a young boy talking on a pay telephone. "Hello, sir, I was calling to see if you needed a lawn boy. Oh, you have one. Well, is he adequate? Oh, he is! Thank you, I was just checking," said the young boy.

The pharmacist then said to the boy, "Sorry you didn't get the job, son."

"Oh, no, sir," said the boy. "I've got the job. I was just calling to check up on myself."

All Debts to Be Paid

The following is copy from an ad that was printed in *The East Africa Standard* in Nairobi, Kenya:

All Debts to Be Paid

I, Allan Alia Waniek Harangui, of P.O. Box 40380, Nairobi, have dedicated my services to the Lord Jesus Christ. I must put right all my wrongs. If I owe you any debt or damage personally or any of the companies I have been director or partner of, i.e.,

Guaranteed Services, Ltd.
Waterpumps Electrical
and General, Co.
Sales and Service, Ltd.

please contact me or my advocates J. L. Kibicho and Company, Advocates, P.O. Box 73137, Nairobi, for a settlement. No amount will be disputed.

God and His Son Jesus Christ be glorified.

Deflower and Devour

When Henry VIII arranged for his illicit marriage to Anne Boleyn, one of those who opposed him was Sir Thomas More, whose life has been dramatized in the play *A Man for All Seasons.* After the marriage was an accomplished fact, it was thought that perhaps Thomas More, as a sensible man, would give up his passive resistance and attend the coronation ceremony.

Two bishops acted as the King's agents, but More declined the invitation, pleading poverty. Promptly they offered to pay for a velvet costume suitable to the ceremony. Again the ex-Lord Chancellor refused. In doing so, he recited a little tale. Once upon a time, it seemed, there was an Emperor who had condemned a maiden to die for some infringement of the law. But the death penalty could not be enforced because she was a virgin and he had previously decreed that no virgin should ever be put to death. His problem was solved by one of his council who said: "Why make you so much ado, my Lords, about so small a matter? Let her first be deflowered, and then after may she be devoured."

"Now, my Lords," said Thomas More to the King's messengers, "it lieth not in my power that they may devour me; but God being my good Lord, I will provide that they shall never deflower me."

John Farrow, The Story of Thomas More *(New York: Image, 1968), 152.*

The Strength of Character

When L. M. Clymer, president of Holiday Inns, resigned his position because of a corporate decision to invest $25 million in a gambling casino in Atlantic City—a decision he had protested on moral grounds—I was impressed. Here was that rare modern man who was willing to sacrifice power and money for his convictions.

So I wrote to Mr. Clymer, expressing my appreciation for his action, and for the ironic way in which he had announced it.

I have now received a reply from which I quote: "You will understand that this was not of my own strength or will, but Christ acting through me. In him all things are possible. The assurance and peace which he has brought me in this decision are the greatest testimony I can give of his love for each of us."

Eutychus VII, Christianity Today, *1 December 1978.*

A Lesson in Integrity

In the book *My Father's House,* Corrie ten Boom recalled the days she spent with her father in his watchmaking shop:

Some of my happiest days came when it was decided that I could work in the shop as an assistant to my kindly, bearded father. I loved being with him and I loved the shop itself.

. . . There were many ups and downs in the watchmaking business. Father loved his work, but he was not a money-maker, and times were often hard. Once I remember we were faced with a real financial crisis. A large bill had to be paid, and there simply wasn't enough money. Then one day a well-dressed gentleman came into the shop and asked to see some very expensive watches. I stayed in the workshop and prayed, with one ear tuned to the conversation in the front room.

"Mmm . . . this is a fine watch, Mr. ten Boom," the customer said, turning a very costly timepiece over in his hands. "This is just what I've been looking for."

I held my breath as I saw the affluent customer reach into his inner pocket and pull out a thick wad of bills. Praise the Lord—cash! (I saw myself paying the overdue bill and being relieved from the burden of anxiety I had been carrying for the past few weeks.)

The customer looked at the watch admiringly and commented, "I had a good watchmaker here in Haarlem . . . His name was van Houten. Perhaps you knew him."

Father nodded his head. He knew almost everyone in Haarlem, especially other watchmakers.

"When van Houten died and his son took over the business, I kept on doing business with the young man. However, I bought a watch from him that didn't run at all. I sent it back three times, but he couldn't seem to fix it. That's why I decided to find another watchmaker."

"Will you show me that watch, please?" Father said.

The man took a large watch out of his vest and gave it to Father.

"Now, let me see," Father said, opening the back of the watch. He adjusted something and handed it back to the customer. "There, that was a very little mistake. It will be fine now. Sir, I trust the young watchmaker. Someday he will be just as good as his father. So if you ever have a problem with one of his watches, come to me. I'll help you out.

Now I shall give you back your money and you return my watch."

I was horrified. I saw Father take back the watch and give the money to the customer. Then he opened the door for him and bowed deeply in his old-fashioned way.

My heart was where my feet should be as I emerged from the shelter of the workshop.

"Papa! How could you?"

Father looked at me patiently through his steel-rimmed glasses.

"Corrie," he said, "you know that I brought the Gospel at the burial of Mr. van Houten."

Of course I remembered. It was Father's job to speak at the burials of the watchmakers in Haarlem. He was greatly loved by his colleagues and was also a very good speaker; he always used the occasion to talk about the Lord Jesus.

"Corrie, what do you think that young man would have said when he heard that one of his good customers had gone to Mr. ten Boom? Do you think the name of the Lord would be honored? As for the money, trust the Lord, Corrie. He owns the cattle on a thousand hills and He will take care of us."

I felt ashamed and I knew that father was right. I wondered if I could ever have that kind of trust instead of blind determination to follow my own stubborn path. Could I really learn to trust God?

"Yes, Father," I answered quietly. Whom was I answering? My earthly father or my Father in Heaven?

Believe What You Believe
See page 302

Right and Wrong Matter More than Life
See page 43

INTELLECTUALS

Above all, we must at all times remember what intellectuals habitually forget: that people matter more than concepts and must come first. The worst of all despotisms is the heartless tyranny of ideas.

Paul Johnson

INTOLERANCE

The New Oppressed

The Office of Student Affairs at Smith College has put out a bulletin listing types of oppression for people belatedly "realizing that they are oppressed." Some samples of the Smith litany of sins:

Oppression of the differently abled by the temporarily able.

Heterosexism: Oppression of those of sexual orientation other than heterosexual, such as gays, lesbians, and bisexuals; this can take place by not acknowledging their existence.

Lookism: The belief that appearance is an indicator of a person's value; the construction of a standard for beauty/attractiveness; and oppression through stereotypes and generalizations of both those who do not fit that standard and those who do.

Arthur M. Schlesinger Jr., The Disuniting of America *(New York: W. W. Norton & Company, 1992), 115.*

The Wrong Combination of Words

See page 242

A Parable of Birds

See page 254

IRRELIGION

The Last Word

"Charles Darwin died in April 1882. He wished to be buried in his beloved village, but the sentiment of educated men demanded a place in Westminster Abbey beside Isaac Newton. As his coffin entered the vast building, the choir sang an anthem composed for the occasion. Its text, from the book of Proverbs, may stand as the most fitting testimony to Darwin's greatness: 'Happy is the man that findeth wisdom, and getteth understanding. She is more precious than rubies, and all the things thou canst desire are not to be compared to her.'"

So wrote Stephen Jay Gould, the eminent Harvard paleontologist, professor of geology, and ardent evolutionist in *Discover* magazine in 1982.

Darwin was not buried in Westminster Abbey because he was a staunch defender of the faith. While he was not a friend of the church, neither was he an atheist. Continues Gould, "He probably retained a belief in some kind of personal god—but he did not grant his deity a directly and continuously intervening role in the evolutionary process."

Darwin was, however, buried in Westminster because of the profound contribution he made to science. Again quoting Gould, "Educated men demanded" he be laid there.

All this is not to name Darwin as the lone culprit responsible for the crisis of faith precipitated by evolutionary science. It is merely an illustration full of ironies and one grand truth.

It is ironic that his final tribute was a scriptural anthem. Likewise ironic is that his final wishes were not honored and he was buried within the church. Even the choice of Scripture in the anthem is ironic: Proverbs, and the pursuit of wisdom.

The grand truth is that Scripture and God literally have the last word. His burial inadvertently acknowledges that the faith reigns supreme over men and their ideas. Even science.

Science is a marvelous tool given by God to discover the secrets of the cosmos and to elicit praise from men. When science is rightly studied within the context of the faith it is an ally, not an enemy. When the scientific pursuit is brought before the face of God, and done under His authority and unto His glory, then it is done *Coram Deo.*

Robert Ingram, ed., "Coram Deo," Tabletalk, *October 1990.*

The UN Meditation Room

The United Nations complex sits on sixteen acres of New York City's choicest real estate, bordering the East River and Manhattan. The lean, immense Secretariat building rises into the sky, the sun reflecting off its window walls. Bright flags of the nations of the world fly in the breezes off the river; the most prominent is the blue and white UN flag, its two white reeds of olive branches surrounding the world.

A visitor is immediately struck by the grandeur of the building, stirred by the sight of dignitaries stepping out of black limousines to cross the massive plaza. He realizes that if this place represents the powers of the world, one might well want to see the place of worship, where the nations bow before the One under whose rule they govern.

The information personnel are bemused. "The chapel? We don't have a chapel. If there is one, I believe it's across the street."

The visitor darts across the thoroughfare, dodging New York's taxis, and successfully arrives at the opposite building's security-clearance desk.

"Well, there's a chapel here," responds the officer, "but it's not associated with the UN." He thumbs through a directory. "Oh, I see, all right, here it is. It's across the street—and tell them you're looking for the meditation room."

Again the visitor dashes across the pavement. An attendant tells him that the room is not open to the public; it's a "nonessential area," and there has been a personnel cutback. But a security guard will escort the visitor through long, crowded hallways and swinging glass doors. Again, there is the pervasive sense of weighty matters being discussed in the noble pursuit of world peace.

The guide pauses at the unmarked door. He unlocks it and gingerly pushes it open. The small room is devoid of people or decoration. The walls are stark white. There are no windows. A few wicker stools surround a large square rock at the center of the room. It is very quiet. But there is no altar, rug, vase, candle, or symbol of any type of religious worship.

Lights in the ceiling create bright spots of illumination on the front wall. One focuses on a piece of modern art: steel squares and ovals. Beyond the abstract shapes, there is nothing in those bright circles of light. They are focused on a void. And it is in that void that the visitor suddenly sees the soul of the brave new world.

Charles Colson, Kingdoms in Conflict *(Grand Rapids, Mich.: William Morrow/Zondervan, 1987), 182–183.*

IRRELIGIOUS

The Wrong Combination of Words

Charles Colson makes this observation: "I discovered that one major U.S. daily, as a matter of policy, will not print the two words *Jesus Christ* together; when combined, the editor says, it represents an editorial judgment."

ISOLATION

Melt Down the Saints

Charles Swindoll reports that when Oliver Cromwell ruled England, the nation experienced a crisis: they ran out of silver and couldn't mint any coins. Cromwell sent his soldiers to the cathedral to see if any silver was available. They reported back that the only silver was in the statues of the saints, to which Cromwell replied, "Let's melt down the saints and get them back into circulation." Sometimes God must do that with us. We must be melted down so that we will get into circulation in the world for Him.

Dynamic Preaching, *vol. 1, no. 4 (January/February 1986): 55.*

Clapping with One Hand

See page 258

J

JEALOUSY

Bring Him Good News

The story is told that in the fourth century, during the time of the desert hermits, some demons were sent to tempt a hermit. They tempted him with every temptation possible: lust to avarice to materialism, and nothing could succeed. Frustrated, the imps returned to Satan and expressed their plight. Satan responded that they had been far too hard on the man. He said: "Send him a message that his brother has just been made bishop of Antioch. Bring him good news."

The demons returned and reported the message, and in that instant, the monk fell to envy and jealousy.

General Preference

General Grant had been for several months in front of Petersburg, apparently accomplishing nothing, while General Sherman had captured Atlanta, and completed his grand "march to the sea." Then arose a strong cry to promote Sherman to Grant's position as lieutenant-general. Hearing of it, Sherman wrote to Grant, "I have written to John Sherman [his brother] to stop it. I would rather have you in command than anyone else. I should emphatically decline any commission calculated to bring us into rivalry." Grant replied, "No one would be more pleased with your advancement than I; and if you should be placed in my position, and I put subordinate, it would not change our relations in the least. I would do all in my power to make your cause win."

James Hastings, ed., The Speaker's Bible, *vol. 17 (Grand Rapids, Mich.: Baker, 1971), 69.*

JOY

It must be said that we can have joy, and therefore will have it, only as we give it to others. . . . There may be cases where a man can be really merry in isolation. But these are exceptional and dangerous.

Karl Barth

JUDGMENT

The Last Word

See page 239

JUSTICE

God is never obliged to treat all men equally. . . . Don't ever ask God for justice—you might get it.

R. C. Sproul

We may see non-justice in God, which is mercy, but we never see injustice in God.

R. C. Sproul

K

KNOWLEDGE

A man ought to read just as inclination leads him; for what he reads as a task will do him little good. A young man should read five hours in a day, and so may acquire a great deal of knowledge.

Samuel Johnson

L

LAUGHTER

During the Civil War, Abraham Lincoln was criticized for his humor. To which he replied, "With the fearful strain that is on me, if I did not laugh I would die."

A Laughing Church

The need for laughter in the church was underlined by missionary statesman Oswald Sanders with these questions:

Should we not see that lines of laughter about the eyes are just as much marks of faith as are the lines of care and seriousness? Is laughter pagan? We have already allowed too much that is good to be lost to the church and cast many pearls before swine. A church is in a bad way when it banishes laughter from the sanctuary and leaves it to the cabaret, the nightclub, and the toastmasters.

J. Oswald Sanders, Spiritual Leadership *(Chicago: Moody, 1967), 60.*

LAW

What was it that I loved in that theft? Was it the pleasure of acting against the law, in order that I, a prisoner under rules, might have a maimed counterfeit of freedom by doing what was forbidden, with a dim similitude of

omnipotence? The desire to steal was awakened simply by the prohibition of stealing.
St. Augustine

Transgression Defined

Chuck Swindoll tells this story about his boyhood. Like many boys, he had a paper route, and like many, he didn't particularly enjoy it. In fact, he used to cut corners in the literal sense of the word. When delivering papers he would ride his bicycle across the lawns of homes that had the misfortune of being on a corner. At one particular place, he had actually worn a narrow trail across the lawn. It wasn't right, but no one seemed to notice. Then one day, as he rode up, he saw a sign that read, "KEEP OFF THE GRASS. NO BIKES." And, you guessed it—he rode right past it anyway on his well-worn trail—right up to the feet of the waiting owner of the sign. And as Swindoll put it, "The man shared with me a few things from his heart." Before, Swindoll's transgression was not fully seen (and in a sense not reckoned); now it was sharply defined and reckoned.

A Matter of History

As a young teenager, Stuart Briscoe was drafted into the Royal Marines during the Korean Conflict. He came under the control of a particularly imposing regimental sergeant major who strode around the barracks leaving a train of tough men quaking in their boots. Briscoe didn't realize how dominant this man had become in his life until the day he was released from the Marines. Clutching his papers in one hand, he was luxuriating in his newfound freedom to the extent of putting the other hand in his pocket, slouching a little, and whistling—sins so heinous that if they had been observed by the sergeant major, they would have landed him in all kinds of trouble! Then Briscoe saw the sergeant major striding toward him. On an impulse he sprang into the posture of a Marine until he realized that he had died to him—the sergeant major and Briscoe no longer had a relationship. He was not dead, and neither was Briscoe; but as far as the sergeant major's domination of his life was concerned, it was all a matter of history. So Briscoe did some reckoning, decided not to yield to the man's tyranny, and demonstrated it by refusing to yield his arms to swinging high and his feet to marching as if on parade and his back to ramrod stiffness. Instead he presented his feet, hands, and back to his newfound freedom as a *former* Marine—and the sergeant major couldn't do a thing about it.

LEADERSHIP

The fundamental requirement of the Christian leader is not a knowledge of where the stream of popular opinion is flowing but a knowledge of where the stream of God's truth lies.
David F. Wells

[Leadership] is not won by promotion but by many prayers and tears. It is attained by confessions of sin, and much heart searching and humbling before God; by self-surrender, a courageous sacrifice of every idol, a bold, deathless, uncompromising and uncomplaining embracing of the cross, and by an eternal, unfaltering looking unto Jesus crucified.
Samuel Logan Brengle

Leadership is like the Abominable Snowman whose footprints are everywhere but [he is] nowhere to be seen.
Warren Bennis

Spiritual leadership is a matter of superior spiritual power, and it can never be self-generated. There is no such thing as a self-made spiritual leader.
J. Oswald Sanders

The Role-Model Debate

Chicago Tribune columnist Mike Royko shared his opinion of public figures as role models in a 1993 column:

There has been a debate about role models lately. It started when Charles Barkley did a Nike commercial saying that he is not a role model, he is a basketball player, and that it's the job of parents to be their children's role models.

This prompted other basketball stars to say, no, Charles is wrong, and that as a public figure, he must accept the responsibility of being a role model.

I agree with Barkley. The ability to jump high and slam-dunk a basketball has entertainment value and pays well; but compared with other skills—such as collecting garbage—it really doesn't make the world a better place to live.

Think about that. Let us say that tomorrow nobody in the United States jumped high and slam-dunked a basketball. So what? Would it affect your life? Of course not.

But if nobody in the United States picked up the garbage, we would really have a stinking mess, with flies and rodents and pestilence and all sorts of unpleasantness.

So one could argue that the guys who work on garbage trucks might be better role models than those who slam-dunk basketballs, even though they don't get contracts to endorse overpriced, Taiwan-made athletic shoes.

But this question is probably best left to philosophers, social scientists and talk show hosts.

What interests me about it is the concept of the public figure as a role model for the young. That's a fairly recent development in our society.

When I was a kid, the phrase *role model* didn't exist. Sure, there were sports heroes. We copied their batting stances, but we didn't think about modeling our lives after them.

Well, there was one exception: Hack Wilson, a great

Cubs home run hitter and legendary drunk. A few older guys in the neighborhood patterned themselves after him. They didn't hit as well as Wilson, but they were his equals in falling off a bar stool.

But before TV kidnapped our brains, athletes and show-biz stars were not an everyday part of our lives. We didn't have the endless parade of celebrities that now roll across the TV screen. Which was probably beneficial. Social values weren't being established by Madonna, fat Roseanne, Magic Johnson, Geraldo, Oprah, David Letterman's guest, MTV, religious hucksters and hop-headed rock stars.

We had the Saturday matinees at the neighborhood movie houses. But as role models, Abbott and Costello, Frankenstein and the Wolfman, and the Three Stooges had limited impact.

That left the family and neighborhood grown-ups—parents, other relatives, neighbors, storekeepers, the beat cop, the bookie, the tavern keeper, precinct captain and maybe a teacher or the school janitor.

Although we didn't know they were role models, and they didn't either, they were pretty good at filling that role.

For one thing, all of the men worked. They had little choice. Government provided almost no safety nets. Not even small cushions. So if a man didn't work, he couldn't buy food or clothing for his family, pay the rent, or buy a pail of beer. Credit cards didn't exist, so he couldn't pile up debt unless he went to a loan shark, who would whack his kneecaps with a bat if he didn't make payments. Working was the only realistic option. Either that or mooching off relatives or becoming a bum or jumping off a bridge. Most preferred work.

So as role models, they did set one excellent example: If you wanted food on the table, a roof over your head, a telephone, a radio, fuel for the stove and maybe the price of a drink or an occasional movie, you found a job and worked. It was as simple as that.

In fact, that was the American dream. Some might find this hard to believe, but the American dream didn't always include owning a $150,000 house with patio, a Japanese car with a CD player, a mini-van, big-screen TV, state-of-the-art stereo, a PC with CD-ROM, graphite-shafted golf clubs, three credit cards and a Club Med vacation. Such objects were not considered entitlements.

Another example they set was that if you wanted to buy a big ticket item—a refrigerator, for example, or a used car—you saved. Remarkably, people saved a bigger piece of their paycheck 50 years ago than they do today. When a rainy day came in those days, if you didn't have your own umbrella, there was no social worker to hand you one. You drowned.

So Barkley is probably right. It's the job of parents—not dunkers, hip-hoppers, rappers and TV babblers—to be role models.

Of course, conditions change. Parents used to be the role models. But that was when you could figure that when the old man left for work in the morning, he'd be home for dinner. Or at least in the corner tavern.

Today, when the male parent leaves the house in the morning, it isn't certain that he'll be back within a year, a decade, or ever.

It's hard to view a phantom as a role model.

Chicago Tribune, *1993.*

LEARNING

Never seem more learned than the people you are with. Wear your learning like a pocket watch and keep it hid-

den. Do not pull it out to count the hours, but give the time when you are asked.
Lord Chesterfield

LEGALISM

He was a good man in the worst sense of the word.
Mark Twain

I reputed legalism intellectually and theologically in 1946, but in 1982 I am still wrestling with it emotionally.
Howard Hendricks

The Skate Debate

The minister of a Scottish Sabbatarian congregation had to travel some distance from his home to the church, where he was to conduct the worship service. It was winter, and the river that flowed past both his home and the church was completely frozen over. Being a good ice skater, the minister decided to skate to the church. Church members were surprised to see their preacher arrive on skates.

The incident gave rise to debate as to whether the minister should have skated on the Sabbath. The elders met and discussed the matter at great length. The argument raged back and forth on the question of whether the practicality of getting to church or the keeping of the Sabbath should be the prime consideration. At last came the vital question to the minister, "Did you enjoy skating up the river?" If the experience brought him pleasure, it was wrong; if it did not, it was permissible.
John W. Drakeford, Humor in Preaching, *Ministry Resources Library (Grand Rapids, Mich.: Zondervan), 17–18.*

LEISURE

Know When to Work and When to Play

What Clarence Jones and his family looked forward to most was their annual holiday at the ocean. (C. W. never could tolerate these missionaries who "boast they have worked twenty-five years without a vacation." He knew how to work, but he also knew how to play.)

Kath would shop for three weeks' supplies, then pack up the children, and in the dark at 6 A.M., board the train for Guayaquil, usually taking along Pedro to help out. John Reed loaned them his fisherman's retreat—a split-bamboo hut on stilts with thatch grass roof, set in an idyllic tropical paradise on the Isle of Puna at the mouth of Guayas River.

For the first three days, Clarence slept; then for three days he read. By that time, the children would have finished exploring the island, C. W. would be rejuvenated, and he gave himself totally to the family in marvelous, glorious, imaginative play.

Lois Neely, Come up to This Mountain *(Wheaton, Ill.: Tyndale, 1980), 118.*

LIBERALISM

Liberalism is not the answer to a heart longing for a vital faith.

Vance Havner

A Parable of Birds

Several species of *Avis religio campus* may be observed this fall. One is the blue-tailed bittern: "I once believed as you do—my father was a fundamentalist preacher. You know, no-fun-all-damn-and-no-mental. But that was before my intellectual enlightenment. And I think you too will find college a fascinating experience . . . if you keep an open mind."

Then there's the spoon-billed humbler: "Have you given up the search for truth? Do you really think you know enough to be able to say, 'I have arrived. I no longer am searching for truth'? Where, my boy, is your humility? Who can ever say he has found that for which humanity has searched for millennia?"

The red-headed-shocker is rare, but not extinct: "I don't care what they taught you in Sunday school or youth meetings back home. What in heaven did you come to college for if you thought you already knew it all? Listen, are you taking zoology? Genetics? Try telling Schleider you believe in a virgin birth. —Now let's begin to construct a mature system of values."

Too often these men are successful in undermining prior convictions. It's a wise student who sees that their negations are as dogmatic as the system they attack, and their theological construction as dependent upon presuppositions—but without the authority of Jesus Christ and God's Word and the Christian Church to support them."

Joseph Bayly, Out of My Mind *(Grand Rapids, Mich.: Zondervan, 1993), 49–50.*

A Celebrity Loser

Barbara Bush, who may have been to the presidency what Lou Holtz was to the Golden Dome at Notre Dame University, was just a celebrity loser to some feminists. Some 150 students at the exclusive Wellesley College in Massachusetts objected to her planned appearance as graduation speaker, contending that she was only a dropout-person who quit college to get married. Said the petition: "To honor Barbara Bush as the commencement speaker . . . is to honor a woman who has gained recognition through the achievements of her husband, which contradicts what we have been taught over our years at Wellesley."

Chicago Tribune, *16 April 1990, sec. 1, p. 14.*

Faith in Faith

See page 150

LIGHT

What You Read in the Light

During the French Revolution political prisoners were

herded into dungeons. In one place a prisoner possessed a Bible. His cell was crammed with men who wanted to hear the Word of God. Once each day for only a few moments, a shaft of light would come through a tiny window near the ceiling. The prisoners devised a plan whereby they would lift the owner of the Bible onto their shoulders and into the sunlight. There, in that position, he would study the Scriptures. Then they would bring him down and say, "Tell us now, friend, what did you read while you were in the light?"

Focal Point *(Denver Seminary), vol. 6, no. 3.*

LISTENING

Listen to your life. See it for the fathomless mystery that it is. In the boredom and pain of it no less than in the excitement and gladness: touch, taste, smell your way to the holy and hidden heart of it because in the last analysis all moments are key moments, and life itself is grace.

Frederick Buechner

We have two ears and one mouth, therefore we should listen twice as much as we speak.

Zeno of Citium, founder of the philosophy known as Stoicism

A Double Fee

Once a young man came to the philosopher Socrates to be instructed in oratory. The moment the young man was introduced he began to talk in an incessant stream. This went on for some time. Socrates finally silenced the man by putting his hand over his mouth. "Young man," he said, "I will have to charge you a double fee."

"A double fee, why is that?"

Socrates replied, "Because I will have to teach you two sciences. First, the science of holding your tongue; and then the science of using it correctly."

Gary Vanderet, "The Skill of Receiving God's Word," Discovery Papers.

The Same Finish Time

In 1963, Adlai E. Stevenson spoke to the students at Princeton University. "I understand I am here to speak and you are here to listen," he said. "Let's hope we both finish at the same time."

Ears for a Cricket

See page 311

LONELINESS

America is one vast terrifying anticommunity. The great organizations to which most people give their working day, and the apartments and suburbs to which they return at night, are equally places of loneliness and alienation . . . protocol, competition, hostility and fear have replaced the warmth of the circle of affection which might sustain man against a hostile universe.

Charles Reich

Nobody needs me, nobody loves me, nobody cares for me. Call you this God's world? To me it seems more like the devil's world.

Orestes Brownson

The bar flourishes, not because most people are alcoholics, but because God has put into the human heart the desire to know and be known, to love and be loved, and so many seek a counterfeit at the price of a few beers.

Harvie M. Conn

There is this cave
In the air behind my body
That nobody is going to touch:
A cloister, a silence
Closing around a blossom of fire.
When I stand upright in the wind,
My bones turn to dark emeralds.

James Wright

Clapping with One Hand

Rose Russel was twenty-five. She was far more successful than most men fifty years of age. She was a partner in a real estate and investment firm in Newport Beach, California, which, next to Beverly Hills, is the place to live in southern California. She was also in partnership on quite a string of properties in the beach area. She drove her own silver Mercedes, and it was paid for. But at twenty-five—with all this apparent success—she went to a motel room, sat down and wrote a plaintive note, and took her own life. Her brief suicide note read simply: "I'm so tired of clapping with one hand."

All Gray Slush

In his poem "A Psalm in a Hotel Room," Joseph Bayly, a Christian author and educator, wrote about his feelings of loneliness that we all can identify with:

I'm alone, Lord, all alone. A thousand miles from home and there is no one here who knows my name, except the clerk and he spelled it wrong. [There is] no one to eat dinner with, laugh at my jokes, listen to my gripes, be happy with me about what happened today and say, "That's great." No one cares. There's just this lousy bed and slush in the streets outside between the buildings. I feel sorry for myself and I have plenty of reason to. Maybe I ought to say I'm on top of it, praise the Lord, things are great. But they're not. Tonight, it's all gray slush.

Joseph Bayly, Psalms of My Life *(Wheaton, Ill.: Tyndale, 1969), 29.*

Rich Without, Poor Within

Elvis Presley owned three jet airplanes, two Cadillacs, a Rolls-Royce, a Lincoln Continental, Buick and Chrysler station wagons, a Jeep, a dune buggy, a converted bus, and three motorcycles. His favorite car was his 1960

Cadillac limousine. The top was covered with pearl white Naugahyde, and its body was sprayed with forty coats of a specially prepared paint that included crushed diamond and fish scales. Nearly all the metal trim was plated with eighteen-karat gold. There were two gold-flake telephones. There was a gold vanity case, containing a gold electric razor and gold hair clippers; an electric shoe buffer; a gold-plated television; a record player; an amplifier; household appliances; and a refrigerator that was capable of making ice in exactly two minutes. Elvis had everything. Once when he had a cold, one of his managers found him in his music room playing the hymn "How Great Thou Art" on the piano. "How do you feel?" the manager asked. "Alone" was Elvis Presley's only response. Rich without, but poor within. Wealth does not satisfy; only Christ can satisfy.

LOVE

Lord, let me live long enough to see those fellows saved who killed our boys, that I may throw my arms around them and tell them I love them because they love my Christ.

T. E. McCully

Faith, like light, should always be simple and unbending; while love, like warmth, should beam forth on every side, and bend to every necessity of our brethren.

Martin Luther

Love is a deep, continuous, growing, and ever-renewing activity of the will, superintended by the Holy Spirit.

Mike Mason

We have found in a total stranger a near and long-lost relative, a true blood relative even closer to us than father or mother.

Mike Mason

Love is gratitude: it is thankfulness for the existence of the beloved; it is the happy acceptance of everything that he gives without the jealous feeling that the self ought to be able to do as much; it is a gratitude that does not seek equality; it is wonder over the other's gift of himself in companionship.

H. Richard Niebuhr

Love is what happens to a man and woman who don't know each other.

Somerset Maugham

When I have learnt to love God better than my earthly dearest, I shall love my earthly dearest better than I do now.

C. S. Lewis

Enough Body to Hold the Soul

During the Revolutionary War a young officer in the British army, before embarking for this country with his regiment, became engaged to a young lady in England. In one of the battles of the Revolution the officer was badly wounded and lost a leg. He accordingly wrote to his affianced bride, telling her how he was disfigured and maimed, and so changed from what had been when she had last seen him and they had plighted their troth that he felt it his duty to release her from all obligation to become his wife. The young lady wrote an answer no less noble than that which she had received from the young man. In this letter she disavowed all thought of refusing to carry out the engagement because of what had happened to her fiancé in battle, and said that she was willing to marry him if there was enough of his body left to hold his soul!

Clarence Edward Macartney, Macartney's Illustrations *(New York: Abingdon, 1956), 306–307.*

The Main Thing Is Not to Love

Here are Sophie Tolstoy's thoughts on her marriage to the great author:

I have always been told that a woman must love her husband and be honorable and be a good wife and mother. They write such things in ABC books, and it is all nonsense. The thing to do is *not* to love, to be clever and sly, and to hide all one's bad points—as if anyone in the world has no faults! And the main thing is *not* to love. See what I have done by loving him so deeply! It is painful and humiliating; but he thinks it is merely silly . . . I am nothing but . . . a useless creature with morning sickness, and a big belly, two rotten teeth, and a bad temper, a battered sense of dignity, and a love which nobody wants and which nearly drives me insane.

Carol Gilligan, In a Different Voice *(Cambridge, Mass.: Harvard University Press), 124.*

Temporary Insanity

Love: temporary insanity curable by marriage.

Ambrose Bierce

Heavy Laden in Body and Soul

This story was told in a letter by Campus Crusade missionaries Clark and Ann Peddicord in Germany:

The former Communist dictator, Erich Honecker, had been released from the hospital where he had been undergoing treatment for cancer. There was probably no single person in all of East Germany who was more despised and hated than he. He had been stripped of all his offices and even his own Communist party had kicked him out. He was booted out of the villa he was living in; the new government refused to provide him and his wife with accommodations. They stood, in essence, homeless on the street. . . . It was Christians who stepped in.

Pastor Uwe Holmer, who was in charge of a Christian help-center north of Berlin, was asked by a church leader if he would be willing to take the Honeckers in. Pastor Holmer and his family decided that it would be wrong to give away a room in the center that could be used for needy people, or an apartment that their staff needed; instead, they took the former dictator and his wife into their own home. It must have been a strange scene when the old couple arrived.

The former absolute ruler of the country was being sheltered by one of the Christians whom he and his wife had despised and persecuted. In East Germany there was a great deal of hate toward the former regime and especially toward Honecker and his wife, Margot, who had ruled the educational system there for 26 years with an iron hand. She had made sure that very few Christian children were able to go on for higher education. There are ten children in the Holmer family and eight of them had applied for further education over the years, and all had been refused a place at college because they were Christians, in spite of the fact that they had good or excellent grades.

Pastor Holmer was asked why he and his family opened their door to such detestable people. . . . Pastor Holmer spoke very clearly, "Our Lord challenged us to follow him and to take in all who are weary and heavy laden—both in soul and in body. . . ." Pastor Holmer also saw that the Lord's command to love one's enemies applied in just such cases as this was. "We have no bitterness in our hearts, because as we followed our Lord, we were able to truly forgive," he said.

Tell Me More about Johnny Brown

Once a young man proposed to his girl as they sat looking over the beautiful lake. "Darling, I want you to know that I love you more than anything else in the world. I want you to marry me. I'm not wealthy; I'm not rich. I don't have a yacht or Rolls-Royce like Johnny Brown, but I do love you with all my heart."

She thought for a minute and then replied, "I love you with all my heart, too, but tell me more about Johnny Brown."

The Pastor's Story File, *no. 21 (July 1986).*

From the Insane Asylum

When we sing the great hymn "The Love of God," most of us do not know that the author found the last verse inscribed on the wall of an insane asylum next to the bed of a man who had evidently found the love of God before he died. Here are the last two verses of the hymn:

The love of God is greater far
Than tongue or pen can ever tell;
It goes beyond the highest star,
And reaches to the lowest hell.
The guilty pair, bowed down with care,
God gave His son to win;
His erring child He reconciled,
And rescued from his sin.

Could we with ink the ocean fill,
And were the skies of parchment made;
Were every stalk on earth a quill,
And every man a scribe by trade;
To write the love of God above
Would drain the ocean dry;
Nor could the scroll contain the whole,
Though stretched from sky to sky.

A Holy Love

Writes a surgeon: I stand by the bed where a young woman lies, her face postoperative, her mouth twisted in palsy, clownish. A tiny twig of the facial nerve, the one to the muscles of her mouth, has been severed. She will be thus from now on. The surgeon has followed with religious fervor the curve of her flesh; I promise you that. Nevertheless, to remove the tumor in her cheek, I had to cut the little nerve.

Her young husband is in the room. He stands on the opposite side of the bed, and together they seem to dwell in the evening lamplight, isolated from me, private. Who are they, I ask myself, he and this wry-mouth I have made, who gaze at and touch each other so generously, greedily? The young woman speaks.

"Will my mouth always be like this?" she asks.

"Yes," I say, "it will. It is because the nerve was cut."

She nods and is silent. But the young man smiles. "I like it," he says. "It is kind of cute."

All at once I know who he is. I understand, and I lower my gaze. One is not bold in an encounter with a God. Unmindful, he bends to kiss her crooked mouth, and I so close can see how he twists his own lips to accommodate to hers, to show her that their kiss still works.

Dr. Richard Selzer, Mortal Lessons *(San Diego, Calif.: Harcourt Brace).*

Love's Willing Sacrifice

Tradition has passed on this story. Cyrus the Mede, the great conqueror of Babylon and the then-known world, had a general under his authority whose wife was accused of treason. The woman was tried before a tribunal, found guilty, and sentenced to death. After the sentence was announced, the general went to Cyrus with this request: "King Cyrus, please let me take her place."

Cyrus, in awe at what the general asked, said to his court, "Can we terminate a love as great as this?" Cyrus relaxed the sentence and paroled the woman to her husband. As the two left the court, the general said to his wife, "Did you see the benevolent look in Cyrus's eyes as he pardoned you?" The wife responded, "I only had eyes for the one who loved me enough that he was willing to die for me."

Friend of Sinners

Early in his life, Jerry McAuley was a thief and counterfeiter. As a result, he spent seven years in prison. Although he was converted there, it was a long time before he experienced the complete victory that is available in Christ. When he did, however, he began witnessing to other men who had sunk deep in sin. Later he opened America's first rescue mission in New York City, where he befriended the worst criminals and downtrodden people of society.

Just before his death in 1884, he said to his wife, "I know that tuberculosis will soon take my life, but I want to die on my knees, still praying for the lost. I'd rather have some poor soul that I led to the Lord put one small rose on my grave than to have the wealth of a millionaire." His wish was granted, for at his funeral, an aged, shabbily dressed man appeared. Handing one of the ushers a few flowers, he asked, in a voice trembling with emotion, that the flowers be placed on the coffin. Then the old man said apologetically, "I hope Jerry, who was my friend, will know that they came from old Joe Chappy." Mrs. McAuley preserved that little bouquet for a long time in remembrance of the fact that her husband had been a true friend of sinners.

Wearing of the Green

A Sunday school teacher asked the five-year-olds in her class to bring in "something green that you love." The next Sunday, they brought in the usual green hats, green sweaters, and green books. One boy entered with an especially big grin on his face. Behind him, wearing a green dress, came his four-year-old sister.

Love, the Great Motivator

When Louis Lawes became warden of Sing Sing Prison in 1920, the inmates existed in wretched conditions. This led him to introduce humanitarian reforms. He gave much of the credit to his wife, Kathryn, however, who always treated the prisoners as human beings. She would often take her three children and sit with the gangsters, the murderers, and the racketeers while they played basketball and baseball. Then in 1937, Kathryn was killed in a car accident. The next day her body lay in a casket in a house about a quarter of a mile from the institution. When the acting warden found hundreds of prisoners crowded around the main entrance of the prison, he knew what they wanted. Opening the gate, he said, "Men, I'm going to trust you. You can go to the house." No count was taken; no guards were posted. Yet not one man was missing that night. Love for one who had loved them made them dependable.

On My Enemy's Behalf

During the Revolutionary War, there was a faithful gospel preacher by the name of Peter Miller. He lived near a fellow who hated him intensely for his Christian life and testimony. In fact, this man violently opposed him and ridiculed his followers. One day the unbeliever was found guilty of treason and sentenced to death. Hearing about this, Peter Miller set out on foot to intercede for the man's life before George Washington. The general listened to the minister's earnest plea but told him he didn't feel he should pardon the minister's friend. "My friend! He is not my friend," answered Miller. "In fact, he's my worst living enemy." "What?" Washington said. "You have walked sixty miles to save the life of your enemy? That, in my judgment, puts the matter in a different light. I will grant your request." With pardon in hand, Miller hastened to the place where his neighbor was to be executed, and arrived just as the prisoner was walking to the scaffold. When the traitor saw Miller, he exclaimed, "Old Peter Miller has come to have his revenge by watching me hang!" But he was astonished as he watched the minister step out of the crowd and produce the pardon that spared his life.

Unselfish Love

A little boy who was quiet and shy moved to a new neighborhood. His name was Steve. One day he came home from school and said, "You know what, Mom? Valentine's Day is coming, and I want to make a valentine for everyone in my class. I want them to know that I love them." His mother's heart sank as she thought, *I wish he wouldn't do that.* Every afternoon she had watched the children coming home from school, laughing and hanging on to each other—all except Steve. He always walked behind them.

She decided to go along with his plans, however, so glue and paper and crayons were purchased, and for three weeks Steve painstakingly made thirty-five valentines. When the day came to deliver the cards, he was very excited. He stacked those valentines under his arm and ran out the door. His mother thought, *This is going to be a tough day for Steve. I'll bake some cookies and have some milk ready for him when he comes home from school. Maybe that will help ease the pain, since he won't be getting many valentines.*

That afternoon she had the warm cookies and the milk ready. She went over to the window, scratched a little of the frost off the glass, and looked out. Sure enough, here came the gang of children, laughing, with valentines tucked under their arms. And there was her Steve. Although still behind the children, he was walking faster than usual, and she thought, *Bless his heart. He's ready to break into tears.* His arms were empty. He didn't have a single valentine.

Steve came into the house, and his mother said, "Sweetheart, Mom has some warm cookies and milk for you, just sit down. . . ." But Steve's face was all aglow. He marched right by her, and all he could say was: "Not a one, not a single one. I didn't forget one. They all know I love them."

Lady Churchill's Second Husband

Winston Churchill once attended a formal banquet in London, when the attending dignitaries were asked the question "If you could not be who you are, who would you like to be?" Naturally everyone was curious as to what Churchill, who was seated next to his beloved Clemmie, would say. After all, Churchill couldn't be expected to say Julius Caesar or Napoleon. When it finally came Churchill's turn, the old man, who was the dinner's last respondent to the question, rose and gave his answer.

"If I could not be who I am, I would most like to be"—and here he paused to take his wife's hand—"Lady Churchill's second husband."

James C. Humes, Churchill: Speaker of the Century *(New York: Stein and Day), 291.*

A Wartime Romance
See page 231

Undying Love
See page 273

Care for the Enemy
See page 68

A Passion for Prisoners
See page 67

LOVE FOR GOD

We must ask, Do I fight merely for doctrinal faithfulness? This is like the wife who never sleeps with anybody else, but never shows love to her own husband. Is that a sufficient relationship in marriage? No, ten thousand times no. Yet if I am a Christian who speaks and acts for doctrinal faithfulness but do not show love to the divine bridegroom, I am in the same place as such a wife. What God wants from us is not only doctrinal faithfulness, but our love day and night.Not in theory, mind you, but in practice.

Francis Schaeffer

We Can Love

This is what King Edward saw on the wall when he visited a home for the deaf:

We cannot shout
We cannot sing
But we can love
Our gracious King

Love Jesus and Nothing Much Can Go Wrong

Here's a letter C. S. Lewis wrote to a girl named Ruth:

Dear Ruth . . . ,

Many thanks for your kind letter, and it was very good of you to write and tell me that you like my books; and what a very good letter you write for your age!

If you continue to love Jesus, nothing much can go wrong with you, and I hope you may always do so. I'm so thankful that you realized [the] "hidden story" in the Narnian books. It is odd, children nearly *always* do, grown-ups hardly ever.

I'm afraid the Narnian series has come to an end, and am sorry to tell you that you can expect no more.

God bless you.

Yours sincerely,

C. S. Lewis

Lyle W. Dorsett and Marjorie Lamp Mead, eds., C. S. Lewis' Letters to Children *(New York: Macmillan, 1985), 111.*

LOVE OF GOD

The worse my state, the greater my need of my Father who loves me.

George Macdonald

Some draw a circle that shuts men out;
Race and position are what they flout;
But Christ in love seeks them all to win,
He draws a circle that takes them in!

Edwin Markham

Love, and do what thou wilt; whether thou hold thy peace, through love hold thy peace; whether thou cry out, through love cry out; whether thou correct, through love correct; whether thou spare, through love do thou spare; let the root of love be within, of this root can nothing spring but what is good.

St. Augustine

The Hound of Heaven

Francis Thompson's early life was one dead end after another. He studied for the priesthood but did not complete his course; he studied medicine and failed; he joined the military and was released after one day; he finally ended up an opium addict in London. Yet he never did escape the pursuit of God, the hunter and initiator, for God loved him. In the midst of his despondency he was befriended by someone who saw his poetic gifts—and as time went on, Thompson was able to put his experience in verse. The poem is "The Hound of Heaven," which Coventry Patmore has called one of the finest odes in the English language. Thompson says it for all of us:

I fled Him, down the nights and down the days;
I fled Him, down the arches of the years;
I fled Him, down the labyrinthine ways
Of my own mind; and in the mist of tears

I hid from Him, and under running laughter.
Up vistaed hopes, I sped;
And shot, precipitated
Down titanic glooms of chasmed fears,
From those strong Feet that followed, followed after.

LOYALTY

I set this down as a fact, that if all men knew what each other said of the other, there would not be four friends in the world.

Blaise Pascal

LUST

At this moment [when lust takes control] God . . . loses all reality. . . . Satan does not fill us with hatred of God, but with forgetfulness of God.

Dietrich Bonhoeffer

The Bigger the Butterfly, the Better

An intriguing entomological experiment shows that a male butterfly will ignore a living female butterfly of his own species in favor of a painted cardboard one, if the cardboard one is big. If the cardboard one is bigger than he is, bigger than any female butterfly ever could be. He jumps the pieces of cardboard. Nearby, the real, living female butterfly opens and closes her wings in vain.

Annie Dillard, The Writing Life *(New York: Harper & Row, 1989), 17–18.*

Slumbering Inclination

See page 409

LYING

Falsehood is the basic fault line in the foundation of the soul, putting all the superstructure in jeopardy. All the believability a person has, his very integrity, totters on

the shifting sand of one lie. Deceit holds hostage all other virtues.
Robertson C. McQuilkin

Lying is a sin that does not go alone; it ushers in other sins.
Thomas Watson

Master Deceivers

In 1991, the *Chicago Tribune* ran this article by Jon Van about lying:

The thing that separates human beings from other animals isn't the ability to reason or use tools, but telling lies and the human capacity for self-deception, scholars said at a major science meeting. . . .

These researchers . . . claimed that proficiency at lying may be the best measure of advancement, with primates much more adept at it than other mammals and human beings the most masterful deceivers on the planet.

Several examples of deception in nature are the virus that tricks a person's immune system to cause a cold and the chimpanzee who misleads its fellow apes to keep bananas to himself and away from dominant animals in the troop.

Even though chimps use deception, tools and imagination, said Robert Sussman, an anthropology professor at Washington University in St. Louis, they employ these devices only for immediate practical purposes, such as getting food. They seem unable to assign any values beyond practical subsistence. . . .

[Says Sussman:] "Deception is socially adaptive for humans. It might also be adaptive to be able to deceive oneself. I don't think animals have a filter through which they see the world, but it is almost a necessity for humans."

Another speaker, Loyal D. Rue, a professor of religion and philosophy at Luther College in Decorah, Iowa, also lent support to the necessity of deception in the world.

"The 'lies' we see in nature and culture are life-support systems," Rue said. "We can't survive without them. Deception is a strategy that we use to save ourselves from social and psychological chaos."

Jon Van, Chicago Tribune, *17 February 1991.*

Undying Love

By the time you swear you're his,
Shivering and sighing,
And he vows his passion is
Infinite, undying—
One of you is lying.

Dorothy Parker, Forbes, *25 November 1991, 240.*

The Truth about Lying

There is a philosophy out there that claims that lying is healthy and not always sinful. That's the implication in Franny Shuker-Haines's article "The Truth about Lying":

One day when I was 7, my 10-year-old sister, Allison, and I decided to make a detour on the way home from school. We headed toward the "downtown" section of our small Midwestern community, with just-received allowances jingling in our pockets. We bought all the forbidden treats we could afford—Hostess Fruit Pies, Twinkies, chocolate chip cookies—and ate as much of them as we could stuff into our greedy little mouths. As we approached the house, I cleverly hid the box of cookies in my long, thin, stocking cap, never realizing that its outline would be comically visible.

When we arrived home, our mother, somewhat frantic, asked where we'd been. "Oh, out playing," Allison and I replied, as we shifted from foot to foot, itching to escape to the safety of our bedroom. "Well, what have you got in your hat?" she asked. "Nothing!" I blurted, as my mother whisked it from my head. I was sure she had x-ray vision—and that I was in big trouble.

Of course, every adult remembers lying as a child. So we shouldn't be surprised when our little ones start to lie to us. All kids do it, and these days, in small, appropriate doses, it's practically considered healthy. "One of the ways that an individual can differentiate himself from another person is with the capacity to have internal secrets, and the ability to deceive that other person," says Clark Ford, M.D., professor of psychiatry at the University of Arkansas at Little Rock. "It's an important part of separation from the parents."

But the fact that some lying is considered normal doesn't mean parents don't have to deal with it. However necessary an occasional fib is to a child's growing sense of self, lying in general should still be discouraged. The best way to handle the issue, however, is no longer with a simple: "Don't you ever lie to me!" Today's parents should come to understand why a variety of responses are necessary—depending on the kind of lie, the age of the teller, and the reasons behind the lie.

Franny Shuker-Haines, "The Truth about Lying," Child, *April 1990, 30.*

Kidnapping of the Brainchild
See page 133

M

MARRIAGE

Marital love is like death—it wants all of us. And who has not been frightened almost to death by love's dark shadow gliding swift and huge as an interstellar shark, swimming mountain, through the deepest waters of our being, through depths we never knew we had?
Mike Mason

Loving your wife is not to love her as a saint, but as a sinner. If we love her for her saintliness, we do not love her at all.
Mike Mason

Marriage is not an achievement which is finished. It is a dynamic process between two people, a relation which is constantly being changed, which grows or dies.
Walter Trobisch

The mystery is this: God did not create the union of Christ and the church after the pattern of human marriage; just the reverse! He created human marriage on the pattern of Christ's relation to the church.
John Piper

To keep a vow, therefore, means not to keep from breaking it, but rather to devote the rest of one's life to

> discovering what the vow means, and to be willing to change and to grow accordingly.
>
> *Mike Mason*

> [A husband must learn] to tolerate his wife's infirmities, because in doing so he either cures her, or makes himself better.
>
> *Jeremy Taylor*

Marriage among the Clergy

The marriages of clergymen and women in the United States fail just as frequently as those of other mortals. This was the finding of a study carried out by the Theological Seminary in Hartford (Connecticut).

According to the survey, conducted in 1993 and 1994, one in four female ministers and one in five male pastors worldwide have been divorced at least once. In the American population as a whole, the same applies to 23 percent of the women and 22 percent of the men.

The church survey indicated that female theologians tended to divorce before their ordination while male theologians tended to divorce after ordination. The divorce rate was found to be higher in liberal churches than it was in conservative churches.

Possessiveness in Marriage

Author Mike Mason has these thoughts on marriage:

When we have bought another person with our whole hearts, we may naturally and truly be said to possess them. Modern couples balk at this idea, and "possessiveness" in marriage has come to be regarded as a cardinal sin. But there is no true marriage without it, and even in the vows there is embedded that curious and potent little phrase "to have and to hold." As Paul says, "the wife's body does not belong to her alone but also to her husband. In the same way, the husband's body does not belong to him alone but also to his wife" (1 Corinthians 7:4). Ownership is expressed in this passage in terms of sexual rights, just as property owners have certain exclusive rights over their land. But the physical is always a sign of something deeper, and in marriage not just the body is given, but the heart. One heart is given in exchange for another, and in this mutual proprietorship is found the deepest and most radical expression of intimacy. It might almost be said that love is the total willingness to be owned.

Mike Mason, The Mystery of Marriage *(Portland, Oreg.: Multnomah, 1978), 87–88.*

Chain Reaction

Other thoughts from Mike Mason on marriage:

We are not simply moving in with someone we think it might be fun to live with. Rather, we are giving our prior assent to the whole chain reaction of trials, decisions, transformations, and personal cataclysms which, once they are done with us, may leave us not only changed beyond recognition, but marked nearly as deeply as by a religious conversion.

Mike Mason, The Mystery of Marriage *(Portland, Oreg.: Multnomah, 1978), 61.*

Not for Anything in the World

Tolstoy came to see marriage not only as a source of great unhappiness but as an obstacle to moral progress. . . . In 1897, in a Lear-like outburst, he told his daughter Tanya:

I can understand why a depraved man may find salvation in marriage. But why a pure girl should want to get mixed up in such a business is beyond me. If I were a girl I would not marry for anything in the world. And so far as being in love is concerned, for either men or women—since I know what it means, that is, it is an ignoble and above all an unhealthy sentiment, not at all beautiful, lofty or poetical—I would not have opened my door to it. I would have taken as many precautions to avoid being contaminated by that disease as I would to protect myself against far less serious infections such as diphtheria, typhus or scarlet fever.

Paul Johnson, Intellectuals *(New York: Harper & Row, 1988), 525–526.*

More Important than Staying Married

How lightly some people take their commitment to marriage. Writes one man, "I hope my wife will never divorce me, because I love her with all my heart. But if one day she feels I am minimizing her or making her feel inferior or in any way standing in the light that she needs to become the person God meant her to be, I hope she'll be free to throw me out even if she's one hundred. There is something more important than our staying married, and it has to do with integrity, personhood, and purpose."

Os Guinness, The Gravedigger Files *(Downers Grove, Ill.: InterVarsity), 100, quoting Peter Williamson and Kevin Perrotta, eds.,* Christianity Confronts Modernity, *12.*

Open Marriage

In their book that advocates open marriage, Nena and George O'Neill contend that "the traditional closed marriage is a form of bondage, for both husband and wife." They list six "psychological commitments" involved in a traditional marriage: "Possession or ownership of the mate . . . Denial of the self . . . Maintenance of the couple-front . . . Rigid role behavior . . . Absolute fidelity . . . Total exclusivity." And they warn: "Subtly, insidiously, often without your even knowing it, the clauses of the closed marriage contract begin to foreclose upon your freedom and your individuality, making you a slave of your marriage."

Out Together

A farmer and his wife were sleeping in bed when a tornado came and swept them and their bed out of the house. There they were, flying through the air together in their bed, when the wife began to cry. The farmer said to her, "This is no time to cry!" She replied, "I can't help it! I'm so happy because this is the first time we've been out together in twenty years."

Married Instead

Snow White and the Seven Dwarfs was the story of the day at the nursery school four-year-old Jane attended. This was the first time she had ever heard the story, so she listened carefully as the teacher told the story of the sweet young girl who was fed a poisoned apple by an old witch, and the predictable result: she fell into a deep sleep and would never wake up unless she received a kiss from the wonderful Prince Charming. Jane couldn't wait to go home and tell her mother this story. At home, Jane said, "Mother, let me tell you this story. You'll never believe it." She began to describe what happened to Snow White. When she got to the end, she said, "And, Mother, Prince Charming kissed her back to life, and guess what happened?" The mother responded, "Well, honey, they lived happily ever after." But the little girl shook her head and replied, "No, they didn't, Mother; they got married!"

A Holy Love
See page 263

Love's Willing Sacrifice
See page 264

Temporary Insanity
See page 261

The Main Thing Is Not to Love
See page 260

MARTYRDOM

A female slave named Felicitas lay in prison; there she bore a child. In her pain, she screamed. The jailers asked her how, if she shrieked at that, she expected to endure death by the beasts. She said: "Now I suffer what I suffer; then another will be in me who will suffer for me, as I shall suffer for him."

Charles Williams, The Descent of the Dove.

When English martyrs Hugh Latimer and Nicholas Ridley were being taken to the stake for burning, Latimer turned to Ridley and said, "Be of good cheer, Brother Ridley; we have lighted such a candle in England as by the grace of God shall never be put out."

Under Fire
See page 397

MATERIALISM

North Americans are consumption mad. Many people go around believing that without things they will simply disappear. North Americans are pleasure minded, self-indulgent, materialistic, and selfish. This vision has captured the hearts of many Christians, young and old. Many Christians try to live according to two visions—to enjoy the best of two worlds—to remain Christians while at the same time pledging to uphold the faith of consumption. Sooner or later, however, one vision, one spiritual force, will gain the upper hand, will become the directing, the determining force in our lives.

R. Kent Hughes

Our thought, our desires, our actions struck no roots in that faith to which we adhered with our lips. With all our strength, we were devoted to material things.

Janine in François Mauriac's Viper's Tangle *(Garden City, N.Y.: Image Books [a division of Doubleday], 1957).*

Consumer religion is an unholy amalgam of convictions and consumption that creates a sacramental materialism in the name of Christ. . . . If consumer religion hadn't

existed already, some American entrepreneur would have been glad to invent it.
Os Guinness

If a man is drunk on wine, you'll throw him out. But if he's drunk on money, you'll make him a deacon.
Os Guinness

The motive of Christian simplicity is not the enjoyment of simplicity itself; that and any other earthly benefit that comes along are part of the "all the rest" (Matthew 6:33). But the sole motive of Christian simplicity is the enjoyment of God himself (and if that be *hedonism,* let's make the most of it!)—it is "the view of the stars."
Vernard Eller

A Token of Gratitude

Neumeister was the chief pastor of the Jacobi-Kirche in Hamburg when Bach applied for the position of organist there in November 1720. It seems clear that the principal reason why Bach failed to receive the appointment was the practice maintained there of expecting the appointee to make a substantial financial contribution to the church. This was, they assured everyone, not to be construed as buying the position, which, as part of the ministry of the church, could be purchased only by running the great danger of the sin of simony. But, according to the minutes of its meeting of 21 November 1720, the search committee that considered Bach and his rivals decided that "if, after the selection has been made, the chosen candidate of his own free will wished to give a token of his gratitude, the latter would be accepted."

Nonetheless, a contemporary narrative, by one Johann Mattheson in *Der Musicalische Patraiot,* leaves no doubt either about the true nature of the financial transaction or about Neumeister's indignant reaction, even though no names are mentioned. Although Bach had "aroused universal admiration for his artistry," one of his rivals "was better at preluding with his thalers [coins] than with his fingers" and got the job. Neumeister was shocked and angered, and he took the occasion of the upcoming Christmas holiday, on the basis of the Gospel story in the second chapter of Luke, to suggest from his pulpit that "even if one of the angels of Bethlehem should come down from Heaven, one who played divinely and wished to become organist of St. Jacobi, but had no money, he might just as well fly away again."

Jaroslav Pelikan, Bach among the Theologians *(Philadelphia, Penn.: Fortress, 1986), 42–43.*

Cold Hard Cash

Rocky Marciano had an irrational greed for cash—not checks, but the green stuff. Frank Saccone, Marciano's accountant and traveling companion, traveled the world with Marciano on hundreds of trips, and he never knew the man to want it any other way. "He had this crazy, crazy need for cash," Saccone says. "He loved the sight of cash. A check was just a little piece of paper. I remember times he'd get a check and lose it. He'd put it somewhere and forget about it. He'd reach in his pocket and pull out checks that were all tattered. I've seen him give away checks for $450,000; $100,000. I'm talking big money. He didn't even associate that with money. To him a check was just a piece of paper. But if he had $40,000 in $10 bills, there was no way he'd give any of that away. He *believed* in the green stuff." . . .

By the time Rocky Marciano died, almost a quarter of a century ago, the life he had created for himself outside the ring was quite as large and unlikely as the figure he had once cut inside it. Of course, Lord only knows what he might be doing today had he somehow survived his endless peregrinations; how many sacks of cash he might have wadded up and squirreled away in his far-flung caches; how big his lending business might have become; or how long he could have avoided arousing the serious curiosity of IRS agents, not only over his out-of-pocket lending business, for which he kept no books or paperwork, but also over his travels around the banquet circuit, where he insisted on payment in cash only. It was a strange, fantastic world he had built for himself, one shaped in considerable part by the obsessive, endless quest for $100 bills.

William Nack, "The Rock," Sports Illustrated, *23 August 1993, 55–56.*

Is It Me or My Money?

John D. Rockefeller suffered from a common problem of the rich—wondering whether friends liked him for himself or for his money. John D. had few golfing partners because "I have made experiments, and nearly always the result is the same. Along about the ninth hole comes some proposition charitable or financial."

Daily Herald, *24 October 1988, sec. 1, p. 8.*

Conspicuous Consumption

Born in Milwaukee in 1919, christened Wladziu Valentino, "Call Me Lee" Liberace became that most hackneyed of all phrases, a legend in his lifetime. Outrageous, flamboyant, he was the highest paid performer anywhere in the world at the height of his fame, netting some five million dollars a year. A great deal of his fortune was spent on such excesses as having his master bedroom in Palm Springs painted as a replica of the *Creation of Man* scene from the Sistine Chapel. Many of the plump pink cherubs winging their way across the ceiling distinctly resemble the baby-faced idol of millions of fans. No, he was not tasteless. But what taste!

Call it compulsive shopping, call it conspicuous consumption, Liberace was certainly conspicuous and certainly compulsive. He finished up with eight warehouses full of stuff that couldn't fit into any of his five residences.

Pan Am Clipper, *vol. 28, no. 4 (April 1988): 13.*

Everything Gets Left Behind

When John D. Rockefeller died, a man was curious about how much he had left behind. Determined to find out, he set up an appointment with one of Rockefeller's highest aides. The man asked the aide how much Rockefeller left behind, and the aide answered, "He left all of it."

Living Well but Not Successfully

In his book *Revolution Now,* Bill Bright gives an example of the art of living well but not successfully: In 1923 a very important meeting was held at the Edgewater Beach Hotel in Chicago. Attending this meeting were nine of the world's most successful financiers: Charles Schwab, steel magnate; Samuel Insull, president of the largest utility company; Howard Hopson, president of the largest gas company; Arthur Cotton, the greatest wheat speculator; Richard Whitney, president of the New York stock exchange; Albert Fall, a member of the president's Cabinet; Leon Fraser, president of the Bank of International Settlements; Jesse Livermore, the great "bear" on Wall Street; and Ivar Krueger, head of the most powerful monopoly.

Twenty-five years later, Charles Schwab had died in bankruptcy, having lived on borrowed money for five years before his death; Samuel Insull had died a fugitive from justice and penniless in a foreign land; Howard Hopson was insane; Arthur Cotton had died abroad, insolvent; Albert Fall had been pardoned so that he could die at home; Leon Fraser, Jesse Livermore, and Ivar Krueger had all died by suicide. All of these men had learned well the art of making a living, but none of them had learned how to live!

Tell Me More about Johnny Brown
See page 262

Small Notes
See page 231

MEEKNESS

The man who is truly meek is the man who is amazed that God and man can think of him as well as they do and treat him as well as they do.

Martyn Lloyd-Jones

MEMORIZATION

A Doer and a Hearer

One day a young Christian came into a mission station in Korea to visit the man who had been instrumental in his conversion to Christ. After the customary greetings, the missionary asked the reason for his coming. "I have been memorizing some verses in the Bible," he said, "and I want to quote them to you." He had walked hundreds of miles just to recite some Scripture verses to his father in the faith.

The missionary listened as he recited without error the entire Sermon on the Mount. He commended the young man for his remarkable feat of memory, then cautioned that he must not only "say" the Scriptures but also practice them. With glowing face, the man responded, "Oh, that is the way I learned them. I tried to memorize them but they wouldn't stick, so I hit on this plan. First, I would learn a verse. Then I would practice what the verse said on a neighbor who was not a Christian. After that I found I could remember it."

Our Daily Bread, *(Grand Rapids, Mich.: Radio Bible Class), March 1992.*

MEMORY

In the practical use of our intellect, forgetting is as important a function as remembering. . . . If we remembered everything, we should on most occasions be as ill as if we remembered nothing.
William James

A good memory is generally joined to a weak judgment.
Montaigne

Incredible Minds

The elder Seneca (c. 55 B.C.–A.D. 37), a famous teacher of rhetoric, was said to be able to repeat long passages of speeches he had heard only once many years before. He would impress his students by asking each member of a class of two hundred to recite a line of poetry, and then he would recite all the lines they had quoted—in reverse order, from last to first. Saint Augustine, who also had begun life as a teacher of rhetoric, reported his admiration of a friend who could recite the whole text of Virgil—backwards!
Daniel J. Boorstin, The Discoverers *(New York: Vintage, 1993), 482.*

There Goes His Memory

See page 3

MERCY

God's mercy hath no relation to time, no limitation in time. . . . Whom God loves He loves to the end; and not only to their end, to their death, but to His end; and His end is, that He might love them still.
John Donne

I do not ask the grace which thou didst give to St. Paul; nor can I dare to ask the grace which thou didst grant to St. Peter; but, the mercy which thou didst show to the Dying Robber, that mercy, show to me.
Copernicus

Not what thou art, nor what thou hast been, doth God regard with his merciful eyes, but what thou wouldst be.
Julian of Norwich

Surprised by Joy

In *Surprised by Joy,* C. S. Lewis comments on his conversion:

I did not then see what is now the most shining and obvious thing; the Divine humility which will accept a convert even on such terms. The Prodigal Son at least walked home on his own feet. But who can duly adore that love which will open the high gates to a prodigal who is brought in kicking, struggling, resentful, and darting his eyes in every direction for a chance of escape. The words *compelle intrare,* compel them to come in, have been so abused by wicked men that we shudder at them; but, properly understood, they plumb the depth of the Divine mercy. The hardness of God is kinder than the softness of men, and His compulsion is our liberation.
C. S. Lewis, Surprised by Joy *(Great Britain: Fontana, 1973), 182–183.*

MIND

The mind today is in profound trouble, perhaps more than ever before. How to order the mind on sound Christian principles, at the heart of where it is formed and informed, is one of the . . . greatest themes that can be considered.
Charles Malik

MINISTRY

To be a true minister to men is always to accept new happiness and new distress.
Phillips Brooks

MONEY

If it be riches that slay you, what matter if it be riches you have or riches you have not.
George Macdonald

I don't think that God despises riches; in fact, He gives them to us. What He despises is the misuse of them, and He rewards stewardship.
Carl F. H. Henry

Money is that something which buys everything but happiness, and takes a man everywhere but heaven.
John Woodbridge Patten

MORALITY

Can law and order survive in a land where justice is determined not by moral principle but by personal expediency?
Charles Colson

Adult movies, and adult situations, are not adult. Adults don't do such things.
R. Kent Hughes

The Greatness of America

In de Tocqueville's classic *Democracy in America,* which scholars feel is probably the greatest book on any national policy and culture, de Tocqueville said:

I sought for the greatness and genius of America in her commodious harbors and her ample rivers, and it was not there. . . .

I sought for the greatness and genius of America in her democratic congress and her matchless constitution, and it was not there.

Not until I went into the churches of America and heard her pulpits flame with righteousness did I understand the secret of her genius and power.

America is great because America is good, and if America ever ceases to be good, America will cease to be great.

Leon Jaworski, Crossroads, *128.*

MORTALITY

A Futile Misadventure

Here is John Updike's observation about his mortality:

Shortly after the insurance report, I was playing basketball—we husbands and fathers were still young enough to play this game of constant motion—and I looked up at the naked, netless hoop: gray sky outside it, gray sky inside it. And as I waited, on a raw rainy fall day, for the opposing touch-football team to kick off, there would come sailing through the air instead the sullen realization that in a few decades we would all be dead. I remember squatting in our cellar making my daughter a dollhouse, under the close sky of the cobwebby ceiling, and the hammer going numb in my hand as I saw not only my life but hers, so recently begun, as a futile misadventure, a leap out of the dark and back.

John Updike, Self-Consciousness *(New York: Fawcett Crest, 1989), 100.*

MOTHERHOOD

All mothers have their favorite child. It is always the same one: the one who needs you at the moment. Who needs you for whatever reason—to cling to, to shout at, to hurt, to hug, to flatter, to reverse charges to, to unload on—but mostly just to be there.

Erma Bombeck

Dear Mother: I wish Mother's Day wasn't always on Sunday. It would be better if it was on Monday so we wouldn't have to go to school.

Note from a nine-year-old girl to her mother

> I did not have my mother long, but she cast over me an influence which has lasted all my life. The good effects of her early training I can never lose. If it had not been for her appreciation and her faith in me at a critical time in my experience, I should never likely have become an inventor. I was always a careless boy, and with a mother of different mental caliber, I should have turned out badly. But her firmness, her sweetness, her goodness, were potent powers to keep me in the right path. My mother was the making of me. The memory of her will always be a blessing to me.
>
> *Thomas Edison*

A Mother's Love

Catherine Booth, the wife of the founder of the Salvation Army, was a woman of immense gifts who had a remarkable public ministry. Writes her son in her biography:

She began her public ministry when I, her eldest child, was five years old. But her own home was never neglected for what some would call—I doubt whether she would have so described it—the larger sphere. Both alike had been opened to her by her God. She saw His purposes in both. In the humble duties of the kitchen table, her hands busy with the food, or in the nursery when the children were going to bed, or at the bedside of a sick child, she was working for God's glory.

Bramwell Booth, These Fifty Years *(London: Cassell and Company, 1929), 25.*

More than a Mother

Most important was the death in July of Mrs. Everest, [Churchill's] old nanny, who was more than his surrogate mother. She was, excepting only his wife, the one in his life who gave him the most unconditional love. At Harrow, to the surprise and sneering gibes of his classmates, he had invited his old nanny down and walked hand in hand with her across the campus, showing her the sights. A classmate wrote years later that it was one of the greatest acts of courage and compassion he had ever seen. For years before her death his nanny had been in retirement, her days brightened by letters from her beloved Winston. He was the only Churchill to attend her funeral. Even though he received only an officer's pay, a meager 120 pounds a year, upon leaving Sandhurst he made an arrangement with a florist for the constant upkeep of her grave. To the end of his life Winston kept her picture on his desk at Chartwell.

James C. Humes, Churchill, Speaker of the Century *(New York: Stein and Day), 28.*

MOTIVATION

He was hard on himself. I couldn't find
That he kept any hours—not for himself.
Daylight and lantern-light were one to him:
I've heard him pounding in the barn all night.
But what he liked was someone to encourage.
Them that he couldn't lead he'd get behind
And drive, the way you can, you know in mowing—
Keep at their heels and threaten to mow their legs off.

Robert Frost, from the poem "The Code"

Inspired Playing

When Lou Little coached football at Georgetown University, he had on his squad a player of average ability who rarely got into the game. Yet the coach was fond of him, and especially liked the way he walked arm-in-arm with his dad on campus.

One day, shortly before the big contest with Fordham, the boy's mother called Mr. Little and said her husband had died that morning of a heart attack. "Will you break the news to my son?" she asked. "He'll take it better from you."

The student went home with a heavy heart that afternoon, but three days later he was back. "Coach," he pleaded, "will you start me in that game against Fordham? I think it's what my father would have liked most."

After a moment's hesitation, Little said, "OK, but only for a play or two." True to his word, he put the boy in—but he never took him out. For 60 action-packed minutes that inspired youngster ran, blocked, and passed like an all-American. After the game the coach praised him, "Son, you were terrific! You've never played like that before. What got into you?"

"Remember how my father and I used to go arm-in-arm?" he replied. "Well, few people knew it, but he was totally blind. I like to think that today was the first time he ever saw me play!"

Bits and Pieces

Love, the Great Motivator

See page 266

N

NARCISSISM

With spiritual narcissism so well advanced, "firm believer" is a matter of aerobics rather than apologetics, of human fitness rather than divine faithfulness. Shapeliness is now next to godliness.

Os Guinness

It is no accident that at the present trends in psychoanalysis are the rediscovery of narcissism. . . . The society is marked by a self-interest and egocentrism that increasingly reduces all relations to one question, "What am I getting out of it?"

Herbert Hendin

O

OBEDIENCE

It is better to go to Troas with God, than anywhere else without Him.

G. Campbell Morgan

Lord, do Thou turn me all into love, and all my love into obedience, and let my obedience be without interruption.

Jeremy Taylor

The Lord of all creation has ordained that he would do his work through us. Our seeing the Spirit's guidance and obeying what he wants us to do and say is the way he works to bless the world.

Lloyd Ogilvie

The Lord will not use us until he has made us ready. Then we thank him for knowing what he is doing.

Lloyd Ogilvie

You have not really learned a commandment until you have obeyed it. . . . Nothing clarifies doctrine like doing. Each new thing learned becomes a *millstone* if we do not make it a *milestone.*

Vance Havner

Counterculture Obedience

To speak positively of obedience today is to be profoundly countercultural. The valid suspicion of talk about obedience is grounded in the experience of authoritarianisms, both past and present. Obedience is confused with "blind obedience," which is morally odious. Obedience is confused with conformity, with going along, with asking no questions. But obedience really means responsiveness; it is related to the Latin *audire,* to hear, to listen, to respond appropriately. Obedience is not the surrender of responsibility but the acceptance of responsibility for what we respond to and how.

Richard John Neuhaus, Freedom for Ministry *(Grand Rapids, Mich.: Eerdmans, 1979), 236–237.*

A Parable of Obedience

Gypsy, a furry wheat-colored collie, found herself mistress of several hundred acres of hill and wood, full of good things like rabbit trails and streams and intriguing burrows, and she delighted in it all. She was given a comfortable bed and good meals, so much so that perhaps she often took them for granted. Obligations there were few, and they were not heavy. She was, to be sure, supposed to worship her Master and be right joyous to be with him. She also knew that she mustn't chase the chickens. While she must obey commands—to follow, to come, to lie down—there were no unreasonable demands, and no tricks. After all, to obey and to worship were natural to her dog nature.

There came a day when, as Gypsy was prowling on the far hill past the string-house and pasture, two things happened simultaneously: The Master called her, and a rabbit fled across the hill. Gypsy wheeled and raced toward the Master; then she stopped. It entered her mind that she didn't have to obey. Perhaps the Master didn't realize about that rabbit. Anyway, these were her acres. The rabbit was hers, really. Very probably, it was all nonsense, the story about everything belonging to the Master. How did she know that the food that appeared in the pan was put there by him? Probably there was some natural explanation. She was a free dog, and that was the end of it. These thoughts went through her mind swiftly as she stood irresolute. Again came the Master's command; the rabbit crossed the top of the hill. Gypsy whirled and raced after the rabbit. She had made a choice; there was nothing to stop her.

Hours later she came home. She saw the Master waiting quietly for her, but she did not rush gladly, leaping and frisking, to him as she had always done. Something new came into her demeanor: guilt. She crawled up to him like a snake on her belly. Undoubtedly she was penitent at the moment. But she had a new knowledge—the knowledge of the possibility of sin, and it was a thrill in her heart and a salt taste in her mouth. Nevertheless she was very obedient the next day and the day after. Eventually though, there was another rabbit—and she didn't even hesitate. Soon it was the mere possibility of a rabbit. And then she dropped the rabbit thing altogether and went her own way.

The Master loved her still, but trusted her no more. In time she lived in a pen and went for walks with a rope around her neck. All her real freedom was gone. But the Master gave her, from time to time, opportunities to obey, again of her own free will. Had she chosen to obey, she would once again have had perfect freedom to wander her hundreds of acres. But she always chose, if she were out of reach, to run. The Master, knowing that hunger would bring her back to her pen, let her run. He could have stopped her; the rifle that would have ended her rebellion with the crack of doom stood in the corner, but while she lived she might choose freedom and obedience.

One day, during a journey by car, Gypsy was taken to the edge of the world. Always Gypsy had limited her disobedience to the hills she knew. But now, coming back to the car, she suddenly felt the old thrill; she turned and fled. The Master called with a note of sharp urgency. Gypsy, her ears dulled to the meanings of the Master, continued her rush into the dark forest. After hours of searching and calling, the Master called once more and then sadly abandoned the lost one and drove home.

Gypsy, if she still lived, wandered the woods and roads an outcast. She became dirty and matted with burrs. No doubt stones were thrown at her and she was often hungry; she had lost the way home. This was the way she chose on the Day of the Rabbit, and continued to choose until there was no more choosing.

OMNIPRESENCE

Do Ants Believe in Becky?

In his book *First Things First,* Frederick Catherwood tells this story about a young woman:

A cheerful American girl called Becky told me that for a long time she couldn't bring herself to believe in God. It was all too fantastic, too unreal. Then one day she was lying on the grass outside her home, and noticed the ants hurrying to and fro. She thought, "I wonder if those ants believe in Becky?" She guessed they probably did not. To them she was a hill, a large shadow. How could they possibly believe in her—she was too different, too complex, too unlike anything they could know about or imagine. She picked up some of the ants and let them run about in her hand. "Even now," she thought, "they don't believe in me. I'm just a surface area. They don't realize I'm looking at them, that I could clap my hands together and kill them."

Then it suddenly dawned on Becky that God might be to her just as she was to the ants. No matter how much she dismissed him, he might still be there, watching her, powerful but waiting. It was that thought which shook her out of her arrogance and made her reflect. It led her to people who could teach her, and bring her to a knowledge of God as Creator and Saviour.

Unlike Becky's ants, we can hear God. He has spoken to the men and women he created. He spoke through prophets and through conscience. He also revealed himself systematically, clearly and logically through the Jewish law, and then face-to-face in Jesus Christ, who was both God and man.

Frederick Catherwood, First Things First *(Tring, England: Lion, 1979).*

Over All Things, All Things Under

Hildebert, archbishop of Tours in the eleventh century, sings of Jehovah's omnipresence in his poem *Alpha et Omega, Magne Deus!* translated by Herbert Kynnaton:

Over all things, all things under,
Touching all, from all asunder;
Centre thou, but not intruded,
Compassing, and yet included;
Over all, and not ascending,
Under all, but not depending;
Over all, the world ordaining,
Under all the world sustaining.

Hildebert (archbishop of Tours), Alpha et Omega, Magne Deus!, *translated by Herbert Kynnaton.*

OMNISCIENCE

God's knowledge of the future is as complete as is His knowledge of the past and the present, and that, because the future depends entirely upon Himself.

A. W. Pink

When we feel as if God were nowhere, He is watching over us with an eternal consciousness, above and beyond our every hope and fear, untouched by the varying faith and fluctuating moods of His children.
George Macdonald

Separating the Good from the Bad
This is a letter from a girl to her pastor:

Dear Pastor,

How does God know the good people from the bad people? Do you tell Him or does He read about it in the newspapers?

Sincerely,
Marie
Age 9

OPPORTUNITY

You cannot buy yesterday back with the tears or prayers or votive offerings of today.
Clarence Edward Macartney

OPTIMISM

The First Home Run Ever
The Little Leaguer put all his sixty pounds into a ferocious swing and connected—barely. The ball scraped by the bottom of the bat, jiggled straight back to the pitcher, who groped and fumbled it. There was still plenty of time to nail the batter at first, but the pitcher's throw soared high over the first baseman's head. The slugger flew on toward second base. Somebody retrieved the ball. The next throw sailed into left field wildly.

The hitter swaggered into third, puffing through a man-sized grin, then continued on to cross the final plate.

"Oh, boy!" he said. "That's the first home run I ever hit in my whole life!"

Paganini and One String
See page 19

ORDINARINESS

God can achieve his purpose either through the absence of human power and resources, or the abandonment of reliance on them. All through history God has chosen and used nobodies, because their unusual dependence on him made possible the unique display of his power and grace. He chose and used somebodies only when they renounced dependence on their natural abilities and resources.

Oswald Chambers

P

PARADOX

A real Christian is an odd number, anyway. He feels supreme love for One whom he has never seen; talks familiarly every day to Someone he cannot see; expects to go to heaven on the virtue of Another; empties himself in order to be full; admits he is wrong so he can be declared right; goes down in order to get up; is strongest when he is weakest, richest when he is poorest and happiest when he feels the worst. He dies so he can live; forsakes in order to have; gives away so he can keep; sees the invisible; hears the inaudible; and knows that which passeth knowledge.

A. W. Tozer

PASSION

Truth without emotion produces dead orthodoxy and a church full (or half-full) of artificial admirers.

John Piper

Be earnest, earnest, earnest—
Mad if thou wilt;
Do what thou dost as if the

stake were Heaven,
And that thy last deed before
the Judgment Day
Charles Kingsley

Free from Clutter

An anecdote survives about Albert Einstein. He was once asked by a student, "Dr. Einstein. How many feet are there in a mile?" To the utter astonishment of the student, Einstein replied, "I don't know."

The student was sure the great professor was joking. Surely Einstein would know a simple fact that every schoolchild is required to memorize. But Einstein wasn't joking. When the student pressed for an explanation of this hiatus in Einstein's knowledge he declared, "I make it a rule not to clutter my mind with simple information that I can find in a book in five minutes."

Albert Einstein was not interested in trivial data. His passion was to explore the deep things of the universe. His passion for mathematical and physical truth made him a pivotal figure in modern world history.

We are called to a similar passion. A passion to know God.

R. C. Sproul, "Right Now Counts Forever," Tabletalk, *vol. 11, no. 3 (June 1987).*

Believe What You Believe

When George Whitefield was getting the people of Edinburgh out of their beds at five o'clock in the morning to hear his preaching, a man on his way to the tabernacle met David Hume, the Scottish philosopher and skeptic. Surprised at meeting Hume on his way to hear Whitefield, the man said, "I thought you did not believe in the gospel." Hume replied, "I don't, but he does."

Clarence Edward Macartney, Preaching Without Notes *(Grand Rapids, Mich.: Baker, 1974), 228.*

The Absolute Demand and Final Succor
See page 150

Parable of the Wild Duck
See page 63

PATIENCE

The hardest thing is that most of us are called to exercise patience, not in the sick bed, but in the street.
George Matheson

You Be Patient

One summer, Pastor Kent Hughes took four of his grandchildren fishing. At age three, Joshua was, shall we say, very active. So Grandpa was constantly saying, "Now, you have to sit still and be patient, Joshua."

Joshua would then say in his antsy way, "I am being patient, huh, Grandpa?" When strangers walked by, Josh would address them—"I'm being patient!"

After an hour, the children's uncle Wil came by, and Joshua handed Uncle Wil the fishing pole and said, "Here, Uncle Wil, you be patient!"

PEACE

Oh what a pearl of great price is the lowest degree of the peace of God.
John Wesley

The Content of God's Rule

In both the Hebrew Bible and the New Testament, peace—the *shalom* of God—is tantamount to salvation. It means the bringing together of what was separated, the picking up of the pieces, the healing of the wounds, the fulfillment of the incomplete, the overcoming of the forces of fragmentation by forgiving love. In short, *shalom* is the content of the rule of God, the promised goal of pilgrim hope.
Richard John Neuhaus, Freedom for Ministry *(Grand Rapids, Mich.: Eerdmans, 1979), 72.*

In Search of Peace

A British cavalry officer who had taken part in the "Charge of the Light Brigade" in the Crimean War was so traumatized by his experience that after the war he resigned his commission. He tried to find peace back home in England, but finally decided to emigrate to America in search of the quiet life. Finally, in the late 1850s, he found the perfect place. He purchased a small farm and retired to a tranquil area in Virginia called Bull Run.

It Is Well with My Soul

H. G. Spafford was a businessman in Chicago. He was a dedicated Christian. He had some serious financial reversals, and during the time of readjustment, he lost his home. He realized his family needed to get away for a vacation. Spafford decided to take the entire family to England. He sent his wife and four daughters ahead on the SS *Ville du Havre.* In midocean the French steamer carrying his loved ones collided with another and sank within twelve minutes; 230 people lost their lives. The four daughters were drowned, but Mrs. Spafford was rescued. She wired her husband, "Saved alone." Mr. Spafford was almost overcome with grief. He had lost his property, his four precious daughters were buried beneath the dark waves of the sea, and his wife was prostrate with grief on the other side of the world. But he put all his trust in God and wrote a song that has comforted thousands since that time:

When peace like a river attendeth my way,
When sorrows like sea-billows roll;
Whatever my lot, Thou hast taught me to say,
"It is well, it is well with my soul."

Truly Happy and Content

See page 77

Transformed Life
See page 346

PERCEPTION

Osler's Observation

A small bottle containing urine sat on the desk of Sir William Osler. He was then the eminent professor of medicine at Oxford University. Sitting before him was a classroom full of young wide-eyed medical students listening to his lecture on the importance of observing details. To emphasize his point, he reached down and picked up the bottle. Holding it high, he announced: "This bottle contains a sample for analysis. It's often possible by testing it to determine the disease from which the patient suffers."

Suiting action to words, he dipped a finger into the fluid and then into his mouth as he continued: "Now I am going to pass this bottle around. Each of you please do exactly as I did. Perhaps we can learn the importance of this technique and diagnose the case."

The bottle made its way from row to row as each student gingerly poked his finger in and bravely sampled the contents with a frown. Dr. Osler then retrieved the bottle and startled his students with these words: "Gentlemen, now you will understand what I mean when I speak about details. Had you been observant, you would have seen that I put my index finger into the bottle but my middle finger into my mouth!"

A Beautiful Distortion
See page 422

PERFECTION

> I have a little sentence which is very helpful to me: In this fallen world, if one will accept only perfection or nothing, one always gets the nothing.
>
> *Francis A. Schaeffer*

Of all the false gods there is probably no greater nuisance in the spiritual world than the "god of one hundred percent." For he is plausible. It can so easily be argued that since God is Perfection, and since He asks the complete loyalty of His creations, then the best way of serving, pleasing and worshipping Him is to set up absolute one-hundred-percent standards and see to it that we obey them. . . . And it has taken the joy and spontaneity out of the Christian lives of many who dimly realize that what was meant to be a life of "perfect freedom" has become an anxious slavery.

J. B. Phillips

PERSECUTION

[Today] the church is not persecuted so much as ignored. Its revolutionary message has been reduced to a toothless creed for bourgeois suburbanites. Nobody opposes it any longer, because really there is nothing to oppose.

John R. W. Stott

Church Growth

A September 22, 1994, *Wall Street Journal* article described the persecution of Christians in China. The author of the article was John S. Barwick:

Beijing—"In the main, religious toleration is a reality. The church is growing and that growth is generally unimpeded," the archbishop of Canterbury said on his recent visit to China.

Archbishop Carey was using a fairly narrow definition of "religious toleration" and an even narrower definition of "church." Congregations that gather secretly in private dwellings throughout China are indeed growing—faster than the official church. Membership in these "house churches"—which contain between five and 500 followers apiece—is conservatively estimated at 20 million, while the official Protestant "Three-Self Patriotic Movement" has seven million members. Likewise, the number of secret Catholics may be twice the four million in the official Catholic Church.

The Protestant house churches have sprung up all over China, and are most numerous in the coastal regions of Henan and Anhui. But their growth is far from "unimpeded." The government does everything from controlling the distribution of Bibles to rounding up and beating these "unofficial" Christians.

Consider an incident earlier this year: After officials in Sian County in the province of Shaanxi got word that five young preachers from neighboring Ankang would be attending a service at a local house church, eight or nine policemen paid it a visit. They beat some people present with their clubs and handcuffed the three male and two female Ankang preachers. The three men were stripped from the waist down and beaten. The 26 other Christians present were then forced to beat the three men 100 times each with a bamboo rod or be beaten themselves.

After this, the three were strung up with rope and beaten unconscious by the cursing police officers. The two women were also harshly beaten, and the officers tore open their clothes and abused them. The beatings continued until dawn, at which time they were all locked in one bare detention room for eight days. One of the men . . . later died.

Every year, thousands of less severe incidents occur, ranging from the fining of Christians who "unlawfully" attend unregistered religious meetings or receive Christian literature from overseas, to the arrest and imprisonment of itinerant evangelists. Most of these cases involve house churches, which are illegal because they are not registered with the government. . . .

The Communists have always regarded religion as a threat to their monopoly on power. But recognizing that banning religion outright is impossible, they sought to capture it within organizations controlled by the party.

Today the Protestant "Three-Self" churches and official Catholic churches are perfectly legal. In principle, they even receive government support and protection—but only in return for compliance with the Communist Party's restrictions on how they practice their faith. That's why their growth has been anemic amid one of the greatest religious revivals the world has ever seen.

From the mouths of the Three-Self leaders themselves, the archbishop heard that their official church received more than 500 complaints about meddling by the party cadres in 1993 alone. He probably wasn't told that the reason these conflicts usually arise is that the party places its sympathizers in positions of authority in the churches to make sure its policies are obeyed. These church leaders are not only corrupt but have a total disregard for the genuine religious sentiments of the vast majority of their congregations.

While party leaders may well fear what China's religious revival portends, Christianity is not the enemy. Religion has never exactly been an opiate for the Chinese masses; history shows it's been more like gunpowder, with governmental misuse providing the spark. While the quasi-Christian Taiping Rebellion nearly toppled the Qing Dynasty in the 1850s, the real cause was the corruption and decay of the imperial order. The rebellion's leader, Hong Xiuquan, was anything but a cat's-paw of foreign missionaries. They denounced him as a heretic.

Christianity is the fastest growing religion in China today, especially among young people. Its dynamism owes much to the passionate commitment and spiritual hunger of Chinese Christians themselves. Their vibrant faith is captured in the words of one female house church leader. When asked if she was afraid of persecution, she smiled and replied, "That would be my time of glory."

Opposition to the Salvation Army

When William Booth began his mission work in east London in 1865, it was to violent opposition, and it grew even more violent in 1878 when Booth's "Christian Mission" became the "Salvation Army" and Booth assumed the title of general. The record challenges our modern sensibilities and credulity. The Salvation Army's historians tell us:

One Salvation Army officer came into a meeting loaded down with dead cats and rats; he explained these had been thrown at him; and that he caught and held the dead animals because if he dropped them the crowd would merely pick them up to be thrown again. Pots of human urine were often dumped on the street preachers. Beatings were not uncommon; in 1889, at least 669 Salvation Army members were assaulted—some were killed and many were maimed. Even children were not immune; hoodlums threw lime in the eyes of a child of a Salvation Army member. The newspapers ridiculed Booth. *Punch* referred to him as "Field Marshal von Booth." Soon a band of thugs and ruffians organized themselves into the "Skeleton Army" and devoted themselves to disrupting the meetings of the Salvation Army. They often attacked Salvation Army members as they paraded through the streets or held open-air meetings. They frequently stormed Salvation Army meeting halls by the hundreds, broke out the window panes, and wrecked the inside of buildings. As first the police did little to stop the "Skeleton Army." Instead of helping they frequently harassed Booth and his followers.

Richard Collier, The General Next to God *(London: Collins, 1965), 175.*

PERSEVERANCE

The Resolve to Return

Peter Cameron Scott was born in Glasgow in 1867 and became the founder of the Africa Inland Mission. But his beginnings in Africa were anything but auspicious. His first trip to Africa ended in a severe attack of malaria that sent him home. He resolved to return after recuperation.

This return was especially gratifying to Scott, because this time his brother John joined him. But before long John was struck down by fever. All alone, Peter buried his brother, and in the agony of those days recommitted himself to preaching the gospel in Africa. Yet again his health gave way and he had to return to England.

How would he ever pull out of the desolation and depression of those days? He had pledged himself to God. But where could he find the strength to go back again to Africa? With man it was impossible!

He found the strength in Westminster Abbey. David Livingstone's tomb is there. Scott entered quietly, found the tomb, and knelt in front of it to pray. The inscription reads,

OTHER SHEEP I HAVE
WHICH ARE NOT OF THIS FOLD;
THEM I ALSO MUST BRING.

He arose from his knees with a new hope. He returned to Africa. And the mission he founded is a vibrant, growing force for the gospel today in Africa.

John Piper, Desiring God *(Portland, Oreg.: Multnomah, 1986), 197–198.*

Holy Burning

See page 126

PERSISTENCE

It is not the critic who counts, nor the man who points out how the strong man stumbled or where the doer of deeds could have done them better. The credit belongs to the man who is actually in the arena, whose face is marred by dust and sweat and blood, who strives valiantly, who errs and comes short again and again, who knows the great enthusiasm, the great devotions, and spends himself in a worthy cause, who at the best knows in the end the triumph of high achievement, and who at the worst, if he fails, at least, fails while daring greatly, so that his place shall never be with those cold and timid souls who know neither victory nor defeat.

Winston Churchill

Nothing in the world can take the place of persistence.

Talent will not; nothing is more common than unsuccessful men with great talent.

Genius will not; unrewarded genius is almost a proverb.

Education will not; the world is full of educated derelicts.

Persistence, determination alone are omnipotent.

Calvin Coolidge

PERSPECTIVE

The greatest thing is to be found at one's post as a child of God, living each day as though it were our last, but planning as though our world might last a hundred years.

C. S. Lewis

Ears for a Cricket

An Indian was in downtown New York, walking along with his friend, who lived in New York City. Suddenly he said, "I hear a cricket."

"Oh, you're crazy," his friend replied.

The Indian insisted, but his friend pointed out, "It's the noon hour. You know there are people bustling around, cars honking, taxis squealing, noises from the city. I'm sure you can't hear it."

The man disagreed. He listened attentively and then walked to the corner, crossed the street, and looked all around. Finally, on the other corner, he found a shrub in a large cement planter. He dug beneath the leaf and found a cricket.

His friend was duly astounded. But the Indian said, "No, my ears are no different from yours. It simply depends on what you are listening to. Here, let me show you."

He reached into his pocket, pulled out a handful of change, and dropped it onto the concrete.

Every head within a block turned.

"You see what I mean?" the Indian said as he began picking up the coins. "It all depends on what you are listening for."

What the People Are Like

One hot day a family traveling down the highway between Johnstown and Jamestown stopped at Farmer Jones's place to ask for a drink of water, which he gladly gave them.

"Where are you headed?" he asked them.

"We're moving from Johnstown to Jamestown to live," they told him. "Can you tell us what the people there are like?"

"Well, what kind of people did you find where you lived before?" Farmer Jones asked.

"Oh, they were the very worst kind!" the people said. "They were gossipy and unkind and indifferent. We are glad to move away."

"Well, I'm afraid you'll find the same in Jamestown," replied Farmer Jones.

The next morning another car stopped, and the same conversation took place. These people were moving to Jamestown too.

"What kind of neighbors will we find there?" they asked.

"Well," said Farmer Jones, "what kind of neighbors did you have where you lived before?"

"Oh, they were the very best! They were so kind and considerate that it almost broke our hearts to move away."

"Well, you'll find exactly the same kind again," Farmer Jones replied.

Kenneth N. Taylor, Romans for the Family Hour *(Chicago: Moody, 1959), 170–171.*

Unselfish Love
See page 267

The First Home Run Ever
See page 299

Right Side Up toward God
See page 129

PESSIMISM

Paganini and One String
See page 19

POLITICS

The main qualification for political office is the ability to foretell what is going to happen tomorrow, next week, next month, and next year—and to have the ability afterwards to explain why it didn't happen.

Winston Churchill

PRAISE

Praise is like horse liniment. It's useful as long as it isn't taken internally.

William Sheppard

I can live for two months on a compliment.

Mark Twain

High Court Praise

Here's a wonderful report of praise from Chuck Colson:

Easter weekend at Walla Walla ended with a fitting postscript, yet another sign of the Kingdom at work. Fred, a young man with a heroin habit and a robbery record, had done time at Walla Walla. The family of one of his robbery victims had prayed for him for years, visited him in prison, and eventually led him to Christ. During a subsequent parole hearing, Fred had confessed to additional crimes of which he had not been convicted, explaining to the startled parole board that as a Christian, he felt he could not do otherwise.

Fred's original conviction was overturned; he was released from prison and began to rebuild his life. He became active in a local church and got involved in a Christian ex-prisoner fellowship while awaiting his retrial.

As it happened, Fred's case was scheduled to be heard on Easter Monday. The Seattle Superior Court was filled with friends, family, and supporters who had already testified on his behalf. Fred had freely confessed his guilt; and now he told Judge Francis Holman that he was prepared to accept whatever punishment the judge deemed appropriate. "For in any event," said Fred, "I am ready to go back to prison and serve Jesus Christ in there."

The judge leaned back in his tall leather chair and ticked off a long list of possible sentences. There was an awkward, drawn-out silence.

Then Judge Holman pounded his gavel. Ten years on each count of robbery—suspended. Fred would be free on probation, providing he would continue in a drug-treatment program and make restitution to his victims at 150 percent of their loss, or $2,200. He looked down at Fred again, his face still solemn: "We send you on your way with best wishes."

For a moment no one moved. Then Fred's pastor

jumped to his feet and gestured to the packed courtroom. "Let's sing it!" he shouted.

A reporter for the *Seattle Times* captured what came next: "Everyone stood up, little old ladies in spring dresses, ex-cons, girls in jeans, men in business suits, a biker with his motorcycle jacket and helmet, prison guards—and they began to sing: 'Praise God from whom all blessings flow. . . .'"

Officials later said that it was the first time a Seattle Superior Court case had ever closed with the Doxology.

Charles Colson, Kingdoms in Conflict *(Grand Rapids, Mich.: William Morrow/Zondervan, 1987), 300–301.*

Sacred Frenzy

See page 132

PRAYER

A good prayer mustn't be too long. Do not draw it out. Prayer ought to be frequent and fervent.

Martin Luther

Some prayers are followed by silence because they are wrong, others because they are bigger than one can understand. It will be a wonderful moment for some of us when we stand before God and find that the prayers we clamoured for in early days and imagined were never answered, have been answered in the most amazing way, and that God's silence has been the sign of the answer.

Oswald Chambers

Anything creative, anything powerful, anything biblical, insofar as we are participants in it, originates in prayer.

Eugene H. Peterson

Listen, my friend! Your helplessness is your best prayer. It calls from your heart to the heart of God with greater effect than all your uttered pleas. He hears it from the very moment that you are seized with helplessness, and He becomes actively engaged at once in hearing and answering the prayer of your helplessness. He hears today as He heard the helpless and wordless prayer of the man sick with palsy.

O. Hallesby

Prayer is not pulling God to my will, but the aligning of my will to the will of God. Aligned to God's redemptive will, anything, everything can happen in character, conduct, and creativeness. The whole person is heightened by that prayer contact. In that contact I find health for my body, illumination for my mind, and moral and spiritual reinforcement for my soul.

E. Stanley Jones

Prayer is one of the means God has etched into the cosmos for the advancement of His purposes.

Carl F. H. Henry

"For all thy blessings, known and unknown, remembered and forgotten, we give thee thanks," runs an old prayer, and it is for the all but unknown ones and the more than half-forgotten ones that we do well to look back over the journeys of our lives because it is their presence that makes the life of each of us a sacred journey.

Frederick Buechner

If I wished to humble anyone, I should question him about his prayers. I know nothing to compare with the topic for its sorrowful confessions.

C. J. Vaughn

In prayer the soul opens up every avenue to the Holy Spirit. God then gently breathes into it that it may become a living soul. He who has ceased to breathe in prayer is spiritually dead.

Sadhu Sunder Singh

Someone once said, "Any discussion of the doctrine of prayer that does not issue in the practice of prayer is not only *not* helpful but harmful."

The great people of the earth today are the people who pray. I do not mean those who *talk about* prayer; nor those who say they *believe in* prayer; nor yet those who can *explain about* prayer; but I mean those people who *take time* and pray.

S. D. Gordon

There is no such thing as private prayer, there is only prayer in private.

Richard John Neuhaus

You can do more than pray after you have prayed, but you cannot do more than pray until you have prayed.

John Bunyan

Communion with God is the one need of the soul beyond all other needs; prayer is the beginning of that communion.

George Macdonald

Prayer is the first thing, the second thing, the third thing necessary to minister. Pray, therefore, my dear brother, pray, pray, pray.

Edward Payson

In prayer we leave the business of time for that of eternity, and intercourse with men for intercourse with God.

Jeremiah Lanphier

When the angel of devotion has gone, the angel of prayer has lost its wings and it becomes a deformed and loveless thing.

E. M. Bounds

The time of business does not differ with me from the time of prayer; and in the noise and clutter of my kitchen, while several persons are at the same time calling

for different things, I possess God in as great tranquillity as if I were on my knees.
Brother Lawrence

Speaking to His Friend
Theodorus said of Martin Luther: "I overheard him in prayer, but good God, with what life and spirit did he pray! It was with so much reverence, as if he were speaking to God, yet with so much confidence as if he were speaking to his friend."
Charles H. Spurgeon, Lectures to My Students *(Grand Rapids, Mich.: Zondervan, 1954), 46.*

The Prayers of the Pilgrims
The Pilgrims regularly employed days of prayer and fasting as part of their way of life to achieve spiritual and earthly goals. For example, in the summer of 1623 their carefully planted crop of corn was threatened by a drought which lasted from May till the middle of July, the corn being almost past saving. So they set apart a day of humiliation to seek the Lord by humble and fervent prayer.

The result: The day was hot and dry, with not a sign of a cloud to be seen. But toward evening God brought a gentle shower which watered the corn perfectly (normally, if rain had come in these conditions it would have been a thunderstorm which would have beaten down the corn and ruined the hope of a harvest). Then in the coming days the Lord provided good showers, mixed with warm, fair weather, bringing about a bountiful harvest.
Derek Prince, Shaping History through Prayer and Fasting *(Old Tappan, N.J.: Fleming H. Revell, 1973), 127–130.*

Answer to Your Own Prayer
In the record of the early life of Hudson Taylor, there is a story of how he became the answer to one of his own prayers. Here's the story in Hudson Taylor's words:

After concluding my last service about ten o'clock that

night, a poor man asked me to go and pray with his wife, saying that she was dying. I readily agreed, and on the way to his house asked him why he had not sent for the priest, as his accent told me he was an Irishman. He had done so, he said, but the priest refused to come without a payment of eighteen pence, which the man did not possess, as the family was starving. Immediately it occurred to my mind that all the money I had in the world was a solitary half-crown, and that it was in one coin; moreover, that while the basin of water gruel I usually took for supper was awaiting me, and there was sufficient in the house for breakfast in the morning, I certainly had nothing for dinner on the coming day.

Somehow or other there was at once a stoppage in the flow of joy in my heart. But instead of reproving myself I began to reprove the poor man, telling him that it was very wrong to have allowed things to get into such a state as he described, and that he ought to have applied to the relieving officer. His answer was that he had done so, and was told to come at eleven o'clock next morning, but that he feared his wife might not live through the night:

"Ah," I thought, "if only I had two shillings and a sixpence instead of this half-crown, how gladly would I give these poor people a shilling!" But to part with the half-crown was far from my thoughts. I little dreamed that the truth of the matter simply was that I could trust God plus one and sixpence, but was not prepared to trust Him only, without any money at all in my pocket.

My conductor led me into a court, down which I followed him with some degree of nervousness. I had found myself there before, and at my last visit had been roughly handled. My tracts had been torn to pieces, and such a warning given me not to come again that I felt more than a little concerned. Still, it was the path of duty, and I followed on. Up a miserable flight of stairs into a wretched room he led me; and oh, what a sight there presented itself! Four or five children stood about, their sunken cheeks and temples all telling unmistakably the story of slow starvation, and lying on a wretched pallet was a poor, exhausted mother, with a tiny infant thirty-six hours old moaning rather than crying at her side, for it too seemed spent and failing.

"Ah," thought I, "if I had two shillings and a sixpence, instead of half a crown, how gladly would they have one and sixpence of it." But still a wretched unbelief prevented me from obeying the impulse to relieve their distress at the cost of all I possessed.

It will scarcely seem strange that I was unable to say much to comfort these poor people. I needed comfort myself. I began to tell them, however, that they must not be cast down; that though their circumstances were very distressing there was a kind and loving Father in heaven. But something within me cried, "You hypocrite! telling these unconverted people about a kind and loving Father in heaven, and not prepared yourself to trust Him without a half a crown."

I was nearly choked. How gladly would I have compromised with conscience, had I a florin and a sixpence! I would have given the florin thankfully and kept the rest. But I was not yet prepared to trust in God alone, without the sixpence.

To talk was impossible under these circumstances, yet strange to say I thought I should have no difficulty in praying. Prayer was a delightful occupation in those days. Time thus spent never seemed wearisome, and I knew no lack of words. I seemed to think that all I should have to do would be to kneel down and pray, and that relief would come to them and to myself together.

"You asked me to come and pray with your wife," I said to the man, "let us pray." And I knelt down.

But no sooner had I opened my lips with "Our Father who art in heaven" than conscience said within, "Dare you mock God? Dare you kneel down and call Him Father with that half-crown in your pocket?"

Such a time of conflict then came upon me as I have never experienced fore or since. How I got through that form of prayer I know not, and whether the words uttered were connected or disconnected I cannot tell. But I arose from my knees in great distress of mind.

The poor father turned to me and said, "You see what a terrible state we are in, sir. If you can help us, for God's sake do!"

At that moment the word flashed into my mind, "Give to him that asketh of thee." And in the word of a King there is power.

I put my hand into my pocket, and slowly drawing out the half-crown, gave it to the man, telling him that it might seem a small matter for me to relieve them, seeing that I was comparatively well off, but that in parting with that coin I was giving him my all; what I had been trying to tell them was indeed true—*God* really was a *Father* and might be trusted. The joy all came back in full flood tide to my heart. I could say anything and feel it then, and the hindrance to blessing was gone—gone, I trust, forever.

Not only was the poor woman's life saved; but my life, as I fully realized, had been saved too. It might have been a wreck—would have been, probably, as a Christian life—had not grace at that time conquered, and the striving of God's Spirit been obeyed.

I well remember how that night, as I went home to my lodging, my heart was as light as my pocket. The dark, deserted streets resounded with a hymn of praise that I could not restrain. When I took my basin of gruel before retiring, I would not have exchanged it for a prince's feast. I reminded the Lord as I knelt at my bedside of His own Word, "He that giveth to the poor lendeth to the Lord"; I asked Him not to let my loan be a long one, or I should have no dinner next day. And with peace within and peace without, I spent a happy, restful night.

James Hastings, ed., The Speaker's Bible, *vol. 17 (Grand Rapids, Mich.: Baker, 1971), 212–214.*

Praying for Others

Praying with other people has been a great encouragement to me: with my wife, when we are alone in the car, with my sons, when I'm driving them to school.

My greatest help [in praying for others] has come from realizing that God can bring to my mind those people and situations for which I ought to pray. He can stir my memory through associations—something I see, something I hear, something I read. If I forget to pray for someone, He can remind me.

A flight attendant on my flight reminds me of a woman whose husband has died. I pray for that woman and her children. The pilot makes me remember to pray for friends who are also airline pilots, and for JAARS and MAF.

Driving the car, I see a street name, a billboard advertisement, a real estate sign, a church: each leads to an association that results in prayer.

A friend mentioned something E. Stanley Jones wrote in connection with prayer; this has been a help to me: If your mind wanders to something else when you're praying, Dr. Jones suggested, pray for that something else.

God can stir our minds to pray: God can bring an image from the past, or from a far distant place, before our mind's eye, and lead us to pray.

Another part of faithfulness in praying for others is not to wait until a convenient, quiet time—rather, to pray in the midst of life's pressure. I think I'm learning this, as well as the rightness of saying, "Let's pray about that now" when someone talks to me about a problem.

We do not pray enough together, as Christian brothers and sisters. We talk, and we forget that our Father is there listening—and that it should be the most natural thing to include Him in our conversation.

Once I said good-bye to Abe Vander Puy at the Quito Ecuador airport. As we stood there with people moving past us, Abe said, "Let's pray." His arm went around me, and he committed me, for the trip and for my life, to the Lord. It's the most satisfying departure from an airport I've ever had. . . .

Prayer may be our children's greatest enlightenment that we have concerns for people and situations beyond our own family circle. . . .

I remember one day early in the Watergate affair when I was driving my two sons, one teen-age, the other on the threshold of teen-age, to school. (A year or so earlier, when the federal judge and former Illinois governor Otto Kerner was on trial, one of them said to me, "But doesn't every-body in public office accept bribes? Do any of them live on their salary?" I was suddenly struck with the image he had—and other children probably had—of public servants.) That morning as we prayed together in the car, I asked God to bring truth to light, to make corruption surface, to judge the guilty and protect the innocent.

Later, looking back, I was glad that I had a part—an infinitesimal part, but a part—in the resolution of Water-gate, by turning to a judge greater than the Senate or the federal court.

Joseph Bayly, Out of My Mind *(Grand Rapids, Mich.: Zondervan, 1993), 140–143.*

We Know Only in Part

Here's an example of when a believer prayed for healing and it didn't happen:

Ponnammal, whose cancer had been discovered in April 1913, became very ill again in the following year. Several times she heard music when no earthly music was being played. Amy Carmichael took it as one of "the many things of life which we may only know in part until for us too the curtain of sense wears thin."

The epistle of James says that the sick should call for the elders of the church to anoint them. Should they do that now? They were not sure. Amy was used to being given some sign to confirm a Scripture verse. So they prayed that if they should, someone who was earnest about following this primitive church custom should come along. He came, an old friend from Madras. It was a solemn meeting around the sickbed, the women dressed as usual in their hand loomed saris, but white ones for this occasion. They laid a palm branch across Ponnammal's bed as a sign of victory and peace. It sounds like a simple formula. It was an act of faith, but certainly accompanied by the anguish of doubt and desire which had to be brought again and again under the authority of the Master.

The answer that came was that Ponnammal, from the very day of the anointing, grew rapidly worse. She lay for days without speaking, her dull eyes half-open, seeming to see nothing. The pain was violent, kept under only by large doses of morphia. "She has been walking through the valley of the shadow of death. I never before watched anyone dying in this slow, terrible way. . . . Nothing was visible but the distress and depression of this most fearful disease."

Once when she seemed to be in unimaginable misery she told Amy how she had longed to be allowed to stay. She thought she could help a little "if the pain did not pass this limit." "It seemed to me the most unselfish word I had ever heard from human lips." Ponnammal touched the limit at last—the limit divinely set to pain—and her "warfare was accomplished" on August 26, 1915. She would never be replaced. She had been among the best. But "we shall have our best again, purified, perfected, assured from change forever." That was the ground of hope.

Elisabeth Elliot, A Chance to Die *(Old Tappan, N.J.: Fleming H. Revell, 1987), 233–234.*

Weed Removal

Chrysostom, a great fourth-century preacher, had this analogy for Christ's work of intercession: A young boy whose father had been away on a long trip wanted to give him a present when he returned. His mother sent him to the garden to gather a bouquet of flowers. The boy gathered flowers as well as weeds, but when his father returned, he received a bouquet of beautiful flowers. The boy's mother had intervened, removing all the weeds.

The prayers of the church, prevailing, acceptable, and fruitful as they are, are not a thing of beauty as they leave the lips of saints. But as they start their way heavenward, they are a mixed bag of weeds with a few stray flowers. When they arrive, however, thanks to the intercession of Christ, they are nothing but beautiful flowers.

Tabletalk, *vol. 24, no. 5 (June 1989): 10.*

Without Breath

Mother Alice Kaholuoluna of Hawaii says this about prayer:

Before the missionaries came, my people used to sit outside their temples for a long time meditating and preparing themselves before entering. Then they would virtually creep to the altar to offer their petition and afterwards would again sit a long time outside, this time to "breathe life" into their prayers. The Christians, when they came, just got up, uttered a few sentences, said Amen and were done. For that reason my people call them haolis, "without breath," or those who fail to breathe life into their prayers.

An Affectionate Pouring of the Heart

From Bedford Prison, John Bunyan wrote this specific definition of prayer:

Prayer is a sincere, sensible, affectionate pouring out of the heart or soul to God, through Christ, in the strength and assistance of the Holy Spirit, for such things as God has promised, or according to the Word of God, for the good of the church, with submission in faith to the will of God.

Aligning My Will to God's

E. Stanley Jones describes the effect of prayer on us like this:

Prayer is not pulling God to my will, but the aligning of my will to the will of God. Aligned to God's redemptive will, anything, everything can happen in character, conduct, and creativeness. The whole person is heightened by that prayer contact. In that contact I find health for my body, illumination for my mind, and moral and spiritual reinforcement for my soul. "Prayer is a time exposure to God," so I expose myself to God for an hour and a half to two hours a day, asking less and less for things and more and more for Himself. For having Him, I have everything. He gives me what I need for character, conduct, and creativeness, so I'm rich with His riches, strong in His strength, pure in His purity, and able in His ability.

E. Stanley Jones, A Song of Ascents *(Nashville: Abingdon, 1968), 383.*

A Nun's Prayer for Malcolm Muggeridge

Sister Mary Paul of the Convent of the Good Shepherd in Liverpool, England, wrote this letter to Malcolm Muggeridge on January 16, 1968:

Dear Mr. Muggeridge,

Forty-three years ago, in Cairo, a young nun read an article in a journal or newspaper which had been sent out to her from home. She sensed that the writer, a young journalist, was rather confused spiritually and she made up her mind that she would pray for him. Every day of that forty-three years the young man's name was mentioned in prayer, and last week after viewing "Panorama" that same sister, now retired from the mission, turned to me and said—"This is what I have been waiting forty-three years for." The name of the young man—now elderly—was Malcolm Muggeridge and the remark on "Panorama" which sister was referring to was " . . . as a confirmed Christian . . ."

Sister doesn't know that I am telling you this, but receiving criticism as so many public figures must do, I thought it would be rather a change to know that you have been the object of the thoughts and prayers of an unknown nun these many years.

Unanswered Prayer

Dr. Howard Hendricks tells of the time when he was a young man, before he was married. He was aware that certain mothers had set their caps for him on behalf of their daughters. One mother even said to him one day, "Howard, I just want you to know that I'm praying that you'll be my son-in-law." Dr. Hendricks always stops at that point in the story and says, very solemnly, "Have you ever thanked God for unanswered prayer?"

The Posture of Prayer

A certain person couldn't find the right posture for prayer. He tried praying on his knees, but that wasn't comfortable; besides, it wrinkled his slacks. He tried praying standing, but soon his legs got tired. He tried praying seated, but that didn't seem reverent. Then one day as he was walking through a field, he fell headfirst into an open well. Did he ever pray!

The Mueller Method

George Mueller was known for his life of prayer and his close walk with God. His rich Christian experience grew out of complete dependence on God's will. Here is his simple method for determining the will of God:

1. I seek to get my heart into such a state that it has no will of its own in a given matter. When we are ready to do the Lord's will—whatever it may be—nine-tenths of the difficulties are overcome.
2. Having done this, I do not leave the result to feeling or simple impression. If I do so, I make myself liable to great delusion.
3. I seek the will of the Spirit of God through, or in connection with, God's Word. The Spirit and the Word must be combined. If I look to the Spirit alone without the Word, I lay myself open to great delusions also. If the Holy Spirit guides us, He will do it according to the Scriptures, never contrary to them.
4. Next I take into account providential circumstances. These often plainly indicate God's will in connection with His Word and Spirit.
5. I ask God in prayer to reveal His will to me.
6. Thus, through prayer, the study of the Word and reflection, I come to deliberate judgment according to the best of my ability and knowledge. If my mind is thus at peace and continues so after two or three petitions, I proceed accordingly. I have found this method always effective in trivial or important issues.

Prayer for the Long Haul

Early in his life, George Mueller made the acquaintance of three men, and he began to pray for their salvation. Mueller lived a long time, but when he died, none of these men had trusted Christ. It is recorded in his diary that he prayed for these men daily during all those years. But that's not the end. The glorious fact is that all three of those men did meet Christ—two of them in their seventies and one in his eighties. In this case, Mueller sowed but someone else reaped. Whether we find ourselves sowing or reaping, our lives are to be impregnated with a sense of urgency. That was part of the secret of Jesus' life—the harvest mentality. We live in a time when we are to be harvesting.

PREACHING

I gave up nothing [a promising medical career]; I received everything. I count it the highest honor that God can confer on any man to call him to be a herald of the gospel.
Martyn Lloyd-Jones

No man is ever going to be able to fill the pulpit adequately unless he spends thousands of hours year after year in the study of God's Word.
Donald Grey Barnhouse

The man who is to thunder in the court of Pharaoh with an imperious "Thus saith the Lord!" must first stand barefoot before the burning bush.
Donald Grey Barnhouse

The Power of John 3:16

According to D. L. Moody, John 3:16 is the verse that brought him to an understanding of the love of God. Early in Moody's ministry he had gone to England. While there, he met a young minister named Henry Morehouse. As they talked, Morehouse said to Moody, "I am thinking of going to America." Moody responded, "Well, if you should ever get to Chicago, come down to my church, and I will give you a chance to preach." Now Moody really did not mean that. He realized after he said it that he hoped this man did not come to America, because Moody had never heard him preach.

Sometime later, after his crusade was over and he had returned to America, Moody received a telegram that read, "Just arrived in New York. Will be in Chicago on Sunday. Morehouse." Moody was perplexed. He had promised the man his pulpit, but he had never heard him preach. After discussing the matter with his wife, and the church leaders, he decided to allow Morehouse to preach once. If he did all right, he could preach again. Moody had to go out of town, and Morehouse came.

After the week was over, Moody returned and asked his wife, "How did the young preacher do?" His wife responded, "He is a better preacher than you are. He is telling sinners that God loves them. You have got to go hear him!" Moody said, "What? He is telling sinners that God loves them? That's not true!" She said, "Well, he has been preaching on John 3:16 all week long." Moody made haste to get down to the church that night. Morehouse stood in the pulpit and began by saying, "I have been hunting for a text all week, and I have not been able to find a better text than John 3:16, so I will just talk about it once more." Later, Moody's own testimony was that on that night he saw the greatness of the love of God as he had never seen it before.

James M. Boice, The Gospel of John, *vol. 1 (Grand Rapids, Mich.: Zondervan, 1975), 279–280.*

Tears for the Lost

A church was looking for a pastor, so they invited several candidates to come and preach for them. One minister spoke on the text, "The wicked shall be turned into hell." The head elder was not in favor of him. A few weeks later, another preacher came and used the same Scripture for his sermon. This time the head elder said, "He's good! Let's call him." The other board members were surprised, and one of them asked, "Why did you like him? He used the same text as the other minister." "True," replied the head elder, "but when the second man emphasized that the lost will be turned into hell, he said it with tears in his eyes and with concern in his voice. The first preacher almost seemed to gloat over it."

Holy Burning
See page 126

The Battle against Criticism
See page 96

PREJUDICE

A believer may risk prison for his own religious beliefs, but he may never build prisons for those of other beliefs.
Charles Colson

If we are not careful, the experiences we have had in the past with a certain individual or with people of whom that individual reminds us become the reality with which we interact.
John Claypool

Parable of the Clown
Somewhere in his writings, Søren Kierkegaard tells about a small circus that traveled from little town to little town in his native Denmark. The pattern of the troupe was to come into a community, hand out announcements of their performance, and then put up a tent on the outskirts of the village for that evening. On one particular occasion, the circus tent caught fire about an hour before the performance was to start. It turned out that the clown was the only member of the troupe who was fully dressed, so he was dispatched into the village to get help as quickly as he could. The clown discharged his responsibility perfectly. He apprised everyone he met of the crisis and begged them to get their water pails and come out to

help. However, the people in this village had had prior experiences with clowns. They had built up in their minds certain expectations about these folks. So, according to Kierkegaard, they heard the clown with their eyes; that is, they assumed that he was on a mission of entertainment and that this was just a new way of drumming up a crowd. Not until they looked on the horizon and saw the ominous red glow did it dawn on them that in this moment what they were encountering was not a clown at all but a human being dressed in a clown's costume bearing an urgent and utterly real message!

Light Green versus Dark Green

Bishop John Reed told the story of how a school bus that carried whites and aborigines had been plagued with fighting. One day, far out in the country, the bus driver stopped and said to the white boys, "What color are you?"

They said, "White."

He said, "No, you are green. Anyone who rides in my bus is green. Now, what color are you?"

And a white boy answered, "Green."

After having all the white boys identify themselves as green, he went to the aborigines and said, "What color are you?"

And they said, "Black."

He said, "No, you are green. Anyone who rides in my bus is green."

So all the aborigines answered that they were green.

After they were several miles down the road, he heard from the back of the bus, "All right, light green on this side; dark green on that side."

Someone's Face

See page 343

PRIDE

Pride is a sin of whose presence its victim is least conscious. [But] nothing is more distasteful to God than self-conceit. This first and fundamental sin in essence aims at enthroning self at the expense of God.
J. Oswald Sanders

The more we have it [pride] ourselves, the more we dislike it in others.
C. S. Lewis

Boasting is the voice of pride in the heart of the strong. Self-pity is the voice of pride in the heart of the weak. Boasting sounds self-sufficient. Self-pity sounds self-sacrificing.
John Piper

I have not yet met a single man who was morally as good as I.
Leo Tolstoy

I know brethren who, from head to foot, in garb, tone, manner, necktie, and boots, are so utterly parsonic that no particle of manhood is visible. . . . Some men appear to have a white cravat twisted round their souls; their manhood is throttled with that starched rag.
Charles H. Spurgeon

The true way to be humble is not to stoop until you are smaller than yourself, but to stand at your real height against some higher nature that will show you what the real smallness of your greatness is.
Phillips Brooks

The earth is strewn with the exploded bladders of the puffed up.
Carl Sandburg

When I want to read a good book, I write one.
Benjamin Disraeli

I often quote myself. It adds spice to my conversation.
George Bernard Shaw

O man, strange composite of heaven and earth!
Majesty dwarfed to baseness! fragrant flower
Running to poisonous seed! and seeming worth
Cloaking corruption! weakness mastering power!
Who never art so near to crime and shame,
As when thou hast achieved some deed of name.
John Henry Newman

The Vainglorious Tailor

Writes Gay Talese in *Unto the Sons:* There were also confrontations in the front of the store in which my father worked, disputes between the customers and the proprietor—the diminutive and vainglorious Francesco Christiani, who took enormous pride in his occupation and believed that he and the tailors under his supervision were incapable of making a serious mistake; or, if they were, he was not likely to acknowledge it.

Once when a customer came in to try on a new suit but was unable to slip into the jacket because the sleeves were too narrow, Francesco Christiani not only failed to apologize to the client but behaved as if insulted by the client's ignorance of the Christiani shop's unique style in men's fashion. "You're not supposed to put your arms *through* the sleeves of this jacket!" Christiani informed his client, in a superior tone, "This jacket is designed to be worn only *over the shoulders!"*

Gay Talese, Unto the Sons *(New York: Alfred A. Knopf, 1992), 97.*

Political Pride

Many years ago, a number of government officials in The Hague, the Netherlands, more fashionable than religious, invited the famous court preacher of Paris, Van Courtonne, of Dutch descent, to preach in their state church chapel. Because he considered their interest more social than spiritual, more a curiosity than a zeal for truth, Van Courtonne declined to come. When the invitation was repeated several times, he agreed to accept, on the condition that all the government officials be present. It was agreed.

The famous Van Courtonne appeared and preached on "The Ethiopian" (Acts 8). His sermon contained four points: (1) A government official who read his Bible—something rare. (2) A government official who acknowledged his ignorance—something rarer still. (3) A government official who asked a lesser person for instruction—something extremely rare. (4) A government official who was converted—the rarest thing of all.

Van Courtonne never received a second invitation.

The Banner, *quoted in* The Wesleyan Advocate.

I'm a Nobody

One is reminded of the story of the pastor who, during Passion week, publicly lamented his sins and declared himself totally unworthy, a nobody. The choir director, not to be outdone, picked up the theme, confessing that he too was a nobody. The sexton, not to be entirely left out, deplored his transgressions, concluding that he too was a nobody. The pastor, turning to the choir director, said, "Now who does he think *he* is to be a nobody?"

Adapted from Richard John Neuhaus, Freedom for Ministry *(Grand Rapids, Mich.: Eerdmans, 1979), 230.*

Aloof Leadership

Chuck Colson vividly recalls a conversation from his White House days:

One brisk December night as I accompanied the president from the Oval Office in the West Wing of the White House to the Residence, Mr. Nixon was musing about what people wanted in their leaders. He slowed a minute, looking into the distance across the South Lawn, and said, "The people really want a leader a little bigger than themselves, don't they, Chuck?" I agreed. "I mean someone like de Gaulle," he continued. "There's a certain aloofness, a power that's exuded by great men that people feel and want to follow."

Jesus Christ exhibited none of this self-conscious aloofness. He served others first; He spoke to those to whom no one spoke; He dined with the lowest members of society; He touched the untouchables. He had no throne, no crown, no bevy of servants or armored guards. A borrowed manger and a borrowed tomb framed His earthly life.

Kings and presidents and prime ministers surround themselves with minions who rush ahead, swing the doors wide, and stand at attention as they wait for the great to pass. Jesus said that He Himself stands at the door and knocks, patiently waiting to enter our lives.

Charles Colson, Kingdoms in Conflict *(Grand Rapids, Mich.: William Morrow/Zondervan, 1987), 85.*

A Sit-Down Strut

Woodrow Wilson, quoting someone else, once described Henry Van Dyke as "the only man he had ever known who could strut sitting down."

More Popular than Jesus

In February 1966, before an American tour, in an interview with Maureen Cleaves of the *London Evening Standard,* John Lennon of the Beatles remarked, "Christianity will go. It will vanish and shrink. I needn't argue about that. I'm right and will be proved right. We're more popular than Jesus Christ right now."

Aesop on Pride

Two ducks were preparing for their annual flight south for the winter, when their friend Mr. Frog informed them of his desire to travel along. "You have no wings," said the ducks.

"No," said Mr. Frog, "but if you two ducks will kindly hold this stick in your mouths, I'll grasp it in the middle with my mouth, and we'll all go along together."

The whole thing was working out quite well. However, as they flew over a pasture, two cows looked up and saw the trio. One of the cows commented, "Now there go a couple of intelligent ducks!"

Mr. Frog heard this and, wanting to get full credit for his idea, said to the cows, "No, it was my id-eee-aaa. . . ."

PRIORITIES

> "If I was consumed with politics, [he explains,] my first priority would be the morning newspapers, not the Bible," but British politician Michael Alison's first priority is not his political career; it is his relationship with God.
>
> *Charles Colson*

A Lousy Mailman

Tony Campolo tells about a friend of his who made a career change:

Some years ago, a friend of mine went to teach English literature at a state college. He was there for three weeks when he went into the dean's office to say that he was quitting.

"I'm not coming back next week, and I thought you ought to know," he said. The dean replied, "If you walk out on your contract, you're not going to teach here again. What's more, you won't teach anywhere, if I can help it."

After my friend left his job, his mother contacted me by phone and said I had to see him. She was sure he had gone crazy and hoped I could talk him into going back to his job.

I found my friend Charlie living in an attic apartment in Hamilton Square, New Jersey. I must admit that his apartment had style: travel posters pasted all over the walls, a good assortment of books scattered around the room, and the stereo playing a Wagnerian opera. I sat down in a bean-bag chair that swallowed me up. After we had exchanged niceties, I came to the point.

"What have you done?" I asked.

"I quit," said Charlie. "I walked out. I don't want to teach anymore. Every time I walked into that classroom, I died a little bit."

I could understand him. I am a teacher, and I know what it is like to go into class and pour out your heart to students, to let every nerve inside you tingle with the excitement of your most profound insights. I know what it is like to passionately share the struggles of your existence, to lay your soul bare in an attempt to communicate your deepest feelings. Then, when it is all over, some student in the back of the room raises his hand and says, "Do we have to know this stuff for the final?"—and I die a little bit too.

It wasn't long before I realized that Charlie was not about to go back into the classroom, so I asked him what he was doing with himself these days. He said, "I'm a mailman."

Reaching back into the value system provided by the Protestant work ethic, I said to him, "Charlie, if you're going to be a mailman, be the best mailman in the world!"

He said, "I am a *lousy* mailman. Everybody else who delivers mail gets back to the post office by about two o'clock. I never get back until six."

"What takes you so long?" I asked.

"I visit," said Charlie. "You'd never believe how many lonely people there are on my route who had never been visited until I became a mailman. What's more, now I can't sleep at night."

"Why can't you sleep at night?" I asked.

"Have you ever tried to sleep after drinking fifteen cups of coffee?" was his reply.

As I sat and looked at my friend Charlie, I envied him. He was alive with the excitement that comes to a person doing something meaningful with his life. Because he moved from being a college professor to being a mailman, he has lost status. But what difference does that make? As Charlie invests himself significantly in the lives of other people, he is finding fulfillment in visiting "orphans and widows in their distress" (James 1:27).

Reverse Order

The founder of McDonald's was once quoted as saying, "I speak of faith in McDonald's as if it were a religion. I believe in God, family and McDonald's—*and in the office that order is reversed.*"

The Price of Advice

A number of years ago a fascinating interview took place. It involved Charles Schwab, then president of Bethlehem Steel, and Mr. Ivy Lee, a management consultant. Lee was a very aggressive and self-confident man who, by stealth, had wangled an interview with Mr. Schwab, who was no less self-assured, being one of the most powerful men in the world.

During the conversation, Mr. Lee asserted that if the management of Bethlehem Steel would follow his advice, the company's operations would be improved and its profits increased. Schwab responded, "Mr. Lee, if you can show us a way to get more things done, I'll be glad to listen; and if it works, I'll pay you whatever you ask within reason."

Lee handed Schwab a blank piece of paper and said: "Write down the most important things you have to do tomorrow." Schwab did so. "Now," Lee continued, "number them in order of importance." Schwab did so.

"Tomorrow morning start on #1 and stay with it until you have completed it. Then go on to #2 and #3 and #4, and so on. Don't worry if you haven't completed everything by the end of the day. At least you will have completed the most important projects. Do this every day. After you have been convinced of the value of this system, have your men try it. Try it as long as you like, and then," concluded Lee, "send me your check for whatever you think the idea is worth."

This was actually a very simple idea. However, a few weeks later Charles Schwab sent Ivy Lee a check for $25,000!—an astronomical amount during the 1930s. He said it was the most profitable lesson he had learned in his long business career.

All-Consuming Choice

See page 429

PROFANITY

Profanity is the linguistical crutch of the inarticulate.

Unknown

Q

QUIET

A Noisy People

Americans are a noisy people, and ours is a noisy culture. Our lives are filled with unremitting racket. Whether we live in a bustling city or the idyllic countryside, whatever our social standing or economic station, Americans seem obsessed by the need for unending sound to accompany their waking hours. . . .

Indeed, silence is usually seen as an anomaly, a digression from the norm, some kind of deviant behavior. "He is so quiet," we say, suggesting something must be wrong, that it is perhaps a symptom of illness.

Church worship leaders have not escaped this frenetic drive to avoid silence. They believe that there must always be some sort of sound. Organists, egged on by pastors and parishioners from the "no dead spots" school of worship, learn to "doodle" until the next sounds can begin. The famous organist E. Power Biggs, once exhorted by a pastor to "play a few chords while I go from here to there," suggested that if he wanted simply some kind of perfunctory noise, the pastor need merely "mumble a few words."

Many consider silence in worship a breach of etiquette,

to be avoided at all costs. Certainly no one would actually plan for moments in which nothing is really happening! And should such moments occur, they are certainly unintentional; the pastor has lost [his] place, the organist can't find the right hymn or someone has expired in the choir loft. From such a perspective, worship becomes continual noise, noise, noise—to be sure, often carefully orchestrated noise, but noise nevertheless. The only exception to this rule is the "moment of prayer," the briefer the better, and best accompanied by soft chords from the organ.

The Christian Century, *23–30 March 1988.*

R

RACISM

Someone's Face

One summer my wife, Barbara, was teaching a class of seven-year-olds. She was using an older version of the Wordless Book that had different colors representing the aspects of salvation. The first page was black for sin, and she asked the children, "What do you think the black page represents?" A little African-American boy raised his hand and said, "Someone's face?" She said, "It could, but here it represents something else."

The Caste System

The social expression of Hinduism is the doctrine, or, more accurately, the practice, of caste, and though its scholars find the subject distasteful, the historical origins of this pernicious system lie in a racism starker than any bigotry found in the veld of South Africa or the red clay of northern Georgia. Over a thousand years before the birth of Christ, the Aryans of uncertain origins conquered the black Dravidian and Munda natives and imposed a hierarchical structure on the entire subcontinent. Brahmanism and its major gods—Siva, Vishnu, Krishna, Rama, and creator Brahma—evolved through successive generations, but the basic principle, or lack of it, endured: the lighter your skin, the higher your caste. Historically, the four great castes are the Brahmins, scholars and priests; Kshatriyas, soldiers and administrators; Vaishyas, merchants; and Sudras, servants and manual laborers. Gandhi was a Vaishya; Nehru, a Kasshmiri Brahmin. But there are countless subcastes, including one for prostitution: if a girl is born into it, she spends her life as a whore; if the child is a boy, he will be a pimp until, having raised another generation of whores and pimps, he dies. You can see his sisters and daughters today, locked in the Cages of Bombay. One caste makes beds, another washes dishes, a third dries them—which is why every British household in the Raj required swarms of servants. . . . There were between sixty and seventy million Untouchables in Gandhi's day. He called them *harijans* ("beloved of God") and worked hard to better their lot, but even Mahatma ("great-souled") Gandhi never suggested the abolition of caste.

James Hastings, ed., The Speaker's Bible, *vol. 17 (Grand Rapids, Mich.: Baker, 1971), 837–838.*

Light Green versus Dark Green
See page 332

REALITY

Just Pretend We Won

Former NBA center and coach Johnny Kerr said his biggest test as a coach came when he coached the then-expanding team the Chicago Bulls and his biggest player was 6' 8" Erwin Mueller.

"We had lost seven in a row, and I decided to give a psychological pep talk before a game with the Celtics," Kerr said. "I told Bob Boozer to go out and pretend he was the best scorer in basketball. I told Jerry Sloan to pretend he was the best defensive guard. I told Guy Rodgers to pretend he could run an offense better than any other guard, and I told

Erwin Mueller to pretend he was the best rebounding, shot-blocking, scoring center in the game.

"We lost the game by 17. I was pacing around the locker room afterward trying to figure out what to say when Mueller walked up, put his arm around me and said, 'Don't worry about it, coach. Just pretend we won.'"

James S. Hewett, ed., Parables, Etc., *vol. 4, no. 2 (Saratoga Press: April 1984).*

REASON

Reason is always a kind of brute force. . . . The real tyranny was the tyranny of aggressive reason over the cowed and demoralized human spirit.

G. K. Chesterton

REDEEMER

The world must be touched at its heart. I seek Him who alone can achieve that victory; and He must Himself be the Heart of hearts, the burning center of all love.

François Mauriac's protagonist in Viper's Tangle *(Garden City, N.Y.: Image Books [a division of Doubleday], 1957).*

REGENERATION

Many people come to listen to the gospel . . . who have always gone to church and Sunday School, . . . yet they may be unregenerate. They need the same salvation as the man who may have come to listen who has never been inside a House of God before. He may have come out of some moral gutter; it does not matter. It is the same way, the same gospel for both, and both must come in the same way. Religiosity is of no value; morality does not count; nothing matters. We are all reduced to the same level because it is "by faith," because it is "by grace."

Martyn Lloyd-Jones

Transformed Life

A great testimony to the power of the Word to beget and sustain faith is found in the story of the conversion and execution of Tokichi Ichii—a man who was hanged for murder in Tokyo in 1918. He had been sent to prison more than twenty times and was known as being cruel as a tiger. On one occasion, after attacking a prison official, he was gagged and bound, and his body suspended in such a way that "my toes barely reached the ground." But he stubbornly refused to say he was sorry for what he had done.

Just before being sentenced to death, Tokichi was sent a New Testament by two Christian missionaries, Miss West and Miss McDonald. After a visit from Miss West, he began to read the story of Jesus' trial and execution. His attention was riveted by the sentence, "And Jesus said, 'Father, forgive them, for they know not what they do.'" This sentence transformed his life.

Wrote Tokichi Ichii: "I stopped: I was stabbed to the heart, as if by a five-inch nail. What did the verse reveal to me? Shall I call it the love of the heart of Christ? Shall I call it His compassion? I do not know what to call it. I only know that with an unspeakable grateful heart I believed."

Tokichi was sentenced to death and accepted it as "the fair, impartial judgment of God." Now the Word that brought him to faith also sustained his faith in an amazing way. Near the end, Miss West directed him to the words of 2 Corinthians 6:8-10 concerning the suffering of the righteous. The words moved him very deeply and he wrote,

"As sorrowing, yet always rejoicing. People will say that I must have a very sorrowful heart because I am daily awaiting the execution of the death sentence. This is not the case. I feel neither sorrow nor distress nor any pain. Locked up in a prison cell six feet by nine in size I am infinitely

happier than I was in the days of my sinning when I did not know God. Day and night . . . I am talking with Jesus Christ.

"As poor, yet making many rich. This certainly does not apply to the evil life I led before I repented. But perhaps in the future, someone in the world may hear that the most desperate villain that ever lived repented of his sins and was saved by the power of Christ, and so may come to repent also. Then it may be that though I am poor myself, I shall be able to make many rich."

The Word sustained him to the end, and on the scaffold with great humility and earnestness he uttered his last words, "My soul, purified, today returns to the City of God."

Faith is born and sustained by the Word of God, and out of faith grows the flower of joy.

John Piper, Desiring God *(Portland, Oreg.: Multnomah, 1986), 120–121.*

D. L. Moody's Two and a Half Conversions
See page 83

It Takes More than a Rhinoceros-Hide Whip
See page 83

Billy Sunday's Conversion
See page 79

The Old Heart
See page 81

REJECTION

The many small rejections of every day—a sarcastic smile, a flippant remark, a brisk denial or a bitter silence may all be quite innocent and hardly worth our attention if they did not constantly arouse our basic fear of being left totally alone with "darkness as our one companion left."

Henri Nouwen

At the Bottom of the Heap

Dr. Erwin Lutzer shares this true story in his book *Failure: The Back Door to Success*:

Discouragement was etched indelibly on Jim's face. He spoke with urgency and only occasionally showed the trace of a smile. "Living for Christ is fine if you are on top of the pile," he surmised with conviction, "but it's a different story when you are at the bottom." Two years before this Jim had accepted Jesus as his Savior while he was in high school. He was so excited, so fresh in his prayers, so real. After high school, Jim was accepted for R.C.M.P. training. And from the first day, he sincerely tried to be a witness to his fellow trainees. He read his Bible and refused to share in immoral conversation and actions. In short, he lived for Christ. And that was the beginning of his troubles. Friends dubbed him "the religious nut." Some simply laughed at him. Others schemed to have him blamed for activities he was not involved in. He was physically thrown out of the games and social events of his companions.

"Perhaps," Jim reasoned, "this is what Christians should expect." But one fact still troubled him. In any group, one person is always first and one is always last. Jim had the latter distinction. He got the lowest score in examinations and barely passed in the practical work. He was not a leader, nor did he have a winsome personality. Worse yet, he commanded little or no respect. "My friends are rejecting Christ," he commented, "but maybe it's just because they don't want to be like me. And on that score I don't blame them. Who'd want to be like me?" He forced a smile to hold back the tears. "I'm a failure and I know it." [Dr. Lutzer mentions that at this point he explained or at least, as he puts it, "tried to explain" that maybe God didn't expect as much from Jim as He did from others. Maybe Jim should accept his limitations and learn to be satisfied with his role in life.] "But," Dr. Lutzer concludes, "my explanation was either deficient or unconvincing, or both. A year later, Jim committed suicide."

Erwin Lutzer, Failure *(Chicago: Moody, 1976).*

RELATIONSHIPS

Next to the blessed sacrament, your neighbor is the holiest object presented to your senses.

C. S. Lewis

RELATIVISM

Moral neutrality slips into moral relativism.

Charles Colson

You believe in a God who plays dice, and I in complete law and order in a world which objectively exists and which I, in a wildly speculative way, am trying to capture.

Albert Einstein, writing to his colleague Max Born

One man's vulgarity is another's lyric.

Justice Harlan

Relativity Became Relativism

At the beginning of the 1920s the belief began to circulate, for the first time at a popular level, that there were no longer any absolutes: of time and space, of good and evil, of knowledge, above all values. Mistakenly but perhaps inevitably, relativity became confused with relativism.

No one was more distressed than [Albert] Einstein by this public misapprehension. . . . Einstein was not a practicing Jew, but he acknowledged God. He believed passionately in absolute standards of right and wrong. His professional life was devoted to the quest not only for truth but also for certitude. . . . He lived to see moral relativism, to him a disease, become a social pandemic, just as he lived to see his fatal equation bring into existence nuclear warfare. There were times, he said at the end of his life, when he wished he had been a simple watchmaker.

Paul Johnson, Modern Times, *revised ed. (New York: HarperCollins, 1991), 456.*

RELIGION

True religion is slow in growth and, when once planted, is difficult of dislodgement; but its intellectual counterfeit has no root in itself; it springs up suddenly, it suddenly withers.

John Henry Newman

REPENTANCE

I regard everything that I taught and wrote before I entrusted my life to Jesus as refuse. I wish to use this opportunity to mention that I have pitched my two books *Gleichnisse Jesu . . .* and *Studien zur Passionsgeschichte,* along with my contributions to journals, anthologies, and *Festschriften.* Whatever of these writings I had in my possession I threw into the trash with my own hands in 1978. I ask you sincerely to do the same thing with any of them you may have on your own bookshelf.

Eta Linnemann

When then? What rests?
Try what repentance can. What can it not?
Yet what can it when one cannot repent?
O wretched state! O bosom black as death!
O limed soul, that, struggling to be free,
Art more engag'd!

William Shakespeare, Hamlet

God's Demand

C. S. Lewis on repentance: Repentance "is not something God demands of you before He will take you back and which He could let you off if He chose; it is simply a description of what going back is like."

Prepared to Live a Truly Christian Life

Before his eventual conversion, when philosopher Mortimer Adler was pressed on his reluctance to become a Christian, he replied, "That's a great gulf between the mind and the heart. I was on the edge of becoming a Christian several times, but didn't do it. I said that if one is born a Christian, one can be lighthearted about living up to Christianity, but if one converts by a clear conscious act of will, one had better be prepared to live a truly Christian life. So you ask yourself, are you prepared to give up all your vices and the weaknesses of the flesh?"

What's Wrong with a Christian Gangster?

Many remember Mickey Cohen, infamous gangster of the postwar era. One night Cohen attended an evangelistic meeting and seemed interested. Realizing what a dramatic impact his conversion could have on the world, many Christian leaders began visiting him. After one long night session, he was urged to open the door and let Christ in, based on Revelation 3:20. Cohen responded.

But as the months passed, people saw no change in his life of crime. When confronted, he responded that no one had told him he would have to give up his work or his friends. After all, there were Christian football players, Christian cowboys, Christian politicians; why not a Christian gangster?

It was only then that he was told about repentance. And at that point he wanted nothing to do with Christianity.

Charles Colson, "Who Speaks for God?" *(Wheaton, Ill.: Crossway, 1985), 153.*

Pardon from the President

A letter was once found in a White House file addressed to former president Grover Cleveland. It was from a nine-year-old girl. In the letter, the girl confessed that she had used two postage stamps a second time because the stamps hadn't been properly canceled. She asked President Cleveland's forgiveness and had enclosed the money for the two stamps.

All Debts to Be Paid
See page 234

REPUTATION

If I take care of my character, my reputation will take care of itself.
Dwight L. Moody

RESPONSIBILITY

There are two eras in American history—the passing of the buffalo and the passing of the buck.
Will Rogers

RESURRECTION

Spring bursts today,
For Christ is risen and all the earth's at play
Christina Rossetti, "Easter Carol"

If a skillful workman can turn a little earth and ashes into such curious transparent glasses as we daily see, and if a little seed that bears no show of such a thing can produce the most beautiful flowers on earth; and if a little acorn can bring forth the great oak; why should we once doubt whether the seed of everlasting life and glory, which is now in the blessed souls with Christ, can by Him communicate a perfection to the flesh that is dissolved into its elements?
Richard Baxter

Every parting gives a foretaste of death; every remeeting a foretaste of the resurrection. That is why even people who are indifferent to each other rejoice so much if they meet again after twenty or thirty years of separation.
Schopenhauer

We are more sure to arise out of our graves than out of our beds.

Thomas Watson

The great Easter truth is not that we are to live newly after death—that is not the great thing—but that we are to be new here and now by the power of the resurrection; not so much that we are to live forever, as that we are to, and may, live nobly now because we are to live forever.

Phillips Brooks

Never Miss the Sun

"I shall rise from the dead," wrote John Donne, Dean of Saint Paul's, "from prostration, from the prosternation of death, and never miss the sun, which shall be put out, for I shall see the Son of God, the Sun of glory, and shine myself as that sun shines. I shall arise from the grave, and never miss this city which shall be nowhere, for I shall see the city of God, the new Jerusalem. I shall look up and never wonder when it shall be day, for the angel will tell me that time shall be no more, and I shall see and see cheerfully that last day of judgment, which shall have no night, never end, and be united the Ancient of Days, to God himself, who had no morning, never began."

Frederick Buechner, The Sacred Journey *(San Francisco, Calif.: Harper San Francisco, 1982), 92–93.*

Thomas Jefferson's Bible

Congress once issued a special edition of Thomas Jefferson's Bible. It was simply a copy of our Bible with all references to the supernatural eliminated. Jefferson, in making his selections from the Bible, confined himself solely to the moral teachings of Jesus. The closing words of Jefferson's Bible are: "There laid they Jesus, and rolled a great stone to the mount of the sepulcher and departed." If our Bible ended like that, it would mean the impossibility of other resurrections. But thank God our Bible does not end like that. And the resurrection of Jesus Christ from the dead is our "living hope."

Walter B. Knight, Knight's Master Book of New Illustrations *(Grand Rapids, Mich.: Eerdmans, 1956), 555–556.*

Don't You Believe It!

Before D. L. Moody's home-going, he said, "Someday you will read in the papers that D. L. Moody is dead. Don't you believe it! At that moment I shall be more alive than I am now; I shall have gone up higher, that is all! I was born of the flesh in 1837; I was born of the Spirit in 1856. That which is born of the flesh may die, but that which is born of the Spirit will live forever!"

Walter B. Knight, Knight's Master Book of New Illustrations *(Grand Rapids, Mich.: Eerdmans, 1956), 559.*

Chocolate Eggs and Jesus Risen

There is a stage in a child's life at which it cannot separate the religious from the merely festal character of Christmas or Easter. I have been told of a very small and very devout boy who was heard murmuring to himself on Easter morning a poem of his own composition which began "Chocolate eggs and Jesus risen." This seems to me, for his age, both admirable poetry and admirable piety. But of course the time will soon come when such a child can no longer effortlessly and spontaneously enjoy that unity. He will become able to distinguish the spiritual from the ritual and festal aspect of Easter; chocolate eggs will no longer be sacramental. And once he has distinguished he must put one or the other first. If he puts the spiritual first he can still taste something of Easter in the chocolate eggs; if he puts the eggs first they will soon be no more than any other sweetmeat. They have taken on an independent, and therefore a soon withering, life.

C. S. Lewis, Reflections on the Psalms *(New York: Harcourt Brace).*

Life in Death Valley

Two hundred miles northeast of Los Angeles is a baked-out gorge called Death Valley—the lowest place in the United States, dropping 276 feet below sea level. It is also the hottest place in the country, with an official recording of 134 degrees. Streams flow into Death Valley only to disappear, and a scant two and a half inches of rain falls on the barren wasteland each year.

But, sometime ago, an amazing thing happened. For nineteen straight days rain fell onto the bone-dry earth. Suddenly all kinds of seed, dormant for years, burst into bloom. In a valley of death there was life!

That is the Easter message. A desert becomes a garden. Beauty transcends the ugly. Love outwits and outlasts hatred. A tomb is emptied. The grim and haunting outline of a cross disappears in the glow of Easter morn.

Floyd Thatcher, The Miracle of Easter, *as submitted by Larry Revert of Trent Church of Christ in Dexter, Oregon.*

Christ Is Risen! He Is Risen Indeed!

About 1930, the Bolshevik, Bukharin, journeyed from Moscow to Kiev. His mission was to address a huge assembly. His subject, atheism. For a solid hour he aimed his heavy artillery at Christianity, hurling argument and ridicule. At last he was finished and viewed what seemed to be the smoldering ashes of men's faith.

"Are there any questions?" Bukharin demanded.

A solitary man arose and asked permission to speak. He mounted the platform and moved close to the Communist. The audience was breathlessly silent as the man surveyed them first to the right, then to the left. At last he shouted the ancient Orthodox greeting, "CHRIST IS RISEN!"

The vast assembly arose as one man, and the response came crashing like the sound of an avalanche, "HE IS RISEN INDEED!"

James S. Hewett, ed., Parables, Etc. *vol. 4, no. 2 (Saratoga Press: April 1984).*

No Voice to Shout, "He Is Risen!"

On the Easter just before he died, D. William Sangster painfully printed a note to his daughter. A deeply spiritual Methodist, he had been spearheading a renewal movement in the British Isles after the Second World War. Then his ministry, except for prayer, was ended by a disease which progressively paralyzed his body, even his vocal chords. But the last Resurrection Sunday he spent on earth, still able to move his fingers, he wrote: "How terrible to wake up on Easter and have no voice to shout, 'He is risen!' Far worse, to have a voice and not want to shout."

James S. Hewett, ed., Parables, Etc. *vol. 4, no. 2 (Saratoga Press: April 1984).*

Make No Mistake: If He Rose at All

Make no mistake: If He rose at all
it was as His body;
if the cells' dissolution did not reverse, the
molecules reknit, the amino acids rekindle,
the Church will fall.

It was not as the flowers,
each soft Spring recurrent;
it was not as His Spirit in the mouths and fuddled
eyes of the eleven apostles;
it was as His flesh: ours.

The same hinged thumb and toes,
the same valved heart

that-pierced-died, withered, paused, and then
regathered out of enduring Might
new strength to enclose.

Let us not mock God with metaphor,
analogy, sidestepping, transcendence;
making of the event a parable, a sign painted
in the faded credulity of earlier ages:
let us walk through the door.

The stone is rolled back, not papier-mâché,
not a stone in a story,
but the vast rock of materiality that in the slow
grinding of time will eclipse for each of us
the wide light of day.

And if we will have an angel at the tomb,
make it a real angel
weight with Max Planck's quanta, vivid with hair,
opaque in the dawn light, robed in real linen
spun on a definite loom.

Let us not seek to make it less monstrous,
for our own convenience, our own sense of beauty,
lest, awakened in one unthinkable hour, we
are embarrassed by the miracle,
and crushed by remonstrance

John Updike, "Seven Stanzas at Easter," in Telephone Poles and Other Poems *(New York: Alfred A. Knopf, 1965).*

The Reality of Christianity

One day a Frenchman brought his new system of religion to Talleyrand and asked, "Why is it that everybody laughs at my religion? It is better than Christianity. What can I do to spread it through the world?" Talleyrand replied, "Go out and live and die serving the people, then on the third day rise from the dead to confirm the hopes of humanity; then the people will listen to you."

I Shall Rise Again

Sir Christopher Wren said in his *Memorials,* a miscellany of writings by himself and his son, that, at the start of work on his new cathedral of St. Paul's, when he and his chief mason had decided where the central point of the crossing should be, over which the dome was to rise, they sent a workman off to bring a stone from the rubble of the old cathedral to mark the spot. The workman chose a fragment at random and brought it to them. It had one word carved on it—*Resurgam* (I shall rise again).

Enough Body to Hold the Soul

See page 260

RETURN OF CHRIST

> The barbarians are coming; the Lord Jesus Christ is coming: *Christians are here now: do they know whether they are coming or going?*
>
> *Carl F. H. Henry*

REVERENCE

Explosive Power

On the whole, I did not find Christians, outside of the catacombs, sufficiently sensible of conditions. Does anyone have the foggiest idea what sort of power we so blithely invoke? Or, as I suspect, does no one believe a word of it? The churches are children playing on the floor with their chemistry sets, mixing up a batch of TNT to kill a Sunday morning. It is madness to wear ladies' straw hats and velvet hats to church; we should all be wearing crash helmets. Ushers should issue life preservers and signal flares; they should lash us to our pews. For the sleeping God may wake someday and take offense, or the waking God may draw us out to where we can never return.

Annie Dillard, Teaching a Stone to Talk *(New York: Harper & Row, 1982), 40–41.*

Not Talking to the President

At one time Bill Moyers served as press secretary to President Lyndon Johnson, who referred to him as "my Baptist preacher" and often called on him to "give thanks for the meal." On one occasion the president, who was having difficulty hearing, interrupted him in the middle of his prayer. "Louder, Bill!" he said. Moyers replied, "I wasn't talking to you, Mr. President."

John W. Drakeford, Humor in Uniform, *Ministry Resources Library (Grand Rapids, Mich.: Zondervan), 33.*

RICHES

Neglected Wealth

Mrs. Bertha Adams was seventy-one years old when she died alone in West Palm Beach, Florida, on Easter Sunday in 1976. The coroner's report read: Cause of death—Malnutrition. After wasting away to fifty pounds she could no longer stay alive. When the state authorities made their preliminary investigation of her place, they found a veritable "pigpen . . . the biggest mess you can imagine." One seasoned inspector declared he'd never seen a dwelling in greater disarray. The woman had begged food from neighbors' doors and what clothes she had were from the Salvation Army. From all outward appearances, she was a penniless recluse, a pitiful and forgotten widow. But such was not the case. Amid the jumble of her unclean, disheveled belongings, two keys were found which led the officials to safety deposit boxes at two different local banks. The discovery was absolutely unbelievable. The first box contained over seven hundred AT&T stock certificates, plus hundreds of other valuable certificates, bonds and solid financial securities . . . not to mention a stash of cash amounting to nearly $200,000. The second box had no certificates, but more money—lots of it, $600,000 to be exact. Adding the net worth of both boxes the woman had well over a million dollars in her possession. This lady, a millionaire, died a stark victim of starvation in a humble hovel many times removed from what she could have been living in.

S

SABBATH

The Jewish understanding of the Sabbath is not connected with the need for relaxation but with the need for intensification, of heightened awareness, that anticipates the hope of cosmic healing.

Richard John Neuhaus

SACRIFICE

Lives that say "my life for yours" are channels of God's grace to a needy world.

R. Kent Hughes

For the support of this declaration, with a firm reliance on the protection of the Divine Providence, we mutually pledge to each other, our lives, our fortunes, and our sacred honor.

The Declaration of Independence

For my own part, I have never ceased to rejoice that God has appointed me to such an office. People talk of the sacrifice I have made in spending so much of my life in Africa. Can that be called a sacrifice which is simply paid back as a small part of a great debt owing to our God, which we can never repay?

David Livingstone

The Signers of the Declaration of Independence

Have you ever wondered what happened to those men who signed the Declaration of Independence? Five signers were captured by the British as traitors and tortured before they died. Twelve had their homes ransacked and burned. Two lost their sons in the Revolutionary Army, another had two sons captured. Nine of the 56 fought and died from wounds or the hardships of the Revolutionary War.

What kind of men were they? Twenty-four were lawyers and jurists. Eleven were merchants, nine were farmers and large plantation owners, men of means, well educated. But they signed the Declaration of Independence knowing full well that the penalty would be death if they were captured.

They signed and they pledged their lives, their fortunes, and their sacred honor.

Carter Braxton of Virginia, a wealthy planter and trader, saw his ships swept from the seas by the British navy. He sold his home and properties to pay his debts and died in rags.

Thomas McKeam was so hounded by the British that he was forced to move his family almost constantly. He served in the Congress without pay, and his family was kept in hiding. His possessions were taken from him, and poverty was his reward.

Vandals or soldiers or both, looted the properties of Ellery, Clymer, Hall, Walton, Gwinnett, Heyward, Rutledge and Middleton.

At the Battle of Yorktown, Thomas Nelson, Jr., noted that the British General Cornwallis had taken over the Nelson home for his headquarters. The owner quietly urged General George Washington to open fire, which was done. The home was destroyed, and Nelson died bankrupt.

Francis Lewis had his home and properties destroyed. The enemy jailed his wife, and she died within a few months.

John Hart was driven from his wife's bedside as she was

dying. Their 13 children fled for their lives. His fields and his grist mill were laid waste. For more than a year he lived in forests and caves, returning home after to find his wife dead, his children vanished. A few weeks later he died from exhaustion and a broken heart.

Lewis Morris and Philip Livingston suffered similar fates.

Such were the stories and sacrifices of the American Revolution. These were not wild-eyed rabble-rousing ruffians. They were soft-spoken men of means and education. Standing tall, straight, and unwavering, they pledged:

"For the support of this declaration, with a firm reliance on the protection of the Divine Providence, we mutually pledge to each other, our lives, our fortunes, and our sacred honor."

"The Price They Paid," Psychology for Living, *July 1991, 7.*

Blazing Bomb

In the late stages of World War II, in the Pacific front, an amazing event took place. Captain Tony Simeral, an air force captain, related the events of the story.

It had happened as they approached the enemy coast, Simeral recalled. They were flying the Pathfinder plane, which drops a phosphorous smoke bomb to assemble the formation before proceeding to the target. On a B-29 this task is performed by the radio operator, back in the waist of the plane. At a signal from the pilot, he releases the bomb through a narrow tube.

The radio operator on Simeral's plane was a young man from Alabama, Staff Sgt. Henry Erwin. His crewmates liked to mimic his soft southern drawl. He always had a smile and was always quiet and courteous. Erwin received the routine order from Simeral, triggered the bomb, and dropped it down the tube. But there was a malfunction. The bomb exploded in the tube and bounced back in Erwin's face, blinding both eyes and searing off an ear. Phosphorous burns with a furious intensity that melts metal like butter. Now the bomb at Erwin's feet was rapidly eating its way through the deck of the plane, toward the full load of incendiaries in their racks below. He was alone, so Erwin took the white-hot bomb in his bare hands and started toward the cockpit, groping his way with elbows and feet.

A folding table was down and blocked the narrow passageway. Erwin hugged the blazing bomb under an arm, feeling it devour the flesh on his ribs, unfastened the spring latch and lifted the table (when the plane was inspected later, the skin of Erwin's entire hand was seared onto the table). He stumbled on, a walking torch. His clothes, hair and flesh were ablaze.

The dense smoke had filled the plane, and Simeral, the pilot, had opened the window beside him to clear the air. Simeral couldn't see Erwin, but he could hear him as he came closer to the cockpit. All Erwin said was, "Pardon me, sir," and reached across to the window and tossed the bomb out. Then Erwin collapsed on the flight deck.

Do the Right Thing
See page 229

All-Out Commitment
See page 116

We Died before We Came
See page 65

A Passion for Prisoners
See page 67

A Few Cents and the Smile of God
See page 76

SALVATION

Helplessness is construed not only as the necessary outcome of living in a fallen world, but also as the great instigator of faith itself.

William Perkins

For as long as men are secure, it is not possible that they should seriously apply their minds unto doctrine, neither without the knowledge and feeling of our sins can we heartily long for Christ.
Richard Greenham

The man that would stand in the favour of God and be saved, must do four things: first, humble himself before God; second, believe in Christ; third, repent of his sins; fourth, perform new obedience unto God.
William Perkins

To say that we are justified by faith is just another way of saying that we are justified not in the slightest measure by ourselves, but simply and solely by the One in whom faith is reposed.
J. Gresham Machen

A Savior for Me

When need awakens the Bible is a new book. When Bishop Butler was dying he was troubled. "Have you forgotten, my lord," said his chaplain, "that Jesus Christ is a Saviour?" "But," said the dying bishop, "how can I know that He is a Saviour for me?" "It is written," said the chaplain, "him that cometh unto Me I will in no wise cast out." And Butler answered, "I have read these words a thousand times, and I never saw their meaning until now. Now I die in peace." The sense of need unlocked for him the treasury of Scripture.
William Barclay, The Gospel of Luke *(Philadelphia, Penn.: Westminster, 1956), 68.*

Checkmated

A famous painting had long hung in a European gallery—no one seemed to know for how long. It showed a chess-board with the devil sitting on a chair on one side, a look of gloating triumph all over his face. Across from him was a dejected, forlorn youth, defeat stamped on a still studying countenance. The title told the story: "Checkmated."

Paul Murphy, the only American chess champion of the world prior to Bobby Fischer, once toured Europe and visited that gallery. He gazed at the painting in silent reflection for a long time. Then excitedly he exclaimed, "Bring me a chessboard; there's one—only one, mind you—but there's one move whereby I can save him!"

Christ, the Lord of the universe, looked down from heaven and saw our plight. The world was checkmated by the devil, but the Redeemer of man made the one move that could free us from gloom in life and doom in eternity—he died to free us from Satan's bondage.

John Wesley White, The Devil *(Wheaton, Ill.: Tyndale, 1971), 163–164.*

Are You Saved?

In the early years of the Victorious Life Testimony, Dr. W. H. Griffith Thomas gave a notable address on the victorious life. He opened by telling the story of a Salvation Army lassie in the city of Durham in the north of England. She met an old gentleman dressed in the garb of a Church of England clergyman and said to him, "Sire, are you saved?" As a Salvation Army soldier she was well instructed in the fact that a man might be a clergyman and yet might not be saved.

The old gentleman looked down with a beautiful smile, characteristic of him, and said to her: "Do you mean *esothen?* or do you mean *sozominos?* or do you mean *sothesomai?"*

She looked up with astonishment and wondered if she were speaking to a foreigner. The clergyman, Dr. Griffith Thomas said, was Bishop Westcott. Reckoned as the greatest Greek scholar in the world, this bishop was also a humble Christian, who dearly loved the Lord. He was using the Greek word for "saved," and he was asking the Salvation Army lassie, "Do you mean, Have I been saved? or do you mean, Am I being saved? or do you mean, Will I be saved?" Dr. Thomas added that before the Salvation Army lassie left she learned more about salvation from the great scholar and humble Christian.

Robertson C. McQuilkin, Joy and Victory *(Chicago: Moody, 1987), 23–24.*

The Most Ungodly Man in St. Louis

Donald Grey Barnhouse's commentary on Romans contains the following story by W. R. Newell:

Years ago in the city of St. Louis, I [Newell] was holding noon meetings in the Century Theatre. One day I spoke on . . . Romans 4:5. "To him that worketh not, but believeth in him who justifieth the ungodly; his faith is reckoned unto him for righteousness." After the audience had gone, I was addressed by a fine looking man of middle age. . . . He immediately said, "I am Captain G—," (a man very widely known in the city). And when I sat down to talk with him, he began: "You are speaking to the most ungodly man in St. Louis." I said, "Thank God!" "What!" he cried. "Do you mean you are glad that I am bad?" "No," I said, "but I am certainly glad to find a sinner that knows he is a sinner." "Oh, you do not know the half! I have been absolutely ungodly for years and years and years. . . ." I could hardly get him quiet enough to ask him: "Did you hear me preach on 'ungodly people' today?" "Mr. Newell," he said, "I have been coming to these noon meetings for six weeks. I do not think I have missed a meeting. But I cannot tell you a word of what you said today. I did not sleep last night. I have hardly had any sleep for three weeks. I have gone to one man after another to find out what I should do. And I do what they say. I have read the Bible. I have prayed. I have given money away. But I am the most ungodly wretch in this town. Now what do you tell me to do? I waited here today to ask you that. I have tried everything; but I am so ungodly!" "Now," I said, "we will turn to the verse I preached on."

I gave the Bible into his hands, asking him to read aloud:

"To him that worketh not." "But," he cried, "how can this be for me? I am the most ungodly man in St. Louis." "Wait," I said, "I beg you to go on reading." So he read, "To him that worketh not, but believeth on him that justifieth the ungodly." "There!" he fairly shouted. "That's what I am—ungodly." "Then, this verse is about you," I assured him. "But please tell me what to do, Mr. Newell. I know I am ungodly; what shall I do?" "Read the verse again, please."

He read: "To him that worketh not"—and I stopped him. "There," I said, "the verse says not to do, and you want me to tell you something to do; I cannot do that." "But there must be something to do; if not I shall be lost forever." "Now listen with all your soul," I said. "There was something to do, but it has been done!" Then I told how that God had so loved him, all ungodly as he was, that He sent Christ to die for the ungodly. And that God's judgment had fallen on Christ, who had been forsaken of God for his, Capt. G—'s sins, there on the cross. Then, I said, "God raised up Christ; and sent us preachers to beseech men, all ungodly as they are, to believe on this God who declares righteous the ungodly, on the ground of Christ's shed blood." He suddenly leaped to his feet and stretched out his hand to me. "Mr. Newell," he said, "I will accept that proposition!" And off he went without another word.

Donald Grey Barnhouse, Romans, *vol. 2 (Fincastle, Va.: Scripture Truth), 232–235.*

As a Child

This is H. A. Ironside's account of D. L. Moody's demonstration of how most people receive Christ when they are young:

When I was only twelve I went into a meeting in an auditorium in Los Angeles. About 10,000 people were gathered in the building which had two galleries, a building that has since been torn down to make way for another. I went to hear D. L. Moody preach. Because I could find no other place, I crawled out on a rafter beneath the ceiling. There was Moody, giving his message. I remember how in the course of his address he said, "I want everyone in this auditorium who is a Christian, who knows he is a Christian, to stand up. Now, remain standing until the ushers can tell me about how many are on their feet." Then he said, "There are between 5,000 and 6,000 people standing. What a testimony—5,000 to 6,000 Christian people in this building! Now," he said, "I want everyone here who became a Christian before he was fifteen to sit down"; and over half of that company sat down. Then he said, "Now how many of those who remain standing accepted Christ before they were twenty?" More than half of those remaining sat down. And then he went on, moving up the years by tens. "All who were saved before they were thirty, be seated"; and a number sat down. "All who were saved before they were forty, be seated"; and a smaller number sat down. And when he got to fifty, there were only about twenty left standing in that great congregation who had trusted Christ after they were fifty years of age! It was an object lesson I have never forgotten.

H. A. Ironside, Lectures on the Book of Acts *(Neptune, N.J.: Loizeaux, 1943), 586–587.*

The Exact Day of Salvation

Once Stuart and Jill Briscoe were at Capernwray Bible School and had to be apart for the day. Stuart had left Jill the car, but he had taken the keys. After being held up for a couple hours, Jill finally borrowed another car. As she was driving down the road, she saw some girls hitchhiking, and she picked them up. They turned out to be three German girls visiting England. Jill just happened to be on her way to a conference for German Christian young people. After some argument and persuasion, she finally got the girls to come to the conference, and one of them was marvelously saved. Jill told the girl's story: "She was a theological student in Germany. She had come under the influence of some teaching that, instead of leading her to an intelligent worship of God, had filled her with much doubt and confusion. She had delivered an ultimatum to the God whose existence she doubted. She told God that if He was there He should show Himself to her in some way. He must do this within three months. If He didn't, she told Him, 'I'll quit my schooling, quit religion, and I *think* I'm going to quit living because there's nothing to live for.'"

After explaining this, she turned to Jill, and with great emotion, said, "The three months end today."

Stuart Briscoe, Bound for Joy *(Ventura, Calif.: Regal), 20–21.*

Get Me In

In 1875 Dr. Charles Berry became pastor of St. George's Road Congregational Church, Bolton, England. The congregation worshiped in a handsome building seating between 1,100 and 1,200 persons. Shortly after his settlement in Bolton, . . . a girl, wearing clogs, and with an old shawl over her head, appeared at his door and begged him to come quickly and visit a dying woman.

At the bedside of this woman, in one of the worst parts of Bolton, Berry attempted to prepare her for eternity. He spoke of the beautiful life that the Lord Jesus had led, and of His influence as an example, a teacher, and a great leader. "Maister, that's no good for me," declared the dying woman firmly. "Maister, I've lived an awfu' sinful life, and I don't want no example and I don't want no leader, but I do want a Saviour. Can't you tell me of the Saviour, and tell me how He can come and get me in?"

There at the bedside of the troubled woman, young Berry realized the great error of his preaching. He had been laying great emphasis upon Jesus Christ the Example, and not upon Jesus Christ the Saviour of sinners. He sat down beside the dying woman and, casting aside all his theories, tried to recall everything that his parents had taught him in his childhood. He told her of man's hopeless nature, conceived and born in sin, of God's great love for mankind, of His gift of His only begotten Son, of the perfect righteousness of Jesus Christ, and of His suffering, death and resurrection for the sins of the human race, and of the gift of redemption through the grace of God and merit of Jesus Christ.

As the day dawned, the old woman died, rejoicing in her Saviour. "I got her in," declared Dr. Berry . . . "And I got in myself."

Webber, A History of Preaching, Part One, *655.*

A Lasting Inheritance

From Patrick Henry's will: "I have now disposed of all my property to my family. There is one thing more I wish I could give them and that is faith in Jesus Christ. If they had that and I had not given them one shilling, they would have been rich; and if they had not that, and I had given them all the world, they would be poor indeed."

Surprised by Joy

See page 287

A Great Debt, Who Can Pay?

See page 15

Thank You, John. I Thank You.

See page 426

SANCTIFICATION

Christ, once known and understood and loved, brings with Him into a man's life a different atmosphere, an atmosphere in which, spontaneously, the evil things begin to droop and the fine things burst to bloom.

David Brainerd

Evelyn Waugh, that superbly gifted but curmudgeonly and extremely malevolent writer, sometimes gave the impression that he positively enjoyed inflicting pain by the sharp and wounding things he said to people, even without provocation. He was once asked a hard question by a brave woman. "Mr. Waugh," she said, "how can you behave as you do, and still remain a Christian?" Waugh replied to her with grim sincerity, "Madam, I may be as bad as you say, but believe me, were it not for my religion, I would scarcely be a human being."

Paul Johnson, "A Historian Looks at Jesus," Charles Colson, Sources: The Problem of Ethics, *Wilberforce Forum: 1992 Prison Fellowship.*

The Force of Life

Shortly after the armistice of World War I, Dr. Donald Barnhouse visited the battlefields of Belgium. In the first year of the war the area around the city of Mons was the scene of the great British retreat; in the last year of the war it was the scene of the greater enemy retreat. For miles west of the city the roads were lined with artillery, tanks, trucks, and other war material that the enemy had abandoned in their hasty flight.

When Dr. Barnhouse was there, it was a lovely spring day; the sun was shining; not a breath of wind was blowing. As he walked along, examining the war material, he noticed that leaves were falling from the great trees that arched along the road. He brushed at a leaf that had fallen against his breast. He pressed the leaf in his fingers, and it disintegrated. He looked up curiously and saw several other leaves falling from the trees. Remember, it was spring, not autumn. Nor was there wind to blow off the leaves. These leaves had outlived the winds of autumn and the frosts of winter.

Yet they were falling that day, seemingly without cause. Then Dr. Barnhouse realized why. The most potent force of all was causing them to fall. It was spring; the sap was beginning to run; the buds were beginning to push from within. From down beneath the dark earth, the roots were taking life and sending it along trunk, branch, and twig, until that life expelled every bit of deadness that remained from the previous year. It was, a great Scottish preacher termed it, "the expulsive power of a new affection."

SCIENCE

Science is a marvelous tool given by God to discover the secrets of the cosmos and to elicit praise from men. When science is rightly studied within the context of the faith it is an ally, not an enemy.

Robert Ingram

SECULARISM

Freud has preempted Calvin as the father of orthodoxy among many pastors. Today's question has changed from "Who were Christ's father and mother?" to "What do you think of your mother?"—but with the same intent: to get material for diagnosis, data to compare with the orthodox model.

Eugene H. Peterson

Things have come to a pretty pass when religion is allowed to invade public life.

Lord Melbourne opposing abolition of the slave trade

A Strike against Tradition

Columnist Cal Thomas notes the drive to erase religious rights from public schools:

Back in 1992 the superintendent of Frederick County, Virginia, public schools Thomas Malcolm issued a memorandum instructing teachers and administrators to no longer refer to Christmas by its traditional name, but to substitute "winter holiday." Christmas parties are OK for schools to hold, but they must be called "holiday parties."

Malcolm did this on his own. He was not responding to a complaint or lawsuit, just the "possibility" that someone might be offended and the traditional references "could" be unconstitutional.

Employees were instructed to refer to Easter as "spring break" or use other terminology that does not convey religious meaning too.

When threatened with lawsuit by The Rutherford Institute, a law firm that argues religious freedom issues in court, Malcolm withheld implementing the policy until a committee he created studies the matter further. But his unilateral strike against a traditional American holiday and the beliefs and practices of an overwhelming majority of Americans is another blow to what remains of this country's heritage.

Malcolm acted at a time when mandatory sex education is the rule in every Virginia public school. Children as young as kindergarten must now be sensitized to AIDS and gay and lesbian lifestyles. But apparently the words "Christmas" and "Easter" are regarded as a more clear and present danger.

With the assistance of pressure groups, government now indulges in the final frontier of bigotry, what writer and Catholic theologian Michael Novak calls "Christophobia." Traditional Christians and Jews are the new counterculture, aliens in a land their forefathers' beliefs and values established. Anything that seems to come from or lead to a world not of this one is deemed offensive, illegal and unwise.

Daily Herald, *13 December 1992.*

Jews for Nothing; Christians for Nothing

This comment was made by Dennis Prager, who is Jewish, in an interview in the November/December 1990 issue of the *Wittenberg Door:*

In public schools, Jews don't meet Christians. Christians don't meet Hindus. Everybody meets nothing. That is, as I explain to Jews all the time, why their children so easily intermarry. Jews don't marry Christians. Non-Jewish Jews marry non-Christian Christians. Jews for nothing marry Christians for nothing. They get along great because they both affirm nothing. They have everything in common—that is exactly what the liberal world wants. They want a bunch of secular universalists with ethnic surnames.

Equal Time

In May 1955, a debate was conducted over the BBC entitled "Christianity vs. Atheism." Churchill objected to the programming. The BBC spokesman responded, "It is our duty to truth to allow both sides to debate."

Churchill shot back, "I suppose then that if there had been the same devices at the time of Christ, the BBC would have given equal time to Judas and Jesus."

James C. Humes, Churchill: Speaker of the Century *(New York: Stein and Day), 286.*

The UN Meditation Room

See page 241

A Mockery of Worship

See page 432

SECURITY

If as a child you have not known a secure home, it is very likely as you go through life regardless of your abode or wherever you are, you will not feel at home. But on the other hand, if as a child you have been secure and at home, wherever you go will be home.

Paul Tournier

SELF

The self is a canvas too narrow, too cramped, to contain the largeness of Christian truth.

David F. Wells

The fascination with the self and with human subjectivity has then become a well-established cultural feature of

> Evangelicalism generally in the latter part of the twentieth century, not simply an ephemeral fashion among the younger generation.
>
> *James Davison Hunter*

> Self-fulfillment is no longer a natural by-product of a life committed to higher ideals but rather is a goal, pursued rationally and with calculation as an end in itself. . . . Self-expression and self-realization compete with self-sacrifice as a guiding life-ethic.
>
> *James Davison Hunter*

Obsessed with Self

Humanity has always gravitated toward sinful self-focus. Shirley MacLaine's famous praise of self-centeredness has become the "primrose path" for multitudes. Says MacLaine:

The most pleasurable journey you take is through yourself . . . the only sustaining love involvement is with yourself. . . . When you look back on your life and try to figure out where you've been and where you are going, when you look at your work, your love affairs, your marriages, your children, your pain, your happiness, when you examine all that closely, what you really find out is that the only person you really go to bed with is yourself. The only person you really dress is yourself. The only thing you have is working to the consummation of your own identity. And that's what I've been trying to do all my life.

Henry Fairlie, The Seven Deadly Sins Today *(South Bend, Ind.: University of Notre Dame Press, 1979), 31–32.*

The Veneration of Self

Both popular and more serious academic scholarship have documented a dramatic turnabout within the larger American culture on this count [attitudes about self] from the mid-1960s. It was a turnabout entailing an accentuation of subjectivity and the virtual veneration of the self, exhibited in deliberate choice to achieve self-understanding, self-improvement, and self-fulfillment. Though it might be supposed that Evangelicalism would be most resistant to change along these lines, traditional assumptions about the self appear to have weakened substantially here as well. There are, in fact, strong indications that a total reversal has taken place in the Evangelical conception of the nature and value of the self. As one might expect, this is particularly prominent within the coming generation of Evangelicals. For example, nearly nine out of every ten Evangelical students (roughly paralleling the number of public university students) agreed that "self-improvement is important to me and I work hard at it." . . . Likewise most (collegians, 68%; seminarians, 52%) agreed that they felt a "strong need for new experiences." The relative significance of these responses is highlighted when they are compared to a national survey of adult Americans conducted by Yankelovich in 1979. The percentage of Evangelical students agreeing with these statements far exceeded the corresponding percentage of the general population on both the importance of self-improvement and the need for new experiences. . . .

On the surface, one might expect college students generally in their special life circumstances to give even greater priority to matters of the self than those adults who work full-time for pay. After all, most college students are single and have only their own present needs and future interests to contemplate. Nevertheless, one would also expect that within the American student population, the Evangelicals would be the least likely to endorse this orientation. They of all groups should be most out of step with dominant cultural patterns. But such is not the case. There is, instead, a very clear parallel between Evangelicals and non-Evangelicals in their attitudes about the self.

James Davison Hunter, Evangelicalism, the Coming Generation *(Chicago: University of Chicago Press, 1987), 65–66.*

The Church as Personal Fulfillment

Sociologist Robert Bellah wrote a book titled *Habits of the Heart*—a phrase he borrowed from de Tocqueville's classic work on American life. Bellah examined the values of several hundred average, middle-class Americans. He came to the conclusion that the reigning ethos in American life in the eighties was what he called "ontological individualism," a radical individualism where the individual is supreme and autonomous and lives for himself or herself. He found that Americans had two overriding goals: vivid personal feelings and personal success.

Bellah tried to find out what people expected from the institutions of society. From business they expected personal advancement. OK, that's fair enough. From marriage, personal development. No wonder marriages are in trouble. And from church, personal fulfillment! The "personal" became the dominant consideration.

Charles Colson, Sources: The Problem of Ethics, *no. 2, Wilberforce Forum: 1992 Prison Fellowship.*

The Leech's Two Daughters

In an unusually graphic illustration, the writer of Proverbs describes the true nature of self. "The leech has two daughters, 'Give,' 'Give'" (Proverbs 30:15). The leech mentioned here, probably as a large and especially repulsive creature, has two forks in its tongue, with which it sucks blood from its victims. It is said that it would often gorge itself until it exploded. Spiritually, this leech is self-love and its two daughters are self-righteousness and self-pity. It is never satisfied, and its insatiable appetite is the enemy of everything around it. It is even its own worst enemy, because self-love can never truly be satisfied.

John MacArthur, Hebrews *(Chicago: Moody, 1983), 425.*

SELF-CENTEREDNESS

We made all this stuff. So thanks for nothing. Amen!
Bart Simpson

SELF-ESTEEM

Justification is thus about our status in the sight of God. It is the way we are viewed by the most significant of all others—God.
Alister McGrath

The Societal Cure-All

The religiouslike belief that a positive self-esteem is a societal cure-all was given its most doctrinaire expression yet by the California State Task Force on Self-Esteem and Personal and Social Responsibility. Despite conflicting scientific evidence, the Task Force's report concluded:

Self-esteem is the likeliest candidate for a *social vaccine,* something that empowers us to live responsibly and that inoculates us against the lures of crime, violence, substance abuse, teen pregnancy, chronic welfare dependency and educational failure.

Jerry Adler, "Hey, I'm Terrific," Newsweek, *17 February 1992, 51.*

Sin Insults the Human Being

The last book by Robert Schuller is particularly noteworthy if only because of its extraordinary circulation—250,000 copies were distributed free of charge to religious leaders across the country. . . . In it Schuller argues that Reformational theology was "imperfect" for it was not a "well-rounded, full-orbed, honestly-interrelated theology system" (pp. 145–146). For nearly 500 years the basic elements of Christian faith have been misunderstood and misapplied. For example, the traditional theological definition of sin (i.e., rebellion against God) "is not incorrect as much as it is shallow and insulting to the human being" (p. 65). "Reformational theology failed to make clear that at the core of sin is a lack of self-esteem" (p. 98). In this light, salvation "means to be permanently lifted from sin (psychological self-abuse with all of its consequences . . .) and home to self-esteem and its God-glorifying human need-meeting, constructive and created consequences. . . . To be saved is to know that Christ forgives me and now I dare to believe that I am somebody and I can do something for God and my fellow human beings" (p. 99). So, too, hell is redefined as the "loss of pride that naturally follows separation from God—the ultimate and unfailing source of our soul's sense of self-respect" (p. 14). . . .

Correspondingly, the "basic problem in our world today" is that "many human beings don't realize who they are. And if we don't know who we are and where we have come from, we will never become what we were meant to be" (p. 62). Given this, Schuller calls upon the church to remodel itself around the mission of addressing these problems. For individual Christians, self-denial will no longer "mean the rejection of that positive emotion we call self-esteem—the joy of experiencing my self-worth—" but will mean a "willingness to be involved in the spiritual and social solutions in society" (pp. 115–116). Likewise the "work-ethic" will become a "person's self-worth ethic" (p. 94).

James Davison Hunter, Evangelicalism, the Coming Generation *(Chicago: University of Chicago Press, 1987), 70–71.*

SELF-IMAGE

I am rough, boisterous, stormy, and altogether warlike, fighting against innumerable monsters and devils. I am born for the removing of stumps and stones, cutting away thistles and thorns, and clearing wild forests.

Martin Luther

A Just-Right Face

A second grader in Tennessee made a good start toward a sense of self-esteem when he submitted an essay entitled "My Face" to his teacher. "My face has two brown eyes," the seven-year-old began. "It has a nose and two cheeks. And two ears and a mouth. I like my face. I'm glad my face is just like it is. It is not bad, it is not good, but just right."

SELFISHNESS

Blessed by unprecedented affluence in the sixties and seventies, Americans rightly concluded there must be more to life than material prosperity, but were beguiled into believing the answers they craved could be found by looking deep enough within. The resultant identity search has paraded under a host of banners: encounter groups, Eastern cults, EST, TM, and a long line of others.
Charles Colson

Living for his own pleasure is the least pleasurable thing a man can do; if his neighbors don't kill him in disgust, he will die slowly of boredom and lovelessness.
Joy Davidman

Monuments to Selfishness

Before the turn of the century, a man named John Davis began work as a hired farmhand in Kansas. Starting with nothing, he eventually amassed a fortune through various enterprises. As his wealth increased he married. His wife's parents objected because they felt she was marrying below her dignity—so he permanently wrote off all his in-laws. Moreover, he cultivated no friends. The Davises were also childless.

As Davis prospered, he was sometimes asked to financially participate in civic projects, but he would have none of it. His rationale was, "I don't owe this town nothing." When he was a very wealthy man, his wife died and John Davis was alone with his money, and he began to spend lavishly.

He hired an artist to design a marble statue for her grave that depicted him and his wife seated at opposite ends of a loveseat. Davis was so pleased that he commissioned a second statue of himself kneeling at her grave. He was again so pleased that he ordered a third statue of his wife kneeling at his future gravesite. It was very expensive because it had to have wings, since she was dead.

Finally, all his money was gone. John Davis had spent $250,000 on tombstones. When he died at the age of ninety-three, he was the resident of a poorhouse, and the monuments, even then, were sinking slowly into the Kansas sod. Eventually, the statues will topple over because of vandalism and neglect. Observers report that when the man was buried, there were very few people in attendance, and only one mourner, a man named Horace England, the tombstone salesman.

Without exaggeration, Mr. Davis's life was one of monumental selfishness!

The Leech's Two Daughters
See page 378

Therapeutic Marriage
See page 134

SELF-REFORM

Don't be angry with yourself that you cannot get the others as you wish them to be, when you cannot get yourself as you wish to be.

Thomas à Kempis

SELF-WORTH

The human being is the only creature made in God's image and likeness. That's pretty good. When sin entered, salvation was offered to mankind only. That's pretty good. Jesus entered our race, wore our flesh, died our death, and took our place. That's pretty good. . . . The next time the devil tells you you're nothing, you tell him who you are.

S. M. Lockerage

SERVANTHOOD

God has three sorts of servants in the world: some are slaves, and serve Him from fear; others are hirelings, and serve for wages; and the last are sons, who serve because they love.

Archbishop Secker

Some of you good people, who do nothing except go to public meetings, and Bible readings, and prophetic conferences, and other forms of spiritual dissipation, would be a good deal better Christians if you would look after the poor and needy around you. If you would just tuck up your sleeves for work, and go and tell the Gospel to dying men, you would find your spiritual health mightily restored, for very much of the sickness of Christians comes through their having nothing to do. All feeding and no working makes men spiritual dyspeptics. Be idle, careless, with nothing to live for, nothing to care for, no sinner to pray for, no backslider to lead back to the cross, no trembler to encourage, no little child to tell of a Savior, no gray-headed man to enlighten in the things of God, no object, in fact, to live for; and who wonders if you begin to groan, and to murmur, and to look within, until you are ready to die of despair.

Charles H. Spurgeon

When I feel I have been least efficient, people have been helped more effectively. It has taken me a long time to learn that the lower my resistances are and the less self-consciousness I have, the more the Word of God comes through.

Lloyd Ogilvie

As in the maiden path she trod,
Fair was the wife foreshewn;
A Mary in the House of God,
A Martha in her own.

Coventry Patmore

God plants His saints in the most useless places. We say, "I should be here because I am so useful." Jesus never estimated His life by the standard of greatest use. God puts His people where they will glorify Him, and we are not capable of judging where that is.

Oswald Chambers

The measure of a man is not how many servants he has, but how many men he serves.

D. L. Moody

You know, Lord, how I serve You
With great emotional fervor
In the limelight. . . .

But how would I react, I wonder
If you pointed to a basin of water
And asked me to wash the calloused feet
Of a bent and wrinkled old woman
Day after day
Month after month
In a room where nobody saw
and nobody knew.

Ruth Harms Calkin

William Booth's Fight to the Finish

See page 116

Aloof Leadership
See page 335

SEX

Once they had sinned, Adam and Eve tried to hide their nakedness from each other and from God, and to one degree or another we have all been hiding it ever since for the reason, I suppose, that we know that our sexuality is yet another good gift from God which as sinners we can nonetheless use to dehumanize both each other and ourselves.

Frederick Buechner

SIMPLICITY

Because of its debts and certain especially Teutonic habits of thought and expression, some modern theology moreover suffers from an exasperating lack of clarity. It sometimes displays all the definition of a fog bank. Suppose a theologian says something like this: "Here we have both an essential and an existential dynamic merged in the concrete, self-transcendent ambiguity of the Now." You feel like saying, "Could you give some examples of that?"

Cornelius Platinga Jr.

The plain things are the main things; and the main things are the plain things.

Alistair Begg

See simplicity and then distrust it.

Alfred North Whitehead

The Gospel's Simplicity

A freshman student once remarked to C. E. Matthews after they had both just heard George W. Truett in chapel, "So, that's George Truett, is it? Huh. He didn't use one word I couldn't understand."

G. Campbell Morgan once read a review of one of his

books that bemoaned its simplicity. It said there were "no flowers of speech, no beauties of expression." He cut out the criticism and pasted it in one of the books with the remark, "Lord, help me to keep it just there."

If our gospel is hidden, it is hidden to the lost. The irony of it all is that we often bury the gospel's simplicity beneath pomp of expression. There's no way to improve the gospel, the sublimity of which is revealed in its simplicity.

SIN

The punishment of sin is sin.
St. Augustine

I am no better than a thief, a prostitute, an adulterer, or a historical-critical theologian. But in the same way that I resist adultery in the name of Jesus, I can also resist historical-critical theology, and appeal to my Savior in time of need.
Eta Linnemann

Celibate priests lose their perceptions. No priest can experience repentance and forgiveness of sin unless he himself falls into sin. Since concupiscence is the most common form of temptation, it is better for him to know something about it.
Willa Cather, Death Comes for the Archbishop

Every time he sins, he is making himself less capable of realizing what sin is, less likely to realize that he is a sinner, for the ugly thing, the really diabolical thing about sin is that it perverts a man's judgment. It stops him from seeing straight.
James Stewart

I have committed many sins in my life. Not one of my sins has ever made me happy. . . . But my sins have brought me pleasure.
R. C. Sproul

When we sin we not only commit treason against God but we do violence to each other. Sin violates people. There is nothing abstract about it.
R. C. Sproul

If all thieves—who nevertheless do not wish to be considered such—were to be hanged from the gallows, the world would soon be desolate, and would be without both executioners and gallows.
Martin Luther

If the sins are deadly to us as individuals, they are no less deadly to our societies. The feebleness of our societies, the steady weakening of all social bonds, is in part a consequence of their own sinning.
Henry Fairlie

It does not matter how small the sins are, provided that their cumulative effect is to edge the man away from the Light and out into nothing. Murder is no better than lies if lying does the trick.
C. S. Lewis, The Screwtape Letters

Sin in a Christian's life makes a coward of him!
Henrietta Mears

Pity Sir Robert Watson-Watt
Strange target of his radar plot.
And thus, with others I could mention,
A victim of his own invention.
Sir Robert Watson-Watt, the man who invented radar

Backed Up by History
I think it was Bishop Fulton Sheen, in paraphrasing G. K. Chesterton, who once said that the doctrine of original sin is the only philosophy empirically validated by 3,500 years of human history. Maybe you dismiss this, too, and say, "this is just the way people are."
Charles Colson, Sources: The Problem of Ethics, *no. 2, Wilberforce Forum: 1992 Prison Fellowship.*

What's Wrong? I Am.

Many years ago there was a famous correspondence in *The Times* under the subject "What is wrong with the world today?" The best letter of all was also the shortest, and read—"Dear Sir, I am. Yours faithfully, G. K. Chesterton." That devastating declaration showed a profound insight into man's universal malaise, and I believe that it can teach us a deeply challenging lesson. I am convinced that throughout the Christian church there are problems, difficulties and frustrations that would begin to dissolve immediately if only some Christians would be honest enough to answer the question—"What's wrong?" with the words "I am!"

John Blanchard, The Truth for Life *(West Sussex, England: H. E. Walter, 1982), 263.*

Symposium on Theft

In a paper presented at a symposium on employee theft, sponsored by the American Psychological Association, the authors pointed out that inventory shortages cost department stores and specialty chains eight billion dollars every year. Of that, 10 percent is attributed to clerical error, 30 percent to shoplifting, and a whopping 60 percent—or sixteen million dollars a day—to theft by employees.

Adam's Fall

Behind the scenes of the nursery rhyme "Humpty Dumpty" there is a profound truth. The rhyme reads:

Humpty Dumpty sat on a wall;
Humpty Dumpty had a great fall.
All the king's horses and all the king's men
Couldn't put Humpty Dumpty together again.

The picture that comes to mind is an egg sitting on a wall. Right? But why? There is nothing in the rhyme that mentions an egg. The one who wrote it probably didn't even have an egg in mind. Here's one idea as to the origin of that rhyme: It was probably born in the mind of a child who learned his ABC's from a book called *The English Primer.* Many children who lived in the 1700s and 1800s learned grammar from that book. Perhaps the child picked up the thought for "Humpty Dumpty" from a verse that was used to teach children the letters *a* and *x*. In the primer, the verse reads:

In Adam's fall
we sinned all.
Xerxes the great did die,
and so must you and I.

In a subtle manner that little verse teaches not only the letters *a* and *x* but also a significant spiritual truth: "In Adam's fall we sinned all." Since the time of Adam, we are born sinners. The one who wrote "Humpty Dumpty" was talking about not an egg that fell but a man. "And all the king's horses and all the king's men" is designed to call together all those kings and people who are frustrated at the bottom of the wall, unable to put their lives together again.

But because Jesus Christ entered history and died for our sins and rose again, we can rewrite "Humpty Dumpty":

Jesus Christ came to our wall.
Jesus Christ died for our fall.
So that regardless of death and despite all our sin
—Through grace, He puts us together again.

The Believer's Duty to Sin

Rasputin, the Russian monk who dominated the Romanov family in their final years, taught that salvation came through repeated experiences of sin and repentance. He argued that because those who sin more require more forgiveness, those who sin with abandon will experience even greater joy as they repent. Therefore, it is the believer's duty to sin.

The Reality of Sin

William Beveridge understood the reality of his sin and his need to repent:

I cannot pray, except I sin;
I cannot preach, but I sin;
I cannot administer, nor receive the holy sacrament, but I sin.
My very repentance needs to be repented of;
And the tears I shed need washing in the blood of Christ.

James Boice, The Gospel of John, *vol. 2 (Grand Rapids, Mich.: Zondervan), 25.*

Royal Water

A chemistry class once learned how acids act on different substances. In the course of an experiment, the professor gave the class a bit of gold and told them to dissolve it. They left it all night in the strongest acid they had. It failed to dissolve. Then they tried various combinations of acids, but in vain.

Finally, they told the professor they thought gold could not be dissolved. He smiled. "I knew you could not dissolve gold," he said. "None of the acids you have there will attack it, but try this," and he handed them a special bottle of acid. They poured some of its contents into the tube that held the piece of gold, and the gold that had resisted all the other acids quickly disappeared in the royal water. The gold at last had found its master.

The next day the professor asked the class, "Do you know why that acid is called 'royal water'?" "Yes," they replied, "it is because it is the master of gold, a substance which can resist almost anything that can be poured on it."

Then he said, "Fellows, I should take time to tell you that there is another substance just as impervious as gold. It cannot be touched or changed though a hundred attempts are made upon it. That substance is the sinful heart. Trial, affliction, riches, honor, imprisonment, or punishment will not soften or master it. Education and culture will not dissolve or purify it. There is but one element that has power over the sin of the human heart—the blood of Christ, the Savior of the soul."

The Deadly Sweetness of Sin

A man lying upon the grass noticed a little plant of sundew when suddenly a tiny fly alighted upon its leaves and tasted one of the tempting glands which grow there.

All at once three crimson-tipped, fingerlike hairs bent over and touched the fly's wings, holding it fast in a sticky grasp. The fly struggled in vain to get free, but the more it struggled the more hopelessly it became besmeared. It still, however, protruded its tongue, feasting as it was being more and more firmly held by additional tentacles. When the captive was entirely at the mercy of the plant, the edges of the leaf folded inwards and formed a closed fist. Two hours later the fly was an empty sucked skin, and the leaf was opening for another unwary visitor.

So often we don't realize the deadly sweetness of sin until it holds us bound.

Pulpit Helps, *December 1977.*

Sin Insults the Human Being
See page 379

You Don't Have to Swallow Depravity
See page 121

The Devil Is a Great Fool
See page 127

Tangle of Vipers
See page 120

SOLITUDE

Anything else will be accepted as a better excuse. If one sets aside time for a business appointment, a trip to the hairdresser, a social engagement, or a shopping expedition, that time is accepted as inviolable. But if one says: I cannot come because that is my hour to be alone, one is considered rude, egotistical or strange. What a commentary on our civilization, when one has to apologize for it, make excuses, hide the fact that one practices it—like a secret vice!

Anne Morrow Lindbergh

SORROW

You that are called born of God, and Christians, if you be not criers, there is no spiritual life in you; if you be born of God, you are crying ones; as soon as He has raised you out of the dark dungeon of sin, you cannot but cry to God.

John Bunyan

SOUL

Is the soul solid, like iron?
Or is it tender and breakable,
like
The wings of a moth in the
beak of the owl?
Who has it, and who doesn't?

Mary Loiver

SOVEREIGNTY OF GOD

Either God is sovereign, or man is sovereign. One of the two must be untrue.

Karl Marx

God is over all things; outside all; within but not enclosed; without but not excluded; above but not raised

up; below but not depressed; wholly above, presiding; wholly beneath, sustaining; wholly within, filling.
Hildebert of Lavardin

The Family Bible

Andrea Wolfe, on staff with The CoMission office in Raleigh, North Carolina, included the following story in one of her Christmas newsletters:

In the 1930s Stalin ordered a purge of all Bibles and all believers. In Stavropol, Russia, this order was carried out with a vengeance. Thousands of Bibles were confiscated, and multitudes of believers were sent to the gulags—prison camps—where most died for being "enemies of the state."

The CoMission once sent a team to Stavropol. The city's history wasn't known at that time. But when the team was having difficulty getting Bibles shipped from Moscow, someone mentioned the existence of a warehouse outside of town where these confiscated Bibles had been stored since Stalin's day.

After much prayer by the team, one member finally got up the courage to go to the warehouse and ask the officials if the Bibles were still there. Sure enough, they were. Then the CoMissioners asked if the Bibles could be removed and distributed again to the people of Stavropol. The answer was, "Yes!"

The next day the CoMission team returned with a truck and several Russian people to help load the Bibles. One helper was a young man—a skeptical, hostile, agnostic collegian who had come only for the day's wages. As they were loading Bibles, one team member noticed that the young man had disappeared. Eventually they found him in a corner of the warehouse, weeping.

He had slipped away, hoping to quietly take a Bible for himself. What he found shook him to the core.

The inside page of the Bible he picked up had the handwritten signature of his own grandmother. It had been her personal Bible. Out of the thousands of Bibles still left in that warehouse, he stole the one belonging to his grandmother—a woman persecuted for her faith all her life.

No wonder he was weeping—God was real. His grandmother had no doubt prayed for him and her city. His discovery of this Bible was only a glimpse into the spiritual realm—and this young man was in the process of being transformed by the very Bible that his grandmother found so dear.

Andrea Wolf, The CoMission, *Raleigh, N.C.*

V. Raymond Edman's Funeral-to-Be

In June 1926 a young missionary in his midtwenties named Raymond Edman fell ill from typhus fever in a mountain village of Ecuador. So grave was his illness that he was carried by train and stretcher from Riobamba to Guayaquil, the port city of Ecuador. Soon his wife followed. When she arrived at the hospital, the attending North American physician told Mrs. Edman that her husband's feet were already cold and that he would soon die. At that, a fellow missionary ordered a black cloth-covered coffin so that they could bury him quickly. And because Mrs. Edman had no black dress, she had her wedding dress dyed black. They even set the time and date of the funeral, 3:00 P.M., July 4. . . .

Meanwhile in Boston, a Dr. Joseph Evans interrupted a prayer meeting that night. "I feel we must pray for Ray Edman in Ecuador." The group prayed desperately, until Evans concluded, "Praise the Lord! The victory is won!"

. . . Years later, 1967 to be exact, Dr. V. Raymond Edman, fourth president of Wheaton College, was addressing the student body in Edman Chapel when at 10:53 A.M. he suddenly stopped speaking and collapsed after a slow half turn—and in the next moments passed into the presence of the King of Kings.

Earle Cairns, In the Presence of the King, 51, 192; *Lois Neely,* Come up to This Mountain *(Wheaton, Ill.: Tyndale, 1980), 65.*

Jesus on the Wheel of the World

Christ's life, especially His death and resurrection, has been interpreted in many different ways. For example, in 1906, Albert Schweitzer published his landmark book, *The Quest for the Historical Jesus.* In it, after reviewing the various historical views of Jesus, Schweitzer concluded that Jesus was a mere man who was dominated by the expectation of the coming of God's kingdom and who finally, in desperation, tried to force its coming by seeking His own death. Schweitzer describes it in this famous quotation:

There is silence all around. The Baptist appears, and cries: "Repent, for the Kingdom of Heaven is at hand." Soon after that comes Jesus, and in the knowledge that He is the coming Son of Man lays hold of the wheel of the world to set it moving on that last revolution which is to bring all ordinary history to a close. It refuses to turn, and He throws Himself upon it. Then it does turn; and crushes Him. Instead of bringing in the eschatological conditions, He has destroyed them. The wheel rolls onward, and the mangled body of one immeasurably great Man, who was strong enough to think of Himself as the spiritual ruler of mankind and to bend history to His purpose, is hanging upon it still. That is His victory and His reign.

Albert Schweitzer, The Quest for the Historical Jesus *(New York: Macmillan, 1906), 370–371.*

Christ Is Everything

See page 49

SPIRITUAL GIFTS

Gifts for Service

When Niccolò Paganini willed his elegant violin to the city of Genoa, he demanded that it never be used. It was a gift designated for preservation but not destined for service.

When the resurrected Christ willed his spiritual gifts to the children of God, he commanded that they be used. They were gifts not destined for preservation but destined for service.

SPIRITUALITY

Many experience displeasure when they see others in possession of spiritual goods. They feel sensibly hurt because others surpass them on this road, and they resent it when others are praised.
St. John of the Cross

The spiritual life which is reached in the work of conversion is a far greater and more glorious effect than mere being and life.
Jonathan Edwards

STRENGTH

It is not our littleness that hinders Christ; but our bigness. It is not our weakness that hinders Christ; it is our strength. It is not our darkness that hinders Christ; it is our supposed light that holds back his hand.
Charles H. Spurgeon

God chose me because I was weak enough. God does not do his great works by large committees. He trains somebody to be quiet enough, and little enough, and then uses him.
Hudson Taylor

Start to Sprint

Ray Buker, an Olympic runner, began his junior year at Bates in the fall of 1920. For the first time since the war the college entered a team for the New England Cross-Country event held in Boston at the Franklin Park course. Ray was a member of that team. It was a strange course, and although it had some gentle slopes it had none of the steep hills that were characteristic of all his cross-country races in Maine. At about a mile from the finish Ray was so far behind the leaders that he was convinced that humanly speaking he could never place, even if he used his sprint for the last part of the race. He prayed, telling the Lord that perhaps it was not His will that he should win, and that he didn't know how he could. The Lord answered, "Start to sprint." Ray replied, "Lord, You know that one can't sprint for a mile." He felt that God's answer entered his soul, "You obey Me and you will see what I can do." Ray began to sprint. He soon drew even with the leaders—and finished first.

Eric Fife, Against the Clock *(Grand Rapids, Mich.: Zondervan).*

Under Fire

Two friends were shut up in prison, and one said to the other, "Oh, I do dread tomorrow morning! I am afraid that when I come to feel the fire, I shall recant. I know that I never was good at bearing pain, and I have heard that the pain of being burned to death is very dreadful." So the other turned round upon him and said, "I am ashamed of you talking like that. You know very well it is for Christ's cause that we are going to die. I am sure that I shall not have any such fear. I could bear a thousand deaths for Christ. I feel such courage in my spirit that I do not dread the pain, and I am ashamed that you do." They both came to be chained to the stake, and the boastful man recanted and saved his skin; but the poor timid man stood bravely in the midst of the fire and burned to death and kept only saying, "Lord, help me! Lord, help me!"

Carry on with Christian Dignity
See page 193

STRESS

You cannot play the fiddle with a loose string.
Vance Havner

Stressed Out

The Rev. H. B. London, Focus on the Family's "pastor to pastors," has spent 31 years in the pulpit and has a thorough understanding of the tremendous pressures that weigh on ministers. London typically receives a call from a pastor who needs to talk to a safe person about the pressures and struggles he is facing. But Rev. London also receives calls from others who care about the pastors close to them.

On more than one occasion, Rev. London has taken a call from a pastor's wife who is upset that her husband has allowed the church to become his mistress.

Once an elderly parishioner phoned, concerned that his pastor was burning out. Rev. London, remembering the group of men he met with every Tuesday morning for 20 years, told him, "Unless your pastor finds a close friend to pray with, he won't escape the cycle that results in burnout."

London . . . is especially concerned about four problems pastors face:

Loneliness. A pastor seldom has anyone to talk to about the pressures of the job, the demands on the family and the sacrifices he has to make. His loneliness also comes from the fear that people would be disillusioned if he talked about the stress.

Feelings of inadequacy. Most pastors say seminary couldn't prepare them for a world that moves this quickly. Also, their wives feel the pressure to find their place. Can they be all things to all people—congregation, husband, children? Forty percent of Rev. London's mail comes from angry, frightened, hurting pastors' wives. And most of them are worried about their husbands' health and emotions.

Another concern is the expectation for the pastor's children to behave well and be involved in all the youth activities.

Insecurity. Rev. London quickly lists four insecure areas for pastors: finances, lack of medical insurance, poor retirement benefits and the fear of forced termination. This does not take into account power structures within the congregation or an attitude resistant to change from some of the church family.

Many pastors are living below the poverty level. One pastor's wife wrote Rev. London that she and her husband cried when they received an unexpected gift of $200. They had never had $200 discretionary income in their entire married life.

"Our goal is to help establish and restore the pastors and their families," says Rev. London, "so they can give their people more than they could in their previously weakened or burned-out condition.

"We believe the church is the first line of defense for the family. When you start messing with the basic fiber of the church, you weaken society."

Focus on the Family, *1 January 1993.*

Pastoral Survey

A 1991 survey of pastors by Fuller Institute of Church Growth revealed that

- 90 percent of pastors work more than forty-six hours per week.
- 80 percent believe that pastoral ministry is affecting their families negatively.
- 33 percent say that "Being in ministry is clearly a hazard to my family."

- 75 percent have reported a significant crisis due to stress at least once in their ministry.
- 50 percent feel unable to meet the needs of the job.
- 90 percent feel they have not been adequately trained to cope with the ministry demands placed on them.
- 40 percent reported a serious conflict with a parishioner at least once a month.
- 70 percent of pastors do not have someone they would consider a close friend.
- 37 percent have been involved in inappropriate sexual behavior with someone in the church.
- 70 percent have a lower self-image after they've pastored than when they started.

Fuller Institute of Church Growth, 1991 survey.

Ready to Break

You may remember the incident at the nuclear power plant at Three Mile Island. There was a fifty-six-foot reactor. Inside of it, on April 1, 1979, a hydrogen bubble occupying the space of a bedroom was present. On April 2, the bubble suddenly grew smaller, to the size of a closet. The best scientists in America didn't know why the bubble developed in the first place or why it shrank or if it would explode. It was against this backdrop that a man wrote a letter to a radio pastor, not about the crisis at Three Mile Island, but about the crisis inside himself and the bubble about to break in his own life. This is what he wrote:

"Apparently everything is going to calm down at Three Mile Island. I'm glad because I live nearby. My own life is kind of a hydrogen bubble about to blow up, or maybe there's going to be a meltdown. My anxiety about my life is just at an unbearable level. I feel such awful guilt about things I've done in the past. Like the accident at Three Mile, it's due to human errors; my errors. Now, just a few sins in my life seem to have triggered something terrible. Frankly, the others here have been worried about Three Mile Island; but I've been worried about my inward life. If the nuclear goes, that might solve my problems . . . but I feel as though I will explode first. I need peace. I haven't lost my mind, my children, or my wife. In fact, they really aren't aware of how far my life has gotten out of hand. Can you understand how I feel?"

SUCCESS

The person who succeeds is not the one who holds back, fearing failure, nor the one who never fails . . . but rather the one who moves on in spite of failure. Far better it is to dare mighty things, to win glorious triumphs, even though checkered by failure, than to take rank with those poor spirits who neither enjoy much nor suffer much because they live in the gray twilight that knows not victory or defeat.

Teddy Roosevelt

God willing, I will push and politick no more. . . . The mountains are too high, history is too long, and eternity is longer. God is too great, man is too small, there are many of God's dear children, and all around there are men going to Hell. And if one man and a small group of men do not approve of where I am and what I do, does it prove I've missed success?

Francis A. Schaeffer

My inclination is to think that Christ meant it in a very literal way when He said to seek the lower seats. That does not mean, as I see it, that we should refuse the higher if the Lord takes us there, but He should do the taking.

Francis A. Schaeffer

> Success exposes a man to the pressure of people and thus tempts him to hold on to his gains by means of fleshly methods and practices, and to let himself be ruled wholly by the dictatorial demands of incessant expansion.
>
> *Charles H. Spurgeon*

The High Cost of Success

In Herman Melville's novel *White Jacket* one of the sailors takes sick with severe stomach pains. Dr. Cuticle, the ship's surgeon, is delighted to have a patient with something more challenging to his art than blisters. He diagnoses appendicitis. Several shipmates are impressed into nursing service. The deckhand is laid out on the operating table and prepared for surgery. Dr. Cuticle goes at his work with verve and skill. He makes his cuts with precision, and, on the way to excising the diseased organ, points out interesting anatomical details to the attendants around the table, who had never before seen the interior of an abdomen. He is absorbed in his work, and obviously good at it. All in all it is an impressive performance, but the sailor attendants are, to a man, not impressed but appalled. The poor patient, by the time he has been sewn up, has been a long time dead on the table. Dr. Cuticle, enthusiastic in his surgery, hadn't noticed. The sailors, shy in their subservience, didn't tell him.

Eugene H. Peterson, Working the Angles *(Grand Rapids, Mich.: Eerdmans, 1987), 74.*

You're Getting ahead of Me

Is it worth obsessing about people getting ahead of you? Take a look at where it can lead:

One day in late 1969, in the research library of the University of California at Berkeley, a young man went berserk. He ran through the library, shouting hysterically at his astonished fellow students, "Stop! Stop! You're getting ahead of me!"

He was arrested. But what was his crime, really? *Being in the wrong decade.* As we all know, the sixties era, and its childish preoccupation with peace, good sex, and battered VW buses, was little more than a black mark, a shameful demerit in the History of Stress.

. . . In the stress-filled eighties, this concept of "getting ahead of me" regained its right place of importance. In fact, it is one of the basic precepts of stress.

Simply stated, *people are getting ahead of you.* All the time.

While you're at your desk, people working out at the gym are getting ahead of you.

While you're at the gym, your coworkers are getting ahead of you.

If a friend gets a promotion at work, she has gotten ahead of you.

If a colleague reads a book you haven't read, he has gotten ahead of you. . . .

The beauty of this concept is that it can be applied across the board, anywhere, anytime.

On the road? Drivers of more expensive cars have gotten ahead of you.

Watching TV? All the writers, actors, and technical crews have gotten ahead of you.

At Marine World? The *dolphins* have gotten ahead of you.

Always judge yourself, and your intrinsic moral worth, in terms of specific achievements as compared to others.

Always judge any situation in relation to how much the people involved have gotten ahead of you, and in what ways.

Doug Sherman and William Hendricks, Your Work Matters to God *(Colorado Springs, Colo.: NavPress, 1987), 37–38.*

A Lousy Mailman

See page 337

Living Well but Not Successfully
See page 284

SUFFERING

God whispers to us in our pleasures, speaks in our conscience, but shouts in our pains: it is His megaphone to rouse a deaf world.
C.S. Lewis

A person can respond to suffering like an egg, or like a potato. A potato goes into the boiling water hard, but comes out pliable. An egg goes into the boiling water soft and comes out hard.
Anonymous

Christ's cross is such a burden as sails are to a ship or wings to a bird.
Samuel Rutherford, writing from prison

Discipleship means allegiance to the suffering Christ, and it is therefore not at all surprising that Christians should be called upon to suffer.
Dietrich Bonhoeffer

One advantage of being thrown on your back is that you face heaven.
Bishop Fulton Sheen

Every person alive fits somewhere onto a scale of suffering that ranges from little to much. However much suffering we have to endure, there are always those below us who suffer less, and those above us who suffer more. The problem is, we usually like to compare ourselves only with those who suffer less. That way we can pity ourselves and pretend we're at the top of the scale. But when we face reality and stand beside those who suffer more, our purple heart medals don't shine so brightly.
Joni Eareckson Tada

Suppose you eliminated suffering, what a dreadful place the world would be. I would almost rather eliminate happiness. The world would be the most ghastly place because everything that corrects the tendency of this unspeakable little creature, man, to feel over-important and over-pleased with himself would disappear. He's bad enough now, but he would be absolutely intolerable if he never suffered.

Malcolm Muggeridge

God pity those who cannot say,
"Not mine but thine," who only pray,
"Let this cup pass," and cannot see
The purpose in Gethsemane.

E. W. Wilcox

The soul would have no rainbow if the eye had no tears.

John Piper

He [Christ] did not come to suffer as little as He could; He did not turn away His face from the suffering; He confronted it, or, as I may say, He breasted it, that every particular portion of it might make its due impression on Him.

John Henry Cardinal Newman

I cannot keep the song of the lark when I get the seal of sonship; I must enter into the pain of my Lord. Yet that pain is better than the world's joy. . . . Put the scar of sympathy in my heart! Let me feel my brother's thorn!

George Matheson

To choose to suffer means that there is something wrong; to choose God's will even if it means suffering is a very different thing. No healthy saint ever chooses suffering; he chooses God's will, as Jesus did, whether it means suffering or not.

Oswald Chambers

Dark Threads the Weaver Needs

Herbert Lockyer wrote a book entitled *Dark Threads the Weaver Needs.* It's a book on human suffering and how we w.restle with it. Mr. Lockyer titled his book after a poem written by an unknown Christian author. The poem reads as follows:

My life is but a weaving, between my Lord and me;
I cannot choose the colours. He worketh steadily.
Ofttimes He weaveth sorrow and I in foolish pride,
forget He sees the upper and I the under side.
Not till the loom is silent and the shuttles cease to fly,
shall God unroll the canvas and explain the reason why,
the dark threads are as needful in the Weaver's skillful hand,
as the threads of gold and silver, in the pattern He has planned.
Unknown

The Pattern of Suffering

The experiences of many East European Christians who lived under Communism portray a pattern of suffering transformed to opportunity and blessing. We need to remember how it was for them.

The experience of Volodia, a Russian believer, illustrates such a divine paradox. In his last year of medical school, when school officials discovered he was a Christian, Volodia was threatened with expulsion from school. "You choose—either God or diploma," the Communist authorities demanded.

Volodia's mentors tried to ensure that Volodia, the best student in his class, would choose to graduate. For several months they conducted indoctrination sessions intended to force the student to renounce his faith.

One day, unannounced, a Communist party official visited Volodia's class and declared, "Strange things have been happening in our university. There is a rumor that some students are trying to believe in God. We want to find out if this is true. I am going to ask Volodia to come forward and clarify this rumor," the official concluded.

Struck by the shock of being summoned, Volodia understood. He was being offered a final chance to renounce his faith. "For twenty minutes I had the opportunity of my lifetime to tell my fellow students about Christ," Volodia, who was soon expelled from university, later told Christians in the West.

Life Goes Better with Affliction
See page 2

Opposition to the Salvation Army
See page 309

Church Growth
See page 306

T

TALENTS

In the battle for existence, talent is the punch, and tact is the clever footwork.
Wilson Mizner

It is my own theory that while talents may diminish with age, gifts only seem to improve and deepen with the passing of years.
Gail MacDonald

TEMPTATION

Thomas Becket: The last temptation is the greatest treason: To do the right deed for the wrong reason.
T. S. Eliot, Murder in the Cathedral

When you flee temptation, leave no forwarding address.
Anonymous

Without temptation no sin would be committed; and without temptation no holiness could be attained. The human wrecks that seem beyond all capacity of repair and refitting, and victorious athletes of righteousness whom their fellowmen adore, are alike the products of temptation.
James Hastings

The Full Force of Temptation

Comments from C. S. Lewis on temptation:

A silly idea is current that good people do not know what temptation means. This is an obvious lie. Only those who try to resist temptation know how strong it is. After all, you find out the strength of the German army by fighting against it, not by giving in. You find out the strength of a wind by trying to walk against it, not by lying down. A man who gives in to temptation after five minutes simply does not know what it would have been like an hour later. That is why bad people, in one sense, know very little about badness. They have lived a sheltered life by always giving in. We never find out the strength of the evil impulse inside us until we try to fight it; and Christ, because He was the only man who never yielded to temptation, is also the only man who knows to the full what temptation means—the only complete realist.

C. S. Lewis, Mere Christianity *(New York: Macmillan, 1952), 124–125.*

Slumbering Inclination

In our members there is a slumbering inclination towards desire which is both sudden and fierce. . . . It makes no difference whether it is sexual desire, or ambition, or vanity, or desire for revenge, or love of fame and power, or greed for money, or finally, that strange desire for the beauty of the world, of nature. Joy in God is in the course of being extinguished in us and we seek all our joy in the creature. At this moment God is quite unreal to us, he loses all reality, and only desire for the creature is real; the only reality is the devil. Satan does not here fill us with hatred of God, but with forgetfulness of God.

Dietrich Bonhoeffer, Temptation *(London: SCM, 1961), 33.*

The Deadly Sweetness of Sin

See page 391

THANKSGIVING

Surely praise and thanksgiving are ever to be the great characteristics of the Christian life.
Martyn Lloyd-Jones

Praise distinguishes the Christian particularly in his prayer and in his worship. . . . The highest point of all worship and prayer is adoration and praise and thanksgiving.
Martyn Lloyd-Jones

No Thanks

Years ago, Northwestern University had a life-saving team that assisted passengers on Lake Michigan boats. On September 8, 1860, the *Lady Elgin* floundered near the campus, and a ministerial student named Edward Spencer personally rescued seventeen people. The exposure from that episode permanently damaged his health and he was unable to continue preparation for the ministry. Some years later when he died, it was noted that not one of the seventeen people he had saved ever came back to thank him.

Warren Wiersbe, Be Complete *(Wheaton, Ill.: Victor, 1981), 43.*

Never-Ending Thanks

An elderly woman once said to Charles H. Spurgeon, "Ah, Mr. Spurgeon, if Jesus Christ does save me, He shall never hear the end of it."

Much Obliged, Lord

Fulton Oursler learned the lesson of a grateful heart from an African-American woman who helped care for him when he was a little boy. Every time she sat down to eat, she would bow her head and say, "Much obliged, Lord." Oursler asked her why she did this, because the food was there for her to enjoy whether she gave thanks or not. She replied, "Sure we get our vittles, but it makes everything taste better to be grateful. Looking for good things is a kind of game an old preacher taught me to play. Take this morning. I woke up and thought, *What's there to praise God for today?* You know what? I couldn't think of a thing! Then from the kitchen came the most delicious odor that ever tickled my nose. Coffee! 'Much obliged, Lord, for the coffee,' I said, 'and much obliged, too, for the smell of it.'"

Many years later, Oursler stood at the bedside of that woman as she lay dying. Seeing her in much pain, he wondered if she could still find something to be grateful for. Just then she opened her eyes. As she saw him and the others gathered around, she folded her hands and said with a smile, "Much obliged, Lord, for such fine friends."

Thank You, John. I Thank You.
See page 426

The Beggar Is a King
See page 19

TIME

Journey into Space

Sergei Krikalev isn't a household name. In April of 1991 he was living a comfortable life in Leningrad earning five hundred rubles a month. Krikalev believed in the Communist party and endorsed the leadership of Mikhail Gorbachev. He dismissed Boris Yeltsin as a political nobody.

Sergei Krikalev, a Russian cosmonaut, was shot into space as part of the Soviet space program. Due to events beyond his control, his five-month journey stretched into ten months before he landed back on earth. When he returned, he entered a new world called the Commonwealth of Independent States. The old Soviet Union had come apart at the seams. His hometown of Leningrad was renamed St. Petersburg. Gorbachev had become a capitalist signing million dollar book deals. The insignificant Yeltsin was now president of

Russia. The Communist party had lost its power and Krikalev's five hundred-rubles-a-month salary couldn't even purchase a pair of scissors to cut the USSR insignia off his tattered uniform. In less than a year, and without warning while Sergei Krikalev circled the earth, a new era began.

Throughout the world new eras have burst upon us. With today's society so vastly different from the recent past, we can identify with Dorothy when she said to her dog in *The Wizard of Oz,* "Toto, I don't think we're in Kansas anymore." New technologies, new attitudes, new groups emerging in our society, force us into a world of constant, unremitting change.

Haddon Robinson, "On Target," Focal Point *(Denver Seminary).*

TOLERANCE

Now, in those days the saints did not say, as the sham saints do now, "We must be largely charitable, and leave this brother to his own opinion; he sees truth from a different standpoint, and has a rather different way of putting it, but his opinions are as good as our own, and we must not say that he is in error." That is at present the fashionable way of trifling with divine truth, and making things pleasant all around.

Charles H. Spurgeon

I never told my own religion nor scrutinized that of another. I never attempted to make a convert, nor wished to change another's creed.

Thomas Jefferson

Suing over Shunning

Witness the instance in which an Amish believer sued his church for censoring his behavior by the discipline the Amish call "shunning." The plaintiff, although he lost in court, won considerable outside sympathy. Not, of course, that the outsiders were interested in the integrity of the beliefs and practices of the Amish community, but because it is thought to be a civil right not to be publicly accused of sin. The demolition of the difference between good and evil is the secularized bastardization of Luther's *simul eustus et peccator.* The pursuit of holiness and the vitality of the churches in our day require a recovery of the practice of Christian discipline.

Richard John Neuhaus, Freedom for Ministry *(Grand Rapids, Mich.: Eerdmans, 1979), 215.*

THE TONGUE

The scorpion carries his poison in his tail, the slanderer carries his in his tongue.

Thomas Watson

To the physician, it is merely a two ounce slab of mucous membrane enclosing a complex array of muscles and nerves that enable our bodies to chew, taste, and swallow. . . . [However] without the tongue no mother could sing her baby to sleep tonight. No ambassador could adequately represent our nation. No teacher could stretch the mind of students. . . . No pastor could comfort troubled souls. No complicated, controversial issue could ever be discussed and solved. Our entire world would be reduced to grunts and shrugs.

Chuck Swindoll

Foul-Mouthed Staffordshire Bill

Staffordshire Bill was foul-mouthed—so much so that even the roughest of his worldly acquaintances were sickened by him—one of the reasons why he always found himself left to his own company, in some deserted corner of the place where they were drinking. With Staffordshire Bill's conversion there came the conviction that he must do something about his foul mouth. He realized that it was dishonoring to God and offensive to man. . . . But he discovered that he was up against something that was too strong for him. He could not speak without swearing, he could not utter a sentence that was not peppered with oaths and blasphemies. He could not help it and he could not stop it.

The truth is that he did not know that he was doing it until the words were out, and then the realization that these horrible terms and words came from his own lips sickened and shamed him and he was driven to a frenzy of despair and to abject misery. . . . He suffered for some weeks, little dreaming that deliverance was at hand.

It came about in this way: he was getting up one morning and gathering his clothes together to get dressed. But there were no socks among his clothes. He went to the bedroom door and shouted to his wife, "I can't find my ——— socks! Where are the ——— things?" As he heard himself, and realized what he had just said, a great horror possessed him and he fell back on the bed in a paroxysm of despair. He cried aloud: "O Lord, cleanse my tongue. O Lord, I can't ask for a pair of socks without swearing. Please have mercy on me and give me a clean tongue."

As he lay there and then got up from that bed, he knew that God had done for him what he could not do for himself. His prayer, his cry of agony was heard and answered. It was his own testimony that from that moment to the end of his days no swear word or foul or blasphemous word ever again passed his lips.

Bethan Lloyd-Jones, Memories of Sandfields *(Carlisle, Penn.: Banner of Truth Trust), 87–88.*

TRANSFORMATION

Caesar hoped to reform men by changing institutions, and laws; Christ wished to remake institutions, and lessen laws by changing men.

Will Durant

TRIALS

If I am told that I am to take a journey that is a dangerous trip, every jolt along the way reminds me that I am on the right road.

F. B. Meyer

A Monument to the Boll Weevil

See page 129

TRUST

An Embarrassing Lesson in Faith

See page 155

TRUTH

In times of war, the truth is so precious, it must be attended by a bodyguard of lies.

Winston Churchill

TYRANNY

Whoever has experienced the power, the unrestrained ability to humiliate another human being . . . automatically loses power over his own sensations. Tyranny is a habit, it has its own organic life, it develops finally into a disease.

Dostoevsky

U

UNBELIEF

It is not enough to say that natural man views God as an enemy. We must be more precise. God is our *mortal* enemy. He represents the highest possible threat to our sinful desires. His repugnance to us is absolute, knowing no lesser degrees.
R. C. Sproul

No one rejects Christ on philosophical grounds, but the rejection of God's light brings the worst darkness.
A. W. Tozer

Phil Donahue Doesn't Get It

Celebrated talk-show host Phil Donahue gave some reasons why he has left his faith:

If God the Father is so all-loving, why didn't He come down and go to Calvary? Then Jesus could have said, "This is my Father in whom I am well-pleased." . . . How could an all-knowing, all-loving God allow His Son to be murdered on a cross in order that He might redeem my sins?

Light Became Dark

Hugh Hefner was raised in a minister's home. Joseph Stalin studied for the priesthood. Mao Tse-tung was raised under missionary teaching. The very light of Christ can become darkness.

Too Late to Rethink the Place of Jesus

Ben Haden tells a story about a hospital visit he made at 3:30 A.M. to see a man he had known for years. The man was dying, and he knew it, so Pastor Haden asked him how it was between him and the Lord.

"Oh," he said, "I've always believed in God, and I know everything is shipshape."

"What do you believe about Jesus?" Haden asked the man.

"I've known God all my life," the man said, "and I've tried to observe godly standards. I've been honest in business, and I haven't made my money crookedly; I've worked for it, and I've worked hard."

"My friend," said Pastor Haden, "and I wouldn't be here if I weren't your friend, answer a straight question: How is it between you and Jesus?"

The man replied: "I've never made a place in my life for Jesus. I don't believe in Jesus. If I were to believe in Jesus, it would upset everything I've thought—my philosophy and my life, and I would have to rethink everything about me."

"By the grace of God," said Pastor Haden, "you have that kind of time; rethink it."

"No," the man said, "I will die without Jesus."

"Why, then, do you think Jesus died?" asked the pastor.

"Oh, I understand He died for sins."

"Your sins," Pastor Haden emphasized.

"Perhaps, perhaps, but it's too late in my life to rethink the place of Jesus. . . . I will die without Jesus." And he did.

Left with Nothing

See page 100

Faith in Faith

See page 150

It Takes More than a Rhinoceros-Hide Whip

See page 83

UNITY

External visible unity is not required for the invisible unity of the church.
Bishop Westcott

Thomas Payne once said as he addressed the First Continental Congress, "If we do not hang together, we will hang separately."

Trespasses or Debts

Two congregations were located only a few blocks from each other in a small community. They thought it might be better if they merged and became one united body, larger and more effective, rather than two struggling churches. Good idea . . . but they weren't able to pull it off. The problem? They couldn't agree on how they should recite the Lord's Prayer. One group wanted "forgive us our trespasses," while the other demanded "forgive us our debts." A newspaper reported that one church went back to its trespasses while the other returned to its debts.

The People Who Love Each Other

Several years ago, Johanne Lukassé of the Belgian Evangelical Mission came to the realization that evangelism in Belgium was going nowhere. The nation's long history of traditional Catholicism, the subsequent disillusionment resulting from *Vatican II,* and the aggression of the cults had left the country seemingly impervious to the gospel. Driven to the Scripture, he read John 1:18-35, and devised a plan. First, he gathered together a heterogeneous group: Belgians, Dutchmen, Americans—whoever would come. Second, he had them rent a house and live together for seven months. As is natural, frictions developed as the believers rubbed against one another. This, in turn, sent them to prayer and victory and love. Finally, they went out and began to see amazing fruit. Outsiders called them, "the people who love each other."

Piano Tuning

A. W. Tozer gave this illustration in his book *The Pursuit of God*:

If you have one hundred concert pianos, and you tune the second piano to the first, and the third piano to the second, and the fourth piano to the third, until you have tuned all one hundred pianos accordingly, you will still have discord and disharmony. But if you tuned each piano to the same tuning fork, you would have unity and harmony. So, too, in the body of Christ. When we each tune ourselves and our lives to Christ's, we will have unity.

A. W. Tozer, The Pursuit of God *(Wheaton, Ill.: Tyndale), 97.*

V

VANITY

If you give a sportsman's cremated remains to Canuck's Sportsman's Memorials, they will, for a price, load the ashes in a shotgun shell, take the shell on a hunting trip and shoot it at a duck or other game animal of your choice. Ashes to ashes, we always say, bucks to ducks.

Dave Barry

A Heart after All

See page 106

VICTORY IN CHRIST

We are not babes in the woods—we are God's people and, no matter how it looks now, we are going to inherit this earth and rule it. The devil may be the prince of this world, but the earth is the Lord's and the fullness thereof, and He will set up His kingdom and His people will be in charge of it.

Vance Havner

VISION

All men dream; but not equally.
Those who dream by night in the dusty
recesses of their minds

Awake to find that it was vanity;
But the dreamers of day are dangerous men,
That they may act their dreams with open
eyes to make it possible.
T. E. Lawrence

The Right to Sell Coca-Cola

You've heard the story about the Atlanta soda fountain where the nerve tonic syrup was mistakenly mixed with carbonated water instead of plain water. The result was the drink now known as Coca-Cola. Among the people who came to Asa Chandler's drugstore to enjoy the new taste was a businessman named B. N. Thomas. Thomas felt that there might be a future in bottling the drink for home consumption, but Chandler thought it a futile idea. So Chandler sold Thomas the right to sell Coca-Cola by the bottle . . . for the grand total of one dollar. Chandler gave away a multimillion dollar industry because he could not see its future. How much of what God has for us do we fail to realize because our vision is so limited?

Dynamic Preaching, *vol. 1, no. 4 (January/February 1986): 55.*

VULNERABILITY

When I got my first TV set, I stopped caring so much about having close relationships. . . . You can only be hurt if you care a lot.

Andy Warhol

WEAKNESS

A Beautiful Distortion

Impressionist painter Claude Monet had cataracts which distorted his perception, but he used this distortion to paint his water lilies, and what we experience in his paintings is delicacy, lightness, beauty, and softness—coming not from perfect eyesight, but from perfect insight into the more subtle characteristics of nature.

Dynamic Preaching, *vol. 5, no. 2 (February 1990): 8.*

WEALTH

All the Pain Money Can Buy

Oh, to be as rich as Christina Onassis. Money can solve so many problems.

For example, say you're living in Europe, and your favorite drink, Diet Coke, is available only in the United States. No problem. Just dispatch your private jet to America once a month for a fresh supply of cola, the way Christina did, at a cost of $30,000 per trip for fuel and pilots' salaries.

Or say you're on a vacation in Austria, and you realize you've left your favorite David Bowie tape back home in Switzerland.

Don't worry—just order your helicopter pilot to fly back

and get it, the way Christina did. And if you crave 24-hour companionship, but your friends complain that they're too busy to spend all their time with you, the solution is simple. Offer them cash (say $20,000 or $30,000 a month) to be your pal, and they'll come running. At least, that's what Christina found.

With an annual income estimated at around $50 million, the heiress daughter of Greek shipping tycoon Aristotle Onassis could buy just about anything she wanted—except, it would seem, happiness. Her childhood was largely rootless and lonely, marred by her parents' divorce and her overbearing but beloved father's frequent absences; her adult years included four ill-advised marriages, periods of depression, and several suicide attempts.

Within two years she lost four family members: Her father died of a degenerative muscular disease; her brother was killed in a plane crash; her mother died of an apparent drug overdose; and her aunt was found dead under suspicious circumstances.

Christina herself died young, at age 37, of a heart attack possibly brought on by repeated bouts of dieting, tremendous weight fluctuations and the overuse of amphetamines and barbiturates.

William Wright, Chicago Tribune, *11 March 1991, sec. 5, p. 3; a book review of* All the Pain That Money Can Buy *(Simon & Schuster). The book is a biography about Christina Onassis.*

WILL

Without Chests

C. S. Lewis wrote an essay called "Without Chests." Observes Chuck Colson:

It's a wonderful article about the will. He [Lewis] said the intellect can't control the passions of the stomach except by means of the will—which is the chest. But we mock honor—and then we are alarmed when there are traitors in our midst. It is like making geldings, he said, and then bidding them to multiply. He was talking abut the loss of character in 1947 and 1948, long before the results we are witnessing today of the loss of character in American life.

Charles Colson, Sources: The Problem of Ethics, *no. 2, Wilberforce Forum: 1992 Prison Fellowship.*

Prepared to Live a Truly Christian Life

See page 351

WITNESSING

If I had been with him any longer, I would have been compelled to be a Christian, and he never spoke to me about it at all.

Sir Henry Stanley on David Livingstone's witness

Bishop John Taylor Smith's One Question

Bishop John Taylor Smith, who was Honorary Chaplain to Queen Victoria and the Chaplain General of the British army during World War I, was a man beloved by all. He was "Everybody's Bishop"—jovial, rotund, saintly, a favorite at Keswick.

Bishop Smith used to ask all the candidates for the chaplaincy one question: "Now, I want you to show me how you would deal with a man. We will suppose I am a soldier who has been wounded on the field of battle. I have three minutes to live and I am afraid to die, because I do not know Christ. Tell me, how may I be saved and die with the assurance that all is well?" If the applicant began to beat around the bush and talk about the true church and ordinances and so on, the good bishop would say, "That won't do. I have only three minutes to live. Tell me what I must do." And as long as Bishop Smith was Chaplain General, unless a candidate could answer that question, he could not become a chaplain in the army.

H. A. Ironside, Lectures on the Book of Acts *(Neptune, N.J.: Loizeaux, 1943), 384.*

Billy Bray's True Happiness

In the last century, Billy Bray, a dynamite Christian, lived across the Atlantic. This Cornish miner was so effervescent, so overflowing with Christ, that wherever he went, men trusted Christ. Each day as he went down into the mines—very dangerous in those days—he would pray with the miners as he went down. "Lord, if any of us must be killed or die today, let it be me. Let not one of these men die, for they are not happy and I am, and if I die today I shall go to be in heaven." It was rumored that at times, when he got to the bottom of those mines, the other miners would all be on their knees.

J. Gilchrist Lawson, Deeper Experiences of Famous Christians *(Chicago: Glad Tidings), 267.*

Divine Appointments

Ian Thomas tells the story of getting on an airplane and being dead tired, so tired that he planned to curl up and sleep. Then he heard a *psssst* and then another *psssst,* and looking in the direction of the sound, he heard a man say, "I'm reading in the Bible about Nicodemus in John 3, and I don't understand it. Do you know anything about the Bible?"

Kent Hughes experienced a similar thing when flying back to Chicago from a missions conference in California. He had been busy the whole week and was looking forward to reading C. S. Lewis's *Letters to Malcolm,* but as he got on the plane he prayed, *Lord, if you want me to share Christ with someone, I'm willing.* When he sat down, the seat next to him was already occupied by a young man who was reading an Isaac Asimov novel. Pastor Hughes took out his book and said, "Are you enjoying your book?" The result? He didn't even remember the jet taking off or the meal as he shared Christ with a young man who lived within five blocks of Pastor Hughes's former residence in California. It was the shortest trip to Chicago he had ever taken. He was so caught up in a divine appointment that he left his copy of *Letters to Malcolm* on the plane.

Thank You, John. I Thank You.

John Albert Broadus was one of the greatest New Testament and homiletics scholars of his day. He was from a small town, where he was converted to Christ. Shortly after his conversion, Broadus witnessed to a friend and classmate named Sandy Jones. He said, "I wish you would become a Christian, Sandy."

"Well, I don't know; perhaps I will," the awkward Sandy replied.

And sure enough, Sandy did accept Christ at the small church in the town. Afterward he walked over to John Broadus, held out his hand, and said, "Thank you, John. I thank you."

John Broadus left the town and launched a distinguished ministry as preacher, seminary president, and teacher of homiletics. Sandy Jones stayed in the small town and became a farmer. However, Broadus returned home often, and every time John and Sandy met, Sandy greeted John with, "Thank you, John. I thank you."

Sandy died before Dr. Broadus did, and Dr. Broadus is reported to have said, "I think the sound sweetest to my ears in heaven, next to the welcome of Jesus, whom I have tried to serve, will be the welcome of Sandy Jones, as he will thrust out his big hand and say, 'Howdy, John; I thank you.'"

Friend of Sinners
See page 265

A Cloud of Witnesses
See page 109

Are You Saved?
See page 366

WORK

This book, being about work, is, by its very nature, about violence—to the spirit as well as to the body. It is about ulcers as well as accidents. About shouting matches as well as fist fights. About nervous breakdowns as well as kicking the dog around. It is, above all (or beneath all), about daily humiliations. To survive the day is triumph enough.

Studs Terkel

Most middle-class Americans tend to worship their work, to work at their play, and to play at their worship. As a result, their meanings and values are distorted. Their relationships disintegrate faster than they can keep them in repair, and their lifestyles resemble a cast of characters in search of a plot.

Gordon Dahl

There is a perennial nobleness, and even sacredness in work . . . A man perfects himself by working. All work, even cotton spinning, is noble. Work alone is noble.

Thomas Carlyle

They talk of the dignity of work, bosh. The dignity is in the leisure.

Herman Melville

We don't consider manual work as a curse, or a bitter necessity, not even as a means of making a living. We consider it as a high human function. As a basis of human life. The most dignified thing in the life of a human

being and which ought to be free, creative. Men ought to be proud of it.
David Ben-Gurion

The laboring man has not leisure for a true integrity day by day. He has no time but to be anything but a machine.
Henry David Thoreau

Possibly the greatest malaise in our country today is our neurotic compulsion to work.
William McNamara

We know that each height, each step, must be gained by patient, laborious toil, and that wishing cannot take the place of working.
Edward Whymper

Sin worketh,
Let me work too.
Sin undoeseth,
Let me do.
Busy as sin
My work I'll ply,
Til I rest in the rest
of Eternity
Andrew Bonar

If anything is worth doing, it is worth doing well.
Anonymous

There are two ways to get to the top of an oak tree: struggle to the top or sit on an acorn until it grows.
Anonymous

Do Not Waste Time

After Michelangelo died, someone found in his studio a piece of paper on which he had written a note to his apprentice, in the handwriting of his old age: "Draw, Antonio, draw and do not waste time."
Annie Dillard, The Writing Life *(New York: Harper & Row, 1989), 79.*

The Best Workers

Walter Sawatsky, in *Soviet Evangelicals Since World War II,* tells this story: He overheard two Soviet factory managers in a Moscow restaurant. One told the other that party officials were pressuring him to fire evangelicals in his plant, but he would not because the evangelicals were his best workers.

The Sears Wish Book

Sears Roebuck Company had trouble keeping employees working in its assembly plant in Panama. The laborers lived in an agrarian, barter economy, but Sears paid them in cash. Thus, the average employee had more cash after a week's work than he had ever seen, and so would quit working. He did not need the job anymore. What was Sears's solution? They gave all their employees a Sears catalog. No one quit after that, because they all wanted the previously undreamed-of things they saw in that book.

All-Consuming Choice

Terence Fox was the president and chief executive officer of Iroquois Brands, Ltd., of Greenwich, Connecticut. They sell liquor. When asked how he had become so successful so quickly he said that at fifteen his most burning ambition was to be wealthy by thirty. At twenty he quit Marquette University and went to work on Wall Street, later getting his degree by attending night school. The six years he spent on Wall Street told him there was no better place to make a lot of money legally. He saw he could make a lot if he worked hard.

And what did that involve? A twenty-four-hours-a-day, seven-days-a-week commitment. "My golf game went from a four to a twelve handicap; I stopped hunting; my marriage faltered after five years. I am never home, I am constantly traveling between our fourteen plants, and on many a Saturday night while I am having dinner alone in a strange airport I say to myself, *You are here because you chose to be.*"

A Bright Idea
See page 125

Personal Responsibility Comes Home
See page 233

A Self-Checkup
See page 234

WORLDLINESS

> Large and influential sections of the world of fundamental Christianity have gone overboard for practices wholly unscriptural, altogether unjustifiable in the light of historic Christian truth, and deeply damaging to the inner life of the individual Christian.
>
> *A. W. Tozer*

WORRY

Never Cross the Fox before You Reach It

When Abraham Lincoln was on his way to Washington to be inaugurated, he spent some time in New York with Horace Greeley and told him an anecdote that was meant to be an answer to the question everybody was asking him: Are we really going to have civil war?

In his circuit-riding days, Lincoln and his companions, riding to the next session of court, had crossed many rivers. But the Fox River was still ahead of them; and they said one to another, "If these streams give us so much trouble, how shall we get over the Fox River?"

When darkness fell, they stopped for the night at a log tavern, where they fell in with the Methodist presiding elder of the district, who rode through the country in all kinds of weather and knew all about the Fox River. They gathered about him and asked him about the present state of the river. "Oh, yes," replied the circuit rider, "I know all about the Fox River. I have crossed it often and understand it well. But I have one fixed rule with regard to the Fox River—I never cross it till I reach it."

WORSHIP

Life is delightfully full of repetitions, and we need them as much as we need complete newness, provided we keep the principle of faith at work in each repetition. Otherwise, we become guilty of vain repetition.
Harold Best

[Worship is] to quicken the conscience by the holiness of God, to feed the mind with the truth of God, to purge the imagination by the beauty of God, to open up the heart to the love of God, to devote that will to the purpose of God.
William Temple

If thou wouldst thus leave thy heart with God on Saturday night, thou shouldst find it with him in the Lord's Day morning.
Puritan preacher George Swinnock

Make all the services of worship spiritual. Let there be a spiritual unction, a reality, throughout all you do or say in God's house, and as his official servant.
Charles Simeon

The Abandonment of Happiness

"Smile, God loves you!" exhorts a little yellow button on a million Christian breasts. Tremble, God loves you! Weep, God loves you! Persevere, God loves you! Repent, God loves you! As Dorothy Day of *Catholic Worker* notoriety kept saying, "God's is a harsh and dreadful love." The celebration that we call worship has less to do with the satisfaction of the pursuit of happiness than with the abandonment of the pursuit of happiness. The Christian proposition is that only as we enter into the pathos and promise of God's love do we discover the peace that surpasses what is understood by happiness.

Richard John Neuhaus, Freedom for Ministry *(Grand Rapids, Mich.: Eerdmans, 1979), 139.*

A Mockery of Worship

The feature article of an October 1978 issue of *Harper's Magazine* entitled "Trendier than Thou" told that the bishop of California, Kilmer Myers, welcomed Bay Area transcendentalists to Grace Cathedral for light shows, guitar liturgies, nature festivals, and pagan ceremonials. Said the article, "In 1971, during one nature ceremony in the cathedral, a decidedly ecumenical audience watched reverently as the poet Allen Ginsberg, wearing a deer mask, joined others similarly garbed to ordain Senators Alan Cranston and John Tunney as godfathers of animals. . . . The cathedral dean was dimly seen through marijuana smoke, wrestling atop the high altar to remove a cameraman, while movie projectors simultaneously cast images of buffalo herds and other endangered species on the walls and ceilings, to the accompaniment of rock music. Although Episcopal priests had protested that this vigil would be a 'profane employment of this sacred house of worship,' Bishop Myers joined in nonetheless and offered prayers for a 'renaissance of reverence for life in America.'"

"Trendier than Thou," Harper's Magazine, *October 1978.*

Adoring Silence

A. W. Tozer, in the preface of his classic book *The Knowledge of the Holy,* explains why he wrote the book:

With our loss of the sense of the majesty has come the further loss of religious awe and consciousness of the divine presence. We have lost our spirit of worship and our ability to withdraw inwardly to meet God in adoring silence.

Modern Christianity is simply not producing the kind of Christian who can appreciate or experience the life in the Spirit. The words, "Be still, and know that I am God," mean next to nothing to the self-confident, bustling worshiper . . . of the twentieth century.

A. W. Tozer, The Knowledge of the Holy *(New York: Harper & Row), 6.*

Devotion to the King . . . of Rock 'n' Roll

Dennis Wise really loved Elvis Presley—so much so that not long after Presley died, Dennis had his face lifted by a plastic surgeon and his hair contoured so that he took on an appearance remarkably similar to Elvis Presley. In fact, for a few months he made a dollar or two making appearances where people loved to see phenomenons like that. When interviewed and asked what would drive a man to reshape his face to look like Elvis Presley, he revealed that Presley had been his model, his idol, for many years. Here's what Dennis Wise told the *Boston Globe* many years ago:

"Yes, sir, Presley's been an idol of mine ever since I was five years old. I have every record he ever made, twice over. Pictures in the thousands. I have books, magazines, pillows, even a couple of books in Chinese and Japanese about him. I even have tree leaves from the front of his house." Wise went on to say, "I never saw Elvis Presley in person. I saw him on stage in the movies four times. Once I stood up on the wall of the Presley mansion and tried to see him. For twelve hours I stood, trying to get a glimpse of him, but he had so many people around him that you would never get close."

Explosive Power

See page 358

YOUTH

The Big Difference

A child is blended of moist, warm elements. . . . A man, when his growth is over, is dry and cold.

Hippocrates

Index of Sources